D1565262

**By the same author**

*Why Religious Tolerance?*
*Why Religion?*
*Do You Believe In Rebirth?*
*Handbook Of Buddhists.*
*Why Worry?*
*Great Personalities On Buddhism.*
*Gems Of Buddhist Wisdom.*
*Whither Mankind?*
*Happy Married Life.*

# *What Buddhists Believe*

## K. Sri Dhammananda

Expanded &
revised edition

*Fifth Edition 1993*

Printed and donated for free distribution by

**The Corporate Body of the Buddha Educational Foundation**

11F., 55 Hang Chow South Road Sec 1, Taipei, Taiwan, R.O.C.

Tel: 886-2-23951198 , Fax: 886-2-23913415

E-mail: overseas@budaedu.org

Website: http: //www.budaedu.org

# TABLE OF CONTENTS

# FOREWORD

THE first edition of this book came into being in 1964 as a result of questions posed by devotees to the Venerable Author in the course of his delivering a prolonged series of Dhamma talks throughout the length and breadth of Malaysia. He felt that a book of this nature should serve as a handy reference book for Buddhists and non-Buddhists alike, presenting in simplified form the beliefs and concepts of Buddhism, and also Buddhist attitude towards other beliefs.

It is ironical but true that there are people who profess this religion and who even claim to be Buddhist leaders, and yet lack the knowledge of the basic principles of Buddhism. Many of them are well-versed with certain rites and rituals but they do not understand the essence of the Master's Teaching. Ignoring the noble Teachings, they have introduced many baseless beliefs and ill-founded traditions, making a mockery of a rational and gentle religion. As a result, many people concerned themselves more with the devotional and ritualistic aspects of Buddhism whilst paying scant attention to true spiritual development which leads to wisdom and understanding.

This is a sad state of affairs brought about by some selfish and misguided religious workers. Driven by ignorance and goaded by mercenary ends, some people have blemished Buddhism as a religion and given the impression that it encourages superstitious beliefs and dependence on charms and omens. Even some monks have lowered themselves to the status of charm peddlars.

*x*

It is ironic that many people do not even know the name of the religion they belong to. There are some who say ' I think I am a Buddhist ' This shows the extent to which they have neglected the Buddhist way of life. Such ignorance of the sublime teachings has encouraged unscrupulous missionaries from other religions to ridicule Buddhism with false accusations and misinterpretation. As a result, Buddhists being ignorant of their own Teachings and unable to refute the false allegations, fall easy prey to the snares of conversion.

It is partly with a view to countering such ignorance that the book ' What Buddhists Believe ' came into being. This book is intended mainly for those who have a genuine desire to know something about the basic Teachings as well as the more difficult aspects of the religion explained in a manner which can be understood in a modern context and without prior knowledge of the subject. The popularity of this book has gone beyond our expectations. It was revised and expanded in 1973 and again in 1982. The demand for this book continues. Chinese, Korean and Indonesian translations of this book are also available.

This year 1987, being the 25th Anniversary of the formation of the Buddhist Missionary Society, it was decided that ' What Buddhists Believe ' should be further revised and enhanced as a ' Special Commemorative Issue ' to celebrate the Silver Jubilee Year of our Society. In this connection, the Venerable Author, with over forty years experience as a missionary, has spent much time on extensive research and compiling suitable new chapters to make the 1987 Reprint of ' What Buddhists Believe ' as *the* Book for all those who seek knowledge about what Buddhism is.

In keeping with the original aim of this book, it is to be emphasized that the Ven. author has no intention whatsoever to denigrate or belittle the beliefs and practices of other religionists and other Buddhist schools of thought. He has repeatedly stressed the Buddha's injunctions in the *Kalama Sutta* to His followers to be open-minded and rational in accepting any teaching. The Buddha in His time never ridiculed the practices and beliefs of other religionists then prevailing but He expounded the truth. It is also not the aim of this book to seek converts, because such a spirit is alien to the spirit of Buddhism. What it does aim at must be reiterated — to inform and educate Buddhists about the basic tenets of their religion and to demonstrate its lofty ideals, making every Buddhist proud to be called a Buddhist. ' What Buddhists Believe ' aims at enlightening others about the pristine Teachings so that with greater and wider understanding they will be good and kind enough to refrain from castigating this Noble Religion which is serving and guiding millions of people to the Right Path.

The Buddha's Teaching is the greatest heritage that man has received from the past. The Buddha's message of non-violence and peace, of love and compassion, of tolerance and understanding, of truth and wisdom, of respect and regard for all life, of freedom from selfishness, hatred and violence, delivered over two thousand five hundred years ago, stands good for today and will stand forever as the Truth. It is an eternal message.

We are in a world torn by strife. The Buddha taught that we must develop the ' Bodhi ' heart of wisdom, a heart of love, a heart of understanding, to overcome the prevailing vices which have plagued man since the beginning of time. ' Overcome anger by non-anger, overcome hatred by love '. Are we practising the advice given by Him? We are responsible for our destiny. We have to cleanse our hearts, scrutinize our own natures and determine to practise the Teachings not only in the letter but, more importantly, in the spirit. It is to be hoped that this publication ' What Buddhists Believe ' will help in guiding many of our Buddhist friends to tread the true path towards Enlightenment.

As the President of the Buddhist Missionary Society, it has been an honour and a pleasure for me to have been closely associated with Venerable Dr. K. Sri Dhammananda, the author, in the production of this book.

I wish to express our sincere thanks and appreciation to Mr. Victor Wee and Mr. Vijaya Samarawickrama for assisting the author in editing the book and for their many useful suggestions which helped to bring the book to its present form. I also like to thank Mrs. Chong Hong Choo who had spent endless hours looking after the innumerable details in the production of the book, from its inception right to its completion. Thanks are also due to Mr H.M.A. de Silva, Misses Lily See, Lee Lai Fong, Quah Pin Pin, Leong Poh Chwee, Tan Kuee Fong and Low Mei Ying for the typing work involved and proof reading, without whose assistance the present book is not possible.

Teh Thean Choo A.M.N.
President
Buddhist Missionary Society

# Author's Note

With so many books available on Buddhism, one may ask if there is need for yet another text. Although books on Buddhism are available on the market, many of them are written for those who have already acquired a basic understanding of the Buddha Dhamma. Some are written in an archaic style, based on a rigid translation of the original texts. Such a style is not appealing to modern readers who might get the impression that Buddhism is a dry subject. There are books by learned scholars who present the teachings in a highly academic and abstruse manner. Except for a few very well-informed readers, these books could create more confusion than clarify, and may even lead the ordinary reader to conclude that Buddhism is too sophisticated for his needs. Some books highlight differences between schools of Buddhism, with the result that the uninitiated reader may be engrossed in the so-called ' intersectarian rivalry ', without realising that there are many more similarities than differences among schools. There are also books written by non-Buddhists who, either deliberately or through their ignorance, distort and misrepresent the true teachings of the Buddha.

This book is written with a specific aim in mind: to introduce the original teaching clearly and without recourse to exaggeration, cultural implications or disparaging of particular schools of Buddhism, so that the reader can understand the Buddha Dhamma in its modern context. There is a growing interest in Buddhism the world over because many informed people have grown rather weary of religious dogmatism and superstitions, on one hand, and greed and selfishness arising from materialism, on the other. Buddhism can teach humanity to walk the Middle Path of moderation and have a better understanding on how to lead a richer life of peace and happiness.

K. Sri Dhammananda
18.3.1987

PART ONE

# LIFE AND MESSAGE
# OF THE BUDDHA

# 1

# LIFE AND NATURE
# OF THE BUDDHA

## Gautama, The Buddha

*The Founder of Buddhism.*

GAUTAMA Buddha, the founder of what came to be known as Buddhism, lived in Northern India in the 6th century B.C. His personal name was Siddhattha, and family name Gotama. The name ' Buddha ' was given to Him after He attained Enlightenment and realized the Truth. It means the ' *Awakened* ' or the ' *Enlightened One* '. He generally called Himself the *Tathagata,* while His followers called Him *Bhagava,* the Blessed One. Others spoke of Him as Gotama or Sakyamuni.

He was born a prince who seemed to have everything. He had a luxurious upbringing and His family was of pure descent on both sides. He was the heir to the·throne, extremely handsome, inspiring trust, stately and gifted with great beauty of complexion and fine presence. At sixteen He married His cousin named Yasodhara who bore Him a son whom they called Rahula. His wife was majestic, cheerful day and night, and full of dignity and grace.

Despite all this, He felt trapped amidst the luxury like a bird in a golden cage. During a visit to the city one day, He saw what is known as the ' Four Sights ', that is, an old man, a sick man, a dead man, and a holy recluse. When He saw the sights, one after another, the realization came to Him that, ' Life is subject to age and death. ' He asked, ' Where is the realm of life in which there is neither age nor death? ' The sight of the recluse, who was calm for having given up the craving for material life, gave Him the clue that the first step in His search for Truth was Renunciation.

Determined to find the way out of these universal sufferings, He decided to leave home to find the cure not for Himself only, but for all mankind. One night in His twenty-ninth year, He bade His sleeping wife and son a silent farewell, saddled His great white horse, and rode off toward the forest.

His renunciation is unprecedented in history. He left at the height of youth, from pleasures to difficulties; from certainty of material security to uncertainty; from a position of wealth and power to that of a wandering ascetic who took shelter in the cave and forest, with His ragged robe as the only protection against the blazing sun, rain and winter winds. He renounced His position, wealth, promise of prestige and power, and a life filled with love and hope in exchange for the search for Truth which no one had found.

For six long years, He laboured to find the Truth. He studied under the foremost masters of the day, and learned all these religious teachers could teach Him. When He could not find what He was looking for, He joined a band of ascetics and tortured His body so as to break its power and crush its interference, since it was believed that Truth could be found this way. A man of enormous energy and will power, He outdid other ascetics in every austerity they proposed. While fasting, He ate so little that when He took hold of the skin of His stomach, He actually touched His spine. He pushed Himself to the extent that no man had done and yet lived: He, too, would have certainly died had He not realised the futility of self mortification, and decided to practise moderation instead.

On the full moon night of the month of Vesakha, He sat under the Bodhi tree at Gaya, wrapped in deep meditation. It was then that His mind burst the bubble of the universe and realised the true nature of all life and all things. At the age of 35 years, He was transformed from an earnest truth seeker into the Buddha, the Enlightened One.

For nearly half a century, the Buddha walked on the dusty paths of India teaching the Dhamma so that those who heard and practised could be ennobled and free. He founded an order of monks and nuns, challenged the caste system, raised the status of women, taught religious freedom and free inquiry, opened the gates of deliverance to all, in every condition of life, high or low, saint or sinner, and ennobled the lives of criminals like Angulimala and courtesans like Ambapali.

He was towering in wisdom and intellect. Every problem was analysed in component parts and then reassembled in logical order with the meaning made clear. None could defeat Him in dialogue. An unequalled teacher, He still is the foremost analyst of the mind and phenomena even up to the present day. For the first time in history, He gave men the power to think for themselves, raised the worth of mankind, and showed that man can reach to the highest knowledge and supreme Enlightenment by his own efforts.

Despite His peerless wisdom and royal lineage, He was never removed from the simple villagers. Surface distinctions of class and caste meant little to Him. No one was too little or low for Him to help. Often when an outcaste, or poor and dejected came to Him, his self-respect was restored and he turned from the ignoble life to that of a noble being.

The Buddha was full of compassion *(karuna)* and wisdom *(panna),* knowing how and what to teach each individual for his own benefit according to his level and capabilities. He was known to have walked long distances to help one single person.

He was affectionate and devoted to His disciples, always inquiring after their well-being and progress. When staying at the monastery, He paid daily visits to the sick wards. His compassion for the sick can be seen from His advice: ' He who attends the sick, attends on me. ' The Buddha kept order and discipline on the basis of mutual respect. King Pasenadi could not understand how the Buddha maintained such order and discipline in the community of monks, when he as a king with the power to punish, could not maintain it as well in his court.

Many miraculous powers were attributed to Him, but He did not consider these important. To Him, the greatest miracle was to explain the Truth and make a man realise it. A teacher with deep compassion, He was moved by human suffering and determined to free men from its fetters by a rational system of' thought and way of life.

The Buddha did not claim to have ' created ' worldly conditions, universal phenomena, or the Universal Law which we call the ' Dhamma '. Although described as *lokavidu* or ' knower of the worlds ', He was not regarded as the sole custodian of that Universal Law. He freely acknowledged that the Dhamma, together with the working of the cosmos, is timeless; it has no creator and is independent in the absolute sense. Every conditioned thing that exists in the cosmos is subject to the operation of Dhamma. What the Buddha did (like all the other Buddhas before Him) was to *rediscover* this infallible Truth and make it known to mankind. In discovering the Truth, He also found the means whereby one could ultimately free oneself from being subjected to the endless cycle of conditioning, with its attendant evils of unsatisfactoriness.

After forty-five years of ministry, the Buddha passed away at the age of eighty at Kusinara, leaving behind thousands of followers, monks and nuns, and a vast treasure store of Dhamma Teaching. The impact of His great love and dedication is still felt today.

In the *Three Greatest Men in History,* H.G. Wells states:

' In the Buddha you see clearly a man, simple, devout, lonely, battling for light, a vivid human personality, not a myth. He too gave a message to mankind universal in character. Many of our best modern ideas are in closest harmony with it. All the miseries and discontents of life are due, he taught, to selfishness. Before a man can become serene he must cease to live for his senses or himself. Then he merges into a greater being. Buddhism in a different language called men to self-forgetfulness 500 years before Christ. In some ways he was nearer to us and our needs. He was more lucid upon our individual importance in service than Christ and less ambiguous upon the question of personal immortality. '

# His Renunciation

*The renunciation of Prince Siddhartha was the boldest step that a man has ever taken.*

CRITICS have condemned Siddhartha for His manner of leaving home and Kingdom. Some described it as a 'callous abandonment of wife and family'. Yet what would have happened if He had not left so stealthily and had approached His loved ones for a formal farewell? They would, of course, have implored him to change His mind. The scene would have been hysterical, and quite possibly the little domain of His father Rajah Suddhodana would have been thrown into turmoil. His intention to seek the truth would have had to be aborted by His father and wife who would prevent Him from His renunciation plans. At the age of 29 years,

Siddhartha was a fullblooded, young man in the prime of life. As it was, the temptation not to abandon all He had known and loved in order to seek the truth must have been formidable. During His final moments in the palace, He visited His bedroom and looked at His slumbering wife and their newborn child. The great impulse to remain and abandon His plan must have caused Him agony. Certainly in those days in India, it was considered a noble thing for a man to forsake home and loved ones to become an ascetic to lead a holy life. All things considered, it would seem that Siddhartha was right in boldly and quickly achieving His plan.

He renounced the world not for His own sake or convenience but for the sake of suffering humanity. To Him the whole of mankind is one family. The renunciation of Prince Siddhartha at that early age was the boldest step that a man could have ever taken.

Detachment is one of the most important factors for the attainment of Enlightenment. The attainment of Enlightenment is by way of non-attachment. Most of life's troubles are caused by attachment. We get angry; we worry; we become greedy and complain bitterly. All these causes of unhappiness, tension, stubbornness and sadness are due to attachment. When we investigate any trouble or worry we have, the main cause is always attachment. Had Prince Siddhartha developed His attachment towards His wife, child, kingdom and worldly pleasures, He would never have been able to discover the remedy for suffering mankind. Therefore, He had to sacrifice everything including worldly pleasures in order to have a concentrated mind free from any distractions, in order to find the Truth that can cure humanity from suffering.

In the eyes of this young Prince, the whole world was burning with lust, anger, greed and many other defilements which ignite the fire of our passions. He saw each and every living being in this world, including His wife and child, suffering from all sorts of physical and mental ailments. So determined was He to seek a solution for the eradication of suffering amongst suffering humanity, that He was prepared to sacrifice everything.

Two thousand five hundred years after His renunciation, some people shed crocodile tears or criticise Him for His action. His wife, however, did not accuse Him for desertion when she realised the purpose of His renunciation. Instead, she gave up her luxurious life to lead a simple life as a mark of respect.

Here is how a well-known poet saw the renunciation of the Buddha:

'Twas not through hatred of children sweet,
'Twas not through hatred of His lovely wife,
Thriller of hearts — not that He loved them less,
But Buddhahood more, that He renounced them all.

*(Dwight Goddard)*

# Nature of the Buddha

*Light of the World*

' Understood are the things to be understood,
Cultivated are the things to be cultivated,
Eradicated are the things to be eradicated,
Therefore Brahmin, I am the Buddha. ' *(Sutta Nipata)*

' As long, brethren, as the Moon and sun have not arisen in the world, just as long is there no shining forth a great light of great radiance. There prevails gross darkness, the darkness of bewilderment. Night is not distinguishable from the day, nor the month, the half-moon and the seasons of the years from each other.

' But, brethren, when the Moon and Sun arise in the world, then a great light of great radiance shines forth. Gross darkness, the darkness of bewilderment, is no more. Then are months and the half-moon and the seasons of years. '

' Just so, brethren, as long as a Buddha, who is an Arahant, a Buddha Supreme, arises not, there is no shining forth a great light of great radiance. But gross darkness, the darkness of bewilderment, prevails. There is no proclaiming, no teaching, no showing forth, no setting up, no opening up, no analysis, no making clear of the Four Noble Truths.

' What Four? The Noble Truth of Suffering, the Arising of Suffering, the ceasing of Suffering, and the approach to the ceasing of Suffering.

' Wherefore, brethren, do you exert yourselves to realize 'This is suffering; this is the arising of Suffering; this is the ceasing of Suffering; this is the approach to the ceasing of Suffering'. '

The above words give us a clear picture of the great value of the arising of the Buddha to the world. The Buddha arose at a time when Western Philosophy as inaugurated by the Greeks, was led by Heraclites who gave a new turn to the early religions of the Olympian gods. It was a time when Jeremiah was giving a new message among the Jews in Babylon.

It was a time when Pythagoras was introducing a doctrine of reincarnation in Italy. It was a time when Confucius was establishing the national life of China by his ethics of conduct.

It was a time when India's social fabric was heavily encrusted with priestcraft, self-mortification, caste distinctions, corrupt feudalism, subjection of women and fear of Brahmanical dominance.

It was at such time that the Buddha, the most fragrant flower of the human race, appeared in the land where saints and sages dedicated their lives in the search for truth.

He was a great man who wielded an extraordinary influence on others even during His life time. His personal magnetism, moral prestige and radiant confidence in His discovery, made Him a popular success. During His active life as a Teacher, the Buddha enlightened many who listened to Him. He attracted the high and low, rich and poor, educated and illiterate, men and

women, householders and ascetics, nobles and peasants. He went
in search of the vicious to teach, while the pure and virtuous came
in search of Him to learn. To all, He gave the gift of the Truth
that He had discovered. His disciples were kings and soldiers,
merchants and millionaires, beggars and courtesans, religious as
well as deluded people. When people were fighting, He made
peace between them. When they were deluded, He enlightened
them. When they were inflamed with rage and lust, He gave them
the cooling water of Truth. When they were forsaken and
wretched, He extended to them the infinite love of His
compassionate heart.

He did not set out to remould the world. He was ' *Lokavidu* '
— ' The knower of the world. ' He knew the world too well to
have any illusions about its nature, or to believe that its laws could
be completely refashioned to suit the desires of man. He knew
that the world does not exist for the pleasure of the man. He
knew about the nature of worldly conditions. He realised the
vicissitude of worldly life. He knew the futility of human
imagination or day-dreaming about the world.

He did not encourage wishful-thinking in terms of establishing
a worldly Utopia. Rather, He told each one of the Way by which
one could later conquer one's own world — the inner subjective
world that is everyone's private domain. In simple language, He
told us that the whole world is within us and the world is led
by the mind and that mind must be trained and cleansed properly.
His Teaching was basically simple and meaningful: ' To put
an end to evil; to fulfil all good; to purify the mind. This is the
advice of all the Buddhas. ' *(Dhammapada, 183)*

He taught the people how to eradicate ignorance. He
encouraged them to maintain freedom in the mind to think freely.
Rigid rituals, rigid dogmas, blind faith and the caste system, all
had no place in His way of life. All people were one in the eyes
of the Buddha.

By every test of what He said, did and was, He demonstrated Himself to be the pre-eminent man in His day. He declared a faith of service, a ministry of sacrifice and achievement. He advised us to start our life from today onwards as if it is the beginning of our life, and to fulfil our endless responsibilities and duties of daily existence here and now without depending on others to do it for us.

He gave the world a new explanation of the universe. He gave a new vision of eternal Happiness, the achievement of perfection in Buddhahood. He pointed out the way to the permanent state beyond all impermanency, the Way to Nibbana, the final deliverance from the misery of existence.

His time was 2,500 years ago. Yet, even today this great Teacher is honoured not only by the religious-minded people, He is also honoured by atheists, historians, rationalists and intellectuals all over the world who have acknowledged Him as the Enlightened, most liberal minded and compassionate Teacher.

' *Sukho Buddhanam Uppado.* '

Happy is the birth of the Buddhas. *(Dhammapada 194)*

# Was Buddha an Incarnation of God?

*Never had the Buddha claimed that He was the son or a messenger of God.*

THE Buddha was a unique human being who was self-Enlightened. He had no one whom He could regard as His teacher. Through His own efforts, He practised to perfection the ten supreme qualities of generosity, discipline, renunciation, wisdom, energy, endurance, truthfulness, determination, goodwill and equanimity. Through His mental purification, He opened the doors to all knowledge. He knew all things to be known, cultivated all things to be cultivated, and destroyed all things to be destroyed. Indeed, no other religious teacher was comparable to Him in terms of cultivation and attainment.

So special was He and so electrifying His message, that many people asked Him ' What (not so much as Who) He was '. Questions on ' Who He was ' would be with respect to His name, origin, ancestry, etc., while ' What He was ' referred to the order of being to which He belonged. So ' godly ' and inspiring was He that even during His time, there were numerous attempts of others to turn Him into a god or a reincarnation of god. Never did He agree to be regarded as such. In the *Anguttara Nikaya,* He said: ' I am not indeed a *deva,* nor a *gandharva,* nor a *yaksa,* nor a *manusya.* Know ye that I am the Buddha. ' After Enlightenment, the Buddha could no longer be classified even as a ' *manusya* ' or an ordinary human being. He belonged to the *Buddha wangsa,* a special race or species of enlightened beings, all of whom are Buddhas.

Buddhas appear in this world from time to time. But some people have the mistaken idea that it is the same Buddha who is reincarnated or appears in the world over and over again. Actually, they are not the same person, otherwise there is no scope for others to attain to Buddhahood. Buddhists believe that anyone can become a Buddha if he develops his qualities to perfection and is able to remove his ignorance completely through his own efforts. After Enlightenment, all Buddhas are similar in their attainment and experience of Nibbana.

In India, the followers of many orthodox religious groups tried to condemn the Buddha because of His liberal teachings which revolutionised the Indian society. Many regarded Him as an enemy when increasing numbers of intellectuals as well as people from all ranks of society took up the religion. When they failed in their attempt to destroy Him, they adopted the reverse strategy of introducing Him as a reincarnation of one of their gods. This way they could absorb Buddhism into their religion. To a certain extent, this strategy worked in India since it had, through the centuries, contributed to the decay and the subsequent uprooting of Buddhism from the land of its origin.

Even today there are certain religionists who try to absorb the Buddha into their beliefs as a way of gaining converts among Buddhists. Their basis for doing so is by claiming that the Buddha Himself had predicted that another Buddha would appear in this world, and that the latest Buddha will become even more popular. One group named a religious teacher who lived 600 years after Gautama the Buddha as the latest Buddha. Another group said that the next Buddha had already arrived in Japan in the 13th century. Yet another group believed that their founder came from the lineage of great teachers (like Gautama and Jesus) and that founder was the latest Buddha. These groups advised Buddhists to give up their old Buddha and follow the so-called new Buddha. While it is good to see them giving the Buddha the same status as their own religious teachers, we feel that these attempts to absorb Buddhists into another faith by misrepresenting the truth are in extreme bad taste.

Those who claim that the new Buddha had already arrived are obviously misrepresenting what the Buddha had said. Although the Buddha predicted the coming of the next Buddha, He mentioned some conditions which had to be met before this can be possible. It is the nature of Buddhahood that the next Buddha will not appear as long as the dispensation of the current Buddha still exists. He will appear only when the Four Noble Truths and the Eightfold Path have been completely forgotten. The people living then must be properly guided in order to understand the same Truth taught by the previous Buddhas. We are still living within the dispensation of Gautama the Buddha. Although the moral conduct of the people has, with very few exceptions, deteriorated, the future Buddha would only appear at some incalculable period when the Path to Nibbana is *completely* lost to mankind and when people are ready to receive Him.

# The Buddha's Service

*The Buddha was born to dispel the darkness of ignorance and to show the world how to be free from suffering.*

THE Buddha was the embodiment of all the virtues that He preached. During His successful and eventful ministry of 45 years, He translated all His words into actions. At no time did He ever show any human frailty or any base passion. The Buddha's moral code is the most perfect the world has ever known.

For more than 25 centuries, millions of people have found inspiration and solace in His Teaching. His greatness still shines today like a sun that outshines the glow of lesser lights. His Teachings still beckon the weary pilgrim to the security and peace of Nibbana. No other person has sacrificed so much of his worldly comfort for the sake of suffering humanity.

The Buddha was the first religious leader in human history to admonish against animal sacrifice for any reason and to appeal to people not to harm any living creature.

To the Buddha, religion was not a bargain but a way to enlightenment. He did not want followers with blind faith; He wanted followers who could think freely and wisely.

The entire human race has been blessed with His presence.

There was never an occasion when the Buddha expressed any unfriendliness towards a single person. Not even to His opponents and worst enemies did the Buddha express any unfriendliness. There were a few prejudiced minds who turned against the Buddha and who tried to kill Him; yet the Buddha never treated them as enemies. The Buddha once said, ' As an elephant in the battle-field endures the arrows that are shot into him, so will I endure the abuse and unfriendly expressions of others. '
*(Dhammapada, 320)*

In the annals of history, no man is recorded as having so consecrated himself to the welfare of all living beings as did the

Buddha. From the hour of His Enlightenment to the end of His Life, He strove tirelessly to elevate mankind. He slept only two hours a day. Though 25 centuries have gone since the passing away of this great Teacher, His message of love and wisdom still exists in its pristine purity. This message is still decisively influencing the destinies of humanity. He was the most Compassionate One who illuminated this world with loving-kindness.

After attaining Nibbana, the Buddha left a deathless message that is still with us. Today we are confronted by the terrible threat to world peace. At no time in the history of the world is His message more needed than it is now.

The Buddha was born to dispel the darkness of ignorance and to show the world how to get rid of suffering and disease, decay and death and all the worries and miseries of living beings.

According to some beliefs, a certain god will appear in this world from time to time to destroy wicked people and to protect the good ones. Buddha did not appear in this world to destroy wicked people but to show them the correct path.

In the history of the world until the Buddha's time, did we ever hear of any religious teacher who was so filled with such all-absorbing sympathy and love for suffering humanity as was the Buddha? At about the same time as the Buddha, we heard of some wise men in Greece: Socrates, Plato and Aristotle and many others. But they were only philosophers and thinkers and seekers after truth; they lacked any inspiring love for the suffering multitudes.

The Buddha's way of saving mankind was to teach them how to find salvation. He was not interested in alleviating a few chance cases of physical or mental distress. He was more concerned with revealing a Path that all people could follow.

Let us take all the great philosophers, psychologists, great thinkers, scientists, rationalists, social workers, reformers and other religious teachers and compare, with an unbiased mind, their greatness, virtues, services and wisdom with the Buddha's virtues, compassion and Enlightenment. One can understand where the Buddha stands amongst all those great people.

# Historical Evidences of the Buddha

*The Buddha is the greatest conquerer the world has ever seen. His Teaching illuminates the way for mankind to cross from a world of darkness, hatred and suffering to a new world of light, love and happiness.*

GAUTAMA the Buddha was not a mythical figure but an actual, historical personality who introduced the religion known today as Buddhism. Evidences to prove the existence of this great religious Teacher are to be found in the following facts:—

1. The testimonies of those who knew Him personally. These testimonies were recorded in the rock-inscriptions, pillars and pagodas made in His honour. These testimonies and monuments to His memory were created by kings and others who were near enough to His time to be able to verify the story of His life.
2. The discovery of places and the remains of buildings that were mentioned in the narratives of His time.
3. The Sangha, the holy order which He founded, has had an unbroken existence to the present day. The Sangha possessed the facts of His life and Teachings which have been transmitted from generation to generation in various parts of the world.
4. The fact that in the very year of His death, and at various times subsequently, conventions and councils of the Sangha were held for the verification of the actual Teachings of the Founder. These verified Teachings have been passed on from teacher to pupil from His time to the present day.

5.  After His passing away, His body was cremated and the bodily relics were divided among eight kingdoms in India. Each king built a pagoda to contain his portion of the relics. The portion given to King Ajata satthu was enshrined by him in a pagoda at Rajagriha. Less than two centuries later, Emperor Asoka took the relics and distributed them throughout his empire. The inscriptions enshrined in this and other pagodas confirmed that those were the relics of Gautama the Buddha.

6.  ' The Mahavansa ', the best and authentic ancient history known to us gives detailed particulars of life as well as details of the life of Emperor Asoka and all other sovereigns related to Buddhist history. Indian history has also given a prominent place to the Buddha's life, activities, Buddhist traditions and customs.

7.  The records which we can find in the Buddhist countries where people received Buddhism a few hundred years after the Buddha's passing away such as Sri Lanka, Burma, China, Tibet, Nepal, Korea, Mongolia, Japan, Thailand, Vietnam, Cambodia and Laos show unbroken historical, cultural, religious, literary and traditional evidence that there was a religious Teacher in India known as Gautama the Buddha.

8.  The Tripitaka, an unbroken record of His 45 years of Teaching is more than sufficient to prove that the Buddha really lived in the world.

9.  The accuracy and authenticity of the Buddhist texts is supported by the fact that they provide information for historians to write Indian history during the 5th and 6th century B.C. The texts, which represent the earliest reliable written records in India, provide a profound insight into the socio-economic, cultural and political environment and conditions during the Buddha's lifetime as well as into the lives of His contemporaries, such as King Bimbisara.

# Salvation Through Arahantahood

*Attaining Nibbana through Arahantahood is not selfish.*

CERTAIN Buddhists believe that to seek salvation by becoming an Arahant is a selfish motive; because everyone, they claim, must try to become a Buddha in order to save others. This particular belief has absolutely no ground in the Teaching of the Buddha. The Buddha never mentioned that He wanted to save every living being in this whole universe. He offered His help only to those who were spiritually matured and willing to accept His Noble way of life.

> ' The doors to the deathless are open!
> Let those who will hear leave wrong doctrine ......
> ' Now shall I turn the Wheel of the Great Law
> For this I go to the Kasian city.
> There shall I beat the drum of deathlessness
> In this world that is groping in the dark. '
> *(Ariya Pariyesana Sutta — Majjhima Nikaya)*

In the Original Teachings of the Buddha, there is no such thing as 'saving others'. According to the method introduced by the Buddha, each and every person must make the effort to train and purify himself to attain his own salvation by following the guidance given by the Buddha. One should not forget the following advice given by the Buddha. ' You yourself make the effort for your salvation, the Buddhas are only Teachers who can show you how to achieve it. ' *(Dhammapada 276)*

The belief that everyone must strive to become a Buddha in order to attain salvation cannot be found in the original Teachings of the Buddha. This belief is just like asking every person to become a doctor in order to cure other people and himself of

---

*For more discussion on self reliance, read ' Do it yourself ' and ' How to save yourself ' in Part III of this book.*

diseases. This advice is most impractical. If people want to cure themselves of their sicknesses they can get medical advice from a qualified doctor. This they can do without waiting until they are all doctors before curing themselves. Nor is there any need for each and every person to be a doctor. If everyone becomes a doctor, who are going to be their patients? In the same way if everyone is going to become Buddhas, who is going to save whom?

Of course, those who wish to become doctors can do so. But they must have intelligence, courage and the means to study medicine. Likewise, it is not compulsory for everyone to become a Buddha to find his salvation. Those who wish to become Buddhas can do so. However, they need the courage and knowledge to sacrifice their comforts and practise all kinds of renunciations in order to attain Buddhahood. Others can be content to be healthy.

To attain Arahantahood, one has to eradicate all greed and selfishness. This implies that while relating with others, an Arahant will act with compassion and try to inspire others to go on the Path leading to Liberation. He is the living proof of the good results that accrue to a person who follows the method taught by the Buddha. The attainment of Nibbana is not possible if one acts with a selfish motive. Therefore, it is baseless to say that striving to become an Arahant is a selfish act.

Buddhahood is indisputably the best and the noblest of all the three ideals (Supreme Buddha, Silent Buddha and Arahant). But not everyone is capable of achieving this highest ideal. Surely all scientists cannot be Einsteins and Newtons. There must be room for lesser scientists who nevertheless help the world according to their capabilities.

# Bodhisatta

*A Bodhisatta is a being devoted to Enlightenment.*

As a ' Compassionate Being ', a Bodhisatta is destined to attain Buddhahood, and become a future Buddha, through the cultivation of his mind.

In order to gain Supreme Enlightenment, he practises transcendental virtues *(Parami)* to perfection. The virtues are generosity, morality, renunciation, wisdom, energy, patience, truthfulness, determination, loving-kindness, and even mindedness. He cultivates these *Parami* with compassion and wisdom, without being influenced by selfish motives or self-conceit. He works for the welfare and happiness of all beings, seeking to lessen the suffering of others throughout the series of his countless lives. In his journey to perfection, he is prepared to practice these virtues, sometimes even at the expense of his own life.

In the Pali scriptures, the designation ' Bodhisatta ' is given to Prince Siddhattha before His Enlightenment and to His former lives. The Buddha Himself used this term when speaking of His life prior to Enlightenment. According to the Pali texts there is no mention of Buddha Bodhi being the only way to attain the final goal of Nibbanic bliss. It was very rare for a disciple during the Buddha's time to forgo the opportunity to attain sainthood and instead declare bodhisattahood as his aspiration. However, there are some records that some followers of the Buddha did aspire to become Bodhisattas to gain ' Buddhahood '

In the Mahayana school of thought, the Bodhisatta cult however, plays an important role. The Mahayana ideal regards the Bodhisatta as a being who, having brought himself to the brink of Nibbana, voluntarily delays the acquisition of his prize so that he may return to the world to make it accessible to others.

He deliberately chooses to postpone his release from Samsara in order to show the path for others to attain Nibbana.

Although Theravada Buddhists respect Bodhisattas, they do not regard them as being in the position to enlighten or save others before their own enlightenment. Bodhisattas are, therefore, not regarded as saviours. In order to gain their final salvation, all beings must follow the method prescribed by the Buddha and follow the example set by Him. They must also personally eradicate their mental defilements and develop all the great virtues.

Theravada Buddhists do not subscribe to the belief that everyone must strive to become a Buddha in order to gain Nibbana. However, the word ' *Bodhi* ' is used to refer to the qualities of a Buddha, or PaccekaBuddha and Arahant in expressions such as Samma Sambodhi, PaccekaBodhi and SavakaBodhi. In addition, many of the Buddhas mentioned in the Mahayana school are not historical Buddhas and are therefore not given much attention by Theravada Buddhists. The notion that certain Buddhas and Bodhisattas are waiting in *Sukhawati* (Pure Abode) for those who pray to them is a notion quite foreign to the fundamental Teachings of the Buddha. Certain Bodhisattas are said to voluntarily remain in *Sukhawati,* without gaining enlightenment themselves, until every living being is saved. Given the magnitude of the universe and the infinite number of beings who are enslaved by ignorance and selfish desire, this is clearly an impossible task, since there can be no end to the number of beings.

Must a Bodhisatta always be a Buddhist? We may find among Buddhists some self-sacrificing and ever loving Bodhisattas. Sometimes they may not even be aware of their lofty aspiration, but they instinctively work hard to serve others and cultivate their pristine qualities. Nevertheless, Bodhisattas are not only found among Buddhists, but possibly among the other religionists as well. The Jataka stories, which relate the previous birth stories of the Buddha, describe the families and forms of existence taken by the Bodhisatta. Sometimes He was born as an animal. It is hard to believe that He could have been born in a Buddhist family in each and every life. But no matter what form He was born as or family he was born into, He invariably strived hard to develop certain virtues. His aspiration to gain perfection from life to life until His final birth when he emerged as a Buddha, is the quality which clearly distinguishes a Bodhisatta from other beings.

# Attainment of Buddhahood

*The attainment of Buddhahood is the most difficult task that a person can pursue in this world.*

THE Buddhahood is not reserved only for chosen people or for supernatural beings. Anyone can become a Buddha. No founder of any other religion ever said that his followers can have the opportunity or potentiality to attain the same position as the founder.

However, attaining Buddhahood is the most difficult task a person can pursue in this world. One must work hard by sacrificing one's worldly pleasures. One has to develop and purify one's mind from all evil thoughts in order to obtain this Enlightenment. It will take innumerable births for a person to purify himself and to develop his mind in order to become a Buddha. Long periods of great effort are necessary in order to complete the high qualification of this self-training. The course of this self-training which culminates in Buddhahood, includes self-discipline, self-restraint, superhuman effort, firm determination, and willingness to undergo any kind of suffering for the sake of other living beings who are suffering in this world.

This clearly shows that the Buddha did not obtain this supreme Enlightenment by simply praying, worshipping, or making offerings to some supernatural beings. He attained Buddhahood by the purification of His mind and heart. He gained Supreme Enlightenment without the influence of any external, supernatural forces but by the development of His own insight. Thus only a man who has firm determination and courage to overcome all hindrances, weaknesses and selfish desires can attain Buddhahood.

Prince Siddhartha did not attain Buddhahood overnight simply by sitting under the Bodhi tree. No supernatural being appeared and revealed anything by whispering into His ear while He was in deep meditation under the Bodhi tree. Behind His Supreme Enlightenment there was a long history of previous births. Many of the Jataka stories tell us how He worked hard by sacrificing His life in many previous births to attain His Supreme Buddhahood. No one can attain Buddhahood without devoting many lifetimes practising the ten perfections or *Paramitas\**. The great period of time needed to develop these ten perfections explains why a Supreme Buddha appears only at very long intervals of time.

Therefore, the Buddha's advice to His followers is that in order to find their salvation it is not necessary for each and every person to wait until he gains his Buddhahood. Aspirants can also find their salvation by becoming *Pacceka Buddhas* (Silent Buddhas) or *Arahantas* — (saints). *Pacceka Buddhas* appear in this world during the period when there is no other Enlightened Buddha. They are also Enlightened. Although their degree of perfection is not similar to that of the Supreme Buddha, they experience the same Nibbanic bliss. Unlike the Supreme Buddha, they do not preach to the masses. They lead a life of solitude.

Arahantas can also experience the same Nibbanic bliss as the Buddhas do. There is no discrimination or status in Nibbana. The only difference is that Arahantas do not have the Supreme

---

*\*The ten virtues are mentioned in the earlier article on 'Bodhisatta'.*

Enlightenment to be able to enlighten others in the same way as the Buddhas do. Arahantas have overcome all their desires and other human weaknesses. They can appreciate the Dhamma which was discovered and taught by the Buddha. They can also show others the correct Buddhist way of life and the Path to salvation.

' *Kiccho Buddhanam Uppado* '

Rare is the appearance of the Buddhas. *(Dhammapada 182)*

# Trikaya — The Three Bodies of the Buddha

*The three bodies of the Buddha consist of Dharma-kaya (Truth body), Sambhoga-kaya (Enjoyment body), and Nirmana-kaya (Manifestation body).*

IN the Mahayana philosophy, the personality of the Buddha is given an elaborate treatment. According to this philosophy, the Buddhas have three bodies *(trikaya),* or three aspects of personality: the *Dharmakaya,* the *Sambhoga-kaya,* and the *Nirmana-kaya.*

After a Buddha has attained Enlightenment, He is the living embodiment of wisdom, compassion, happiness and freedom. At the beginning, there was only one Buddha in the Buddhist tradition. He is the historical Sakyamuni the Buddha. However, even during His lifetime, He made the distinction between Himself as the enlightened, historical individual, on one hand, and Himself as the Embodiment of Truth, on the other. The enlightened personality was known as the ' *Rupakaya* ' (Form-body) or ' *Nirmana-kaya* ' (Manifestation-body). This was the physical body of the Buddha who was born among men, attained Enlightenment, preached the Dhamma and attained *Maha Parinibbana.* The Manifestation-body or physical body of Buddhas are many and differ from one another.

On the other hand, the principle of Enlightenment which is embodied in Him is known as *Dharma-kaya* or Truth-body. This is the essence of the Buddha and is independent of the person realising it. ' Dhamma ' in this expression means ' Truth ', and does not refer to the verbal teachings which were recorded down in scriptures. The teaching of the Buddha also emanates from this ' Essence ' or ' Truth '. So the real, essential Buddha is Truth or the principle of Enlightenment. This idea is clearly stated in the original Pali texts of the Theravada. The Buddha told Vasettha that the Tathagata (the Buddha) was *Dharma-kaya,* the ' Truth-body ' or the ' Embodiment of Truth ', as well as *Dharmabhuta,* ' Truth-become ', that is, ' One who has become Truth ' *(Digha Nikaya).* On another occasion, the Buddha told Vakkali: ' He who sees the Dhamma (Truth) sees the Tathagata; he who sees the Tathagata sees the Dhamma *(Samyutta Nikaya).* That is to say, the Buddha is equal to Truth, and all Buddhas are one and the same, being no different from one another in the *Dharma-kaya,* because Truth is one.'

In the Buddha's lifetime, both the *Nirmana-kaya* and the *Dharma-kaya* were united in Him. However, after His *Parinibbana,* the distinction became more pronounced, especially in the Mahayana philosophy. His Manifestation-body was dead and enshrined in the form of relics in stupas: His Dhamma-body is eternally present.

Later, the Mahayana philosophy developed the ' *Sambhoga-kaya* ', the Enjoyment-body. The *Sambhoga-kaya* can be considered as the body or aspect through which the Buddha enjoyed Himself in the Dhamma, in teaching the Truth, in leading others to the realisation of the Truth, and in enjoying the company of good, noble people. This is a selfless, pure, spiritual enjoyment, not to be confused with sensual pleasure. This ' Enjoyment-body ' is not categorically mentioned in Theravada texts although it can be appreciated without contradiction if understood in this context. In Mahayana, the Enjoyment-body of the Buddha, unlike the impersonal, abstract principle of the *Dharma-kaya,* is also considered as a person, though not a human, historical person.

Although the terms *Sambhoga-kaya* and *Dharma-kaya* found in the later Pali works come from Mahayana and semi-Mahayana works, scholars from other traditions did not show hostility towards them. Ven. Buddhaghosa in his *Visuddhi Magga* referred thus to the bodies of the Buddha:

' The Buddha is possessed of a beautiful *rupakaya* adorned with eighty minor and thirty-two major signs of a great man, and possessed of a *Dharmakaya* purified in every way and glorified by *Sila, Samadhi,* ... full of splendour and virtue, incomparable and fully enlightened. '

Though Buddhaghosa's conception was realistic, he was not immune from the religious bias of attributing superhuman power to the Buddha. In the *Atthasallini,* he said that during the three months' absence of the Buddha, when He was engaged in preaching the *Abhidhamma* to His mother in the *Tusita* heaven, He created some *Nimmita-buddhas* as exact replicas of Himself. These *Nimmita-buddhas* could not be distinguished from the Buddha in voice, words and even the rays of light that issued forth from His body. The ' created Buddha ' could be detected only by the gods of the higher realms of existence and not by ordinary gods or men. From this description, it is clear that the early Theravadins conceived Buddha's *Rupakaya* or *Sambhoga-kaya* as that of a human being, and His *Dharma-kaya* as the collection of His Dhamma, that is, doctrines and disciplinary rules, collectively.

# 2
# HIS MESSAGE

## Message for All

*Buddha, the flower of mankind, is no more in this world but the sweet fragrance of His peace message remains forever.*

BUDDHISM is one of the oldest religions still being practised in the world today. While the names of many other religions which existed in India have been forgotten today, the teachings of the Buddha, (better known as the Dhamma) are still relevant to the needs of today's society. This is because the Buddha has always considered himself as a *human* religious teacher whose message was meant to promote the happiness and well-being of other human beings. The Buddha's primary concern was to help His followers to live a normal life without either going to the extremes of self-denial or totally surrendering to sensual desires.

The practical nature of the Buddha's teaching is revealed in the fact that not everyone is expected to attain exactly the same goal in one lifetime, since the mental impurities are deeply rooted. Some people are spiritually more advanced than others and they can proceed to greater heights according to their state of development. But every single human being has the ultimate potential to attain the supreme goal of Buddhahood if he has the determination and will to do so.

Even now does the soft, sweet voice of the Buddha ring in our ears. And sometimes we perhaps feel a little ashamed because we do not understand Him fully. Often we only praise His Teaching and respect Him, but do not try to practise what He preached. The Buddha's Teaching and message have had their effect on all people for thousands of years whether they believe in religion or not. His message is for all.

Though the Buddha, the flower of mankind, is no longer in this world, the sweet fragrance and exquisite aroma of His Teachings have spread far and wide. Its balmy, diffusing fragrance has calmed and soothed millions. Its ambrosial perfume has heartened and cheered every nation which it has penetrated. The reason that His Teachings have captured millions of hearts is because they were spread (not by weapons or political power) but by love and compassion for humanity. Not a drop of blood stains its pure path. Buddhism wins by the warm touch of love, not by the cold claws of fear. Fear of the supernatural and the doctrine of everlasting hell-fire have no place in Buddhism.

During the last 25 centuries since the appearance of the Buddha, many changes have taken place in this world. Kingdoms have risen and fallen; nations have prospered and perished. However, the world today has forgotten many of these past civilisations. But the name of the Buddha remains alive and fresh in the minds of millions of people today. The Kingdom of Righteousness that He built is still strong and steady. Although many temples, pagodas, images, libraries and other religious symbols erected in His honour were destroyed, His untainted Noble Name and the message He gave remain in the minds of cultured people.

The Buddha taught man that the greatest of conquests was not the subjugation of others but of the self. He taught in the *Dhammapada,* ' Even though a man conquers ten thousand men in battle, he who conquers but himself is the greatest of conquerors '.

Perhaps the best example of how the gentle message of the Compassionate One could rehabilitate the most savage of men is the case of the Emperor Asoka. About two hundred years after the Buddha, this king waged fierce battles across India and caused great anguish and fear. But when he absorbed the Dhamma, he regretted the evil that he had done. We remember and honour him today because after his conversion to the path of peace, he embarked on another battle: a battle to bring peace to mankind. He proved without doubt that the Buddha was right when He asserted that true greatness springs from love, not hatred, from humility, not pride; from compassion, not cruelty.

The Emperor Asoka's conversion from cruelty to kindness was so complete that he forbade even the killing of animals in his kingdom. He realised that his subjects stole because of want and he set out to reduce want in his kingdom. But above all, he instructed the followers of the Buddha to remember the Master's teaching never to force their beliefs on others who were loyal to other religious leaders. In other cases we have heard of kings who, upon conversion, diverted their thirst for blood by spreading their new religion by the sword! Only Buddhism can take pride in a king who has never been equalled in such greatness before or ever since.

The Buddha's Teachings were introduced in order that societies could be cultured and civilized and live in peace and harmony. All of life's most difficult problems can be better understood if we but try to learn and practise His teachings. The Buddha's approach to the problems and suffering of mankind is straight-forward and direct.

The Buddha was the greatest conqueror the world has ever seen. He conquered the world with His infallible weapons of love and truth. His Teaching illuminates the Way for mankind to cross from a world of darkness, hatred, and suffering, to a new world of light, love and happiness.

# Miraculous Power

*If a wicked man can become a pure religious man, this according to Buddhism, is a practical miracle.*

IN every religion we hear of miracles being performed by either the founders of these religions or by some of their disciples. In the case of the Buddha, miracles occurred from the day of His birth until His passing away into *Nibbana*. Many of the psychic powers (so-called miraculous powers in other religions) of the Buddha were attained through His long and intense training in meditation. The Buddha meditated and passed through all the highest stages of contemplation that culminated in pure self-possession and wisdom. Such attainments through meditation are considered nothing miraculous but fall within the power of any trained ascetic.

Using meditation on the night of His Enlightenment, there arose within the Buddha a vision of His previous births, the many existences with all their details, He remembered His previous births and how He had made use of these births to gain His Enlightenment. Then the Buddha had a second and wider vision in which He saw the whole universe as a system of *Kamma* and *Rebirth*. He saw the universe made up of beings that were noble and wicked, happy and unhappy. He saw them all continually ' passing away according to their deed ', leaving one form of existence and taking shape in another. Finally, He understood the nature of Suffering, the cessation of Suffering and the Path that leads to the cessation of Suffering. Then a third vision arose within the Buddha. He realised that He was completely free from all bondages, human or divine. He realised that He had done what had to be done. He realised He had no more re-birth to go through because He was living with His final body. This knowledge destroyed all ignorance, all darkness, and light arose within Him. Such is the psychic power and the wisdom that arose within the Buddha as He sat meditating under the Bodhi tree.

The Buddha had a natural birth; He lived in a normal way. But He was an extraordinary man, as far as His Enlightenment was concerned. Those who have not learnt to appreciate His Supreme Wisdom  try to explain His greatness by peeping into His life and looking for miracles. However, the Buddha's Supreme Enlightenment is more than enough for us to understand His greatness. There is no need to show His greatness by introducing any miraculous power.

The Buddha knew of the power that could be developed by training the human mind. He also knew that His disciples could acquire such powers through mental development. Thus the Buddha advised them not to exercise such psychic power in order to convert less intelligent people. He was referring to the ' miraculous ' power to walk on water, to exorcise spirits, raise the dead and perform the so-called supernormal practices. He was also referring to the ' miracles of prophesy ' such as thought-reading, sooth-saying, fortune-telling, and so on. When the uneducated believers see the performance of such powers, their faith deepens. But the nominal converts who are attracted to a religion because of these powers embrace a faith, not because they realise the truth, but because they harbour hallucinations. Besides, some people may pass remarks that these miracles are due to certain charms. In drawing people to listen to the Dhamma, the Buddha appealed to their reasoning power.

The following story illustrates the Buddha's attitude towards miraculous powers. One day the Buddha met an ascetic who sat by the bank of a river. This ascetic had practised austerities for 25 years. The Buddha asked him what he had received for all his labour. The ascetic proudly replied that, now at last, he could cross the river by walking on the water. The Buddha pointed out that this gain was insignificant for all the years of labour, since he could cross the river using a ferry for one penny!

In certain religions, a man's miraculous performance can help him to become a saint. But in Buddhism, miracles can be a hindrance for a person to attain sainthood, which is a gradual personal attainment and individual concern. Each person himself must work for his sainthood through self-purification and no one else can make another person a saint.

The Buddha says that a person can gain miraculous power without gaining spiritual power. He teaches us that if we first gain spiritual power, then we automatically receive the miraculous or psychic powers too. But if we develop miraculous powers without spiritual development, then we are in danger. We can misuse this power for worldly gain *(Pataligama-Udana)*. There are many who have deviated from the right path by using their miraculous powers without having any spiritual development. Many people who are supposed to have obtained some miraculous powers succumbed to the vain glory of obtaining some worldly gain.

Many so-called miracles talked about by people are merely imaginations and hallucinations created by their own minds due to a lack of understanding of things as they truly are. All these miracles remain as miracles as long as people fail to know what these powers really are.

The Buddha also expressly forbade His disciples to use miracles to prove the superiority of His teachings. On one occasion He said that the use of miracles to gain converts was like using dancing girls to tempt people to do something. Anyone with the proper mental training can perform miracles because they are simply an expression of the superiority of mind over matter.

According to the Buddha, the *miracle of realisation* is a real miracle. When a murderer, thief, terrorist, drunkard, or adulterer is made to realise that what he had been doing is wrong and gives up his bad, immoral and harmful way of life, this change can be regarded as a miracle. The change for the better arising from an understanding of Dhamma is the highest miracle that any man can perform.

# The Buddha's Silence

*When the questioner himself was not in a position to understand the real significance of the answer to his question and when the questions posed to Him were wrong, the Buddha remained silent.*

THE scriptures mention a few occasions when the Buddha remained silent to questions posed to Him. Some scholars, owing to their misunderstanding of the Buddha's silence, came to the hasty conclusion that the Buddha was unable to answer to these questions. While it is true that on several occasions the Buddha did not respond to these metaphysical and speculative questions, there are reasons why the Buddha kept noble silence.

When the Buddha knew that the questioner was not in a position to understand the answer to the question because of its profundity, or if the questions themselves were wrongly put in the first place, the Blessed One remained silent. Some of the questions to which the Buddha remained silent are as follows:

1.  Is the universe eternal?
2.  Is it not eternal?
3.  Is the universe finite?
4.  Is it infinite?
5.  Is soul the same as the body?
6.  Is the soul one thing and the body another?
7.  Does the Tathagata exist after death?

8.   Does He not exist after death?

9.   Does He both (at the same time) exist and not exist after death?

10.  Does He both (at the same time) neither exist nor not exist?

The Buddha who had truly realised the nature of these issues observed noble silence. An ordinary person who is still unenlightened might have a lot to say, but all of it would be sheer conjecture based on his imagination.

The Buddha's silence regarding these questions is more meaningful than attempting to deliver thousands of discourses on them. The paucity of our human vocabulary which is built upon relative experiences cannot hope to convey the depth and dimensions of Reality which a person has not himself experienced through Insight. On several occasions, the Buddha had very patiently explained that human language was too limited and could not describe the Ultimate Truth. If the Ultimate Truth is absolute, then it does not have any point of reference for worldlings with only mundane experiences and relative understanding to fully comprehend it. When they try to do so with their limited mental conception, they misunderstand the Truth like the seven blind men and the elephant. The listener who had not realised the Truth could not fathom the explanation given, just like a man who was blind since birth will have no way of truly understanding the colour of the sky.

The Buddha did not attempt to give answers to all the questions put to Him. He was under no obligation to respond to meaningless questions which reflected gross misunderstanding on the part of the questioner and which in any case had no relevance to one's spiritual development. He was a practical Teacher, full of compassion and wisdom. He always spoke to people fully understanding their temperament, capability and capacity to comprehend. When a person asked questions not with the intention to learn how to lead a religious life but simply to create an opportunity for splitting hairs, the Blessed One did not answer these questions. Questions were answered to help a person towards self-realisation, not as a way of showing His towering wisdom.

According to the Buddha, there are several ways of answering various types of questions. The first type of question is one that requires a definite answer, such as a ' yes ' or ' no '. For example, the question, ' Are all conditioned things impermanent? ' is answered with a ' Yes '. The second type of question is one requiring an analytical answer. Suppose someone says that Angulimala was a murderer before he became an ' Arahant '. So is it possible for all murderers to become arahants? This question should be analysed before you can say ' Yes ' or ' No '. Otherwise, it will not be answered correctly and comprehensively. You need to analyse what conditions make it possible for a murderer to become a saint within one life-time.

The third type of question is one where it is necessary to ask a counter question to help the questioner to think through. If you ask, ' Why is it wrong to kill other living beings? ' the counter question is, ' How does it feel when others try to kill you? ' The fourth kind of question is one that should be dropped. It means that you should not answer it. These are the questions which are speculative in nature, and any answer to such questions will only create more confusion. An example of such a question is, ' Does the universe have a beginning or not? ' People can discuss such questions for years without coming to a conclusion. They can only answer such questions based on their imagination, not on real understanding.

Some answers which the Buddha gave have close parallels to the kind responses which are given in nuclear science. According to Robert Oppenheimer, 'If we ask, for instance, whether the position of the electron remains the same, we must say ' no '; if we ask whether the electron is at rest, we must say ' no '; if we ask whether it is in motion, we must say ' no '. The Buddha has given such answers when interrogated as to the conditions of a man's self after his death; but they are not familiar answers in accordance with the tradition of seventeenth and eighteenth century science.'

It is important to note however that the Buddha did give answers to some of these questions to His most intellectually developed disciples after the questioner had left. And in many cases, His explanations are contained in other discourses which show us, who live in an age of greater scientific knowledge, why these questions were not answered by the Buddha just to satisfy the inquisitive minds of the questioners.

# The Buddha's Attitude Towards Worldly Knowledge

*Worldly knowledge can never help one to lead a pure religious life for gaining peace and emancipation.*

WORLDLY knowledge is useful for worldly ends. With such knowledge, mankind learns how to use the earth's resources to improve the standard of living, grow more food, generate power to run factories and to light up streets and houses, manage factories and businesses, cure sickness, build flats and bridges, cook exotic dishes, and so on. Worldly knowledge can also be used for harmful purposes such as building missiles with nuclear warheads, manipulating the stock market, cheating ' legally ', and inflaming political anxiety and hatred. Despite the rapid expansion of worldly knowledge, especially in the twentieth century, mankind has been brought no nearer to the solution of his spiritual problems and pervasive unsatisfactoriness. In all likelihood, it never will solve mankind's universal problems and bring peace and happiness because of the premises on which such knowledge, discoveries and inventions are built.

While Buddhism can bring greater understanding on how to lead a good, worldly life, its main focus is how to gain spiritual liberation through the development of wisdom and mental culture. For ordinary human beings, there is no end to the search for worldly knowledge, but in the final analysis it does not really matter. For as long as we are ignorant about the Dhamma, we will forever be trapped in Samsara. According to the Buddha:

' For a long time, Brothers, have you suffered the death of a mother; for a long time, the death of a father; for a long time, the death of a son; for a long time, the death of a daughter; for a long time, the death of brothers and sisters; for a long time have you undergone the loss of your goods; for a long time have you been afflicted with disease. And because you have experienced the death of a mother, the death of a father, the death of a son, the death of a daughter, the death of brothers and sisters, the loss of goods, the pangs of disease, company of the undesired, you have truly shed more tears upon this long way — hastening from birth to death, from death to birth — than all the waters that are held in the four great seas. ' *(Anguttara Nikaya)* Here the Buddha is describing the Suffering of continuous births and deaths in the world. He was interested in one simple thing: to show people the Way out of all this Suffering.

Why did the Buddha speak in this manner to His disciples? And why did He not make an attempt to solve the problems as to whether the world is eternal or not, whether it is finite or not? Such problems might be exciting and stimulating to those who have the curiosity. But in no way do these problems help a person to overcome Suffering. That is why He swept these problems aside as useless, for the knowledge of such things would not tend to one's wellbeing.

The Buddha, foresaw that to speak on things which were of no practical value, and which were lying beyond the power of comprehension, was a waste of time and energy. He foresaw that to advance hypotheses about such things only served to divert thoughts from their proper channel, hindering spiritual development.

Worldly knowledge and scientific research should be complemented by religious and spiritual values. Otherwise such worldly knowledge does not in any way contribute to one's progress in leading a pure, religious life. Man has come to the stage where his mind, fed by the instruments and fruits of technological advancements, has become obsessed with egoism, craving for power, and greed for material wealth. Without religious values, worldly knowledge and technological advancement can lead to man's downfall and destruction. They will only inflame man's greed which will take on new and terrifying dimensions. On the other hand, when worldly knowledge is harnessed for moral ends, it can bring maximum benefit and happiness for mankind.

# The Last Message of the Buddha

*' When I am gone, my Teaching shall be your Master and Guide. '*

THREE months before His passing away the Buddha addressed His disciples and said; ' I have delivered sermons to you during these forty-five years. You must learn them well and treasure them. You must practise them and teach them to others. This will be of great use for the welfare of the living and for the welfare of those who come after you '

' My years are now full ripe; the life span left is short. I will soon have to leave you. You must be earnest. O monks, be mindful and of pure virtue! Whoever untiringly pursues the Teaching, will go beyond the cycle of birth and death and will make an end of Suffering. '

When Ananda asked the Buddha what would become of the Order after He passed away, the Buddha replied, ' What does the Order expect of me, Ananda? I have preached the Truth without any distinction; for in regard to the Truth, there is no clenched hand in the Teachings of the Buddha.... It may be, Ananda, that to some among you, the thought will come 'The Master's words will soon end; soon we will no longer have a master.' But do not think like this, Ananda. When I am gone, my Teaching and the disciplinary code shall be your Master. '

The Buddha further explained: ' If there is anyone who thinks, 'It is I who will lead the brotherhood', or 'The Order is dependent on me, it is I who should give instructions', the Buddha does not think that He should lead the Order or that the Order is dependent on Him. I have reached the end of my days. Just as a worn-out cart can only be made to move with much additional care, so my body can be kept going only with much additional care. Therefore, Ananda, be a lamp and refuge unto yourselves. Look for no other refuge. Let the Truth be your lamp and your refuge. Seek no refuge elsewhere. '

At the age of eighty, on His birthday, He passed away without showing any worldly supernatural powers. He showed the real nature of component things even in His own life.

When the Buddha passed away into Nibbana, one of His disciples remarked, ' All must depart — all beings that have life must shed their compounded forms. Yes, even a Master such as He, a peerless being, powerful in Wisdom and Enlightenment, even He must pass away. '

The parting words of the Buddha:
' *Appamadena Sampadetha Vaya Dhamma Sankhara* '.
'Work diligently. Component things are impermanent.'

*(Maha Parinibbana Sutta)*

# 3

# AFTER THE BUDDHA

## Does the Buddha Exist After His Death?

*The question: 'Does the Buddha exist after His death or not', is not a new question. The same question was put to the Buddha during His lifetime.*

WHEN a group of ascetics came and asked the same question from certain disciples of the Buddha, they could not get a satisfactory answer from them. Anuradha, a disciple, approached the Buddha and reported to Him about their conversation. Considering the understanding capacity of the questioners, the Buddha usually observed silence at such questions. However in this instance, the Buddha explained to Anuradha in the following manner:

' O Anuradha, what do you think, is the form *(Rupa)* permanent or impermanent? '

' Impermanent, Sir. '

' Is that which is impermanent, painful or pleasant? '

' Painful, Sir. '

' Is it proper to regard that which is impermanent, painful and subject to change as: 'This is mine; this is I, this is my soul or permanent substance? '

' It is not proper, Sir. '

' Is feeling permanent or impermanent? '

' Impermanent, Sir. '

' Is that which is impermanent, painful or pleasant? '

' Painful, Sir. '

' Is it proper to regard that which is impermanent, painful and subject to change as ' This is mine, this is I, this is my soul '? '

' It is not proper, Sir. '

' Are perception, formative tendencies and consciousness, permanent or impermanent? '

' Impermanent, Sir. '

' Is that which is impermanent, painful or pleasant? '

' Painful, Sir. '

' Is it proper to regard that which is impermanent, painful and subject to change as: ' This is mine, this is I, this is my soul' ? '

' It is not proper, Sir. '

' Therefore whatever form, feeling, perception, formative tendencies, consciousness which have been, will be and is now connected with oneself, or with others, gross or subtle, inferior or superior, far or near; all forms, feelings, perceptions, formative tendencies and consciousness should be considered by right knowledge in this way: ' This is not mine; this is not I; this is not my soul. ' Having seen thus, a noble, learned disciple becomes disenchanted with the form, feeling, perception, formative tendencies and consciousness. Becoming disenchanted, he controls his passion and subsequently discards them.'

' Being free from passion he becomes emancipated and insight arises in him: ' I am emancipated. ' He realizes: ' Birth is destroyed, I have lived the holy life and done what had to be done. There is no more birth for me. '

' What do you think, Anuradha, do you regard the form as a Tathagata? '

' No, Sir. '

' O Anuradha, what is your view, do you see a Tathagata in the form? '

' No, Sir. '

' Do you see a Tathagata apart from form? '

' No, Sir. '

' Do you see a Tathagata in feeling, perception, formative tendencies, consciousness? '

' No, Sir. '

' O Anuradha, what do you think, do you regard that which is without form, feeling, perception, formative tendencies and consciousness as a Tathagata? '

' No, Sir. '

' Now, Anuradha, since a Tathagata is not to be found in this very life, is it proper for you to say: 'This noble and supreme one has pointed out and explained these four propositions:

A Tathagata exists after death;

A Tathagata does not exist after death;

A Tathagata exists and yet does not exist after death;

A Tathagata neither exists nor does not exist after death? '

' No Sir. '

' Well and good, Anuradha. Formerly and now also I expound and point out only the truth of Suffering and the cessation of Suffering. ' *(Anuradha Sutta — Samyutta Nikaya.)*

The above dialogue between the Buddha and Anuradha may not be satisfactory to many, since it does not satisfy the inquiring mind of the people. Truth is such that it does not give satisfaction to the emotion and intellect. Truth happens to be the most difficult thing for man to comprehend. It can only be fully comprehended by Insight. Buddhahood is nothing but the embodiment of all the great virtues and supreme enlightenment. That is why Buddhas who could enlighten others are very rare in this world.

# A Successor to the Buddha

*Buddhahood is the highest of all achievements.*

MANY people ask why the Buddha did not appoint a successor. But can any one appoint another to take the place of the Supreme Enlightened One? Attaining Buddhahood is the highest of all achievements that only the wisest man can reach. He is the flower of mankind. To attain this highest position, one must have the qualifications such as self-training, self-discipline, moral background, supreme knowledge, and extra-ordinary compassion towards every living being. Therefore, a person himself must take the trouble to qualify himself in order to attain Buddhahood. For example, a doctor cannot appoint even his own son as doctor unless the son has qualified himself to be a doctor. A lawyer cannot appoint another person as a lawyer unless that person obtains the necessary qualifications. A scientist cannot appoint another person as a scientist unless that person possesses the knowledge of a scientist.

Therefore, the Buddha did not appoint a successor. On the other hand, even if He had done that, the person who was to succeed Him would not have the real qualities of the Buddha and would certainly misuse the authority and mislead the public.

Authority over a religion must be exercised by a person or persons possessing a clear mind, proper understanding, perfection and leading a holy life. Authority should not be exercised by worldly-minded people who have become slaves to sensual pleasures or who crave for worldly material gain or power. Otherwise the sacredness, freedom and truth in a religion could be abused.

# The Future Buddha

*'I am not the first Buddha to come upon this earth; nor shall I be the last. Previously, there were many Buddhas who appeared in this world. In due time, another Buddha will arise in this world, within this world cycle.'*

WHEN the Buddha was about to pass away, Ven. Ananda and many other disciples wept. The Buddha said, ' Enough, Ananda. Do not allow yourself to be troubled. Do not weep. Have I not already told you that it is in the very nature of things that they must pass away. We must be separated from all that is near and dear to us. The foolish man conceives his idea of Self; the wise man sees there is no ground on which to build the Self. Thus the wise man has a right conception of the world. He will conclude that all component things will be dissolved again; but the Truth will always remain. '

The Buddha continued: ' Why should I preserve this body when the body of the excellent law will endure? I am resolved. I have accomplished my purpose and have attended to the work set upon me. Ananda, for a long time you have been very near to me in thoughts, words and acts of much love beyond all measure. You have done well, Ananda. Be earnest in effort and you too will soon be free from bondages! You will be free from sensuality, from delusion, and from ignorance. ' Suppressing his tears, Ananda said to the Buddha, ' Who shall teach us when You are gone? ' And the Buddha advised him to regard His Teaching as the Master.

The Buddha continued again: ' I am not the first Buddha to come upon earth; nor shall I be the last. In due time, another Buddha will arise in this world, a Holy One, a Supremely Enlightened One, endowed with wisdom, in conduct auspicious, knowing the universe, an incomparable leader of men, a master of devas and men. He will reveal to you the same Eternal Truths which I have taught you. He will proclaim a religious life, wholly perfect and pure; such as I now proclaim. '

' How shall we know him? ' asked Ananda. The Buddha replied, ' He will be known as *Maitreya* which means kindness or friendliness. '*

Buddhists believe that those people who at present are doing meritorious deeds by leading a religious life will have a chance to be reborn as human beings in the time of *Maitreya Buddha* and will obtain *Nibbana* identical with that of Gautama Buddha. In this way they will find salvation through the guidance of His Teaching. His Teaching will become a hope of the remote future for everybody. However, according to the Buddha devout religious people can gain this Nibbanic bliss at any time if they really work for it irrespective of whether a Buddha appears or not.

' As long as my disciples lead a pure religious life, so long the world will never become empty of Arahantas. '

*(Maha Parinibbana Sutta)*

---

*In *Buddha Vansa,* 28 names of the previous Buddhas are mentioned, including Gautama the Buddha.

PART TWO

# BUDDHISM: ESSENCE AND COMPARATIVE APPROACHES

# 4

# TIMELESS TRUTH
# OF THE BUDDHA

## The Lion's Roar

*After hearing the Buddha, many decided to give up the wrong
views they previously held regarding their religious way of life.*

BUDDHISM is a beautiful gem of many facets, attracting people
of diverse personalities. Every facet in this gem has tested methods
and approaches that can benefit the Truth seekers with their
various levels of understanding and spiritual maturity.

The Buddha Dhamma is the fruit resulting from a most
intensive search conducted over a long period of time by a
compassionate noble prince whose mission was to help suffering
humanity. Despite being surrounded by all the wealth and luxuries
normally showered on a crown prince, He renounced His luxurious

life and voluntarily embarked on a tough journey to seek the Truth and to find a panacea to cure the sickness of the worldly life with its attendant suffering and unsatisfactoriness. He was bent on finding a solution to alleviate all suffering. In His long search, the prince did not rely on or resort to divine guidance or traditional beliefs as was fashionable in the past. He did an intensive search with a free and open mind, guided solely by His sincerity of purpose, noble resolution, inexhaustible patience, and a truly compassionate heart with the ardent wish to relieve suffering. After six long years of intensive experiment, of trial and error, the noble prince achieved His aim — He gained Enlightenment and gave the world His pristine teachings known as Dhamma or Buddhism.

The Buddha once said, ' Monks, the lion, king of beasts, at eventide comes forth from his lair. He stretches himself. Having done so, he surveys the four quarters in all directions. Having done that, he utters thrice his lion's roar. Having thrice uttered his lion's roar, he sallies forth in search of prey.

' Now, monks, whatever animals hear the sound of the roaring of the lion, king of beasts, for the most part, they are afraid; they fall to quaking and trembling. Those that dwell in holes seek them; water-dwellers make for the water; forest-dwellers enter the forest; birds mount into the air.

' Then whatsoever ruler's elephants in village, town or palace are tethered with stout leather bonds, they burst out and rend those bonds asunder; void their excrements and in panic run to and fro. Thus potent, is the lion, king of beasts, over animals. Of such mighty power and majesty is he.

' Just so, monks, is it when a Buddha arises in the world, an Arahant, a Perfectly Enlightened One, perfect in wisdom and in conduct, wayfarer, Knower of the worlds, the unsurpassed trainer of those who can be trained, teacher of gods and men, a Buddha, an Exalted One. He teaches the Dhamma: 'Such is the nature of concept of Self; this is the way leading to the ending of such a Self. '

'Whatsoever gods there be, they too, on hearing the Dhamma of the *Tathagata,* for the most part are afraid: they fall to quaking and trembling, saying: 'We who thought ourselves permanent are after all impermanent: that we who thought ourselves stable are after all unstable: not to last, though lasting we thought ourselves. So it seems that we are impermanent, unstable, not to last, compassed about with a Self.' Thus potent is a *Tathagata* over the world of gods and men. *(Anguttara Nikaya).*

# What is Buddhism?

*Buddhism is nothing but the NOBLE TRUTH.*

WHAT is Buddhism? This question has puzzled many people who often enquire if Buddhism is a philosophy, a religion, or a way of life. The simple answer is that Buddhism is too vast and too profound to be neatly placed in any single category. Of course, Buddhism includes philosophy and religion and a way of life. But Buddhism goes beyond these categories.

The categories or labels given to Buddhism are like signboards to let the people know what is being presented. If we compare Buddhism to a medicine shop, it will be clear that the signboard on the medicine shop will not cure a person of his sickness. If the medicine is effective, then you can use it to heal yourself without being concerned as to the signboard that merely gives a label for the medicine. Likewise, if the Teaching of the Buddha is effective, then use it and do not be concerned about the label or signboard. Do not try to slip Buddhism into any single category or limit it under any signboard.

Different people living at different times and in different places have given different labels and interpretations to Buddhism. To some people, Buddhism might appear to be only a mass of superstitious practices. To another group of people, Buddhism might be a convenient label to be used for temporal gains. To another group, it is old fashioned. To yet another group, Buddhism will have significance as a system of thought for intellectuals only. To some others, it is a scientific discovery. To the pious and devout Buddhist, Buddhism means his entire life, the fulfilment of all he holds near and dear to him.

Some intellectuals see Buddhism as a product of its Indian environment or as an outgrowth of another kind of Indian religious teaching. Buddhism is nothing but the Noble Truth. It is an intellectual approach to reality. The Buddha's realisation of universal problems did not come through a purely intellectual or rational process but through mental development and purification. The intellectual stance reminiscent of the scientific attitude, surely makes the Buddha absolutely unique among religious teachers of all time. Of course, the high standard of intellectual inquiry and ethical endeavour prevailing at the time in India were prime conditions for the re-emergence of the light of the Dhamma from the darkness of oblivion. Thousands of years of religious and philosophical development had left on the intellectual soil of India a rich and fertile deposit of ideas and ideals which formed the best possible environment into which the seed of the Dhamma could fall. Greece, China, Egypt and Babylonia, for all their loftiness of thought, had not attained the same quality of vision as the forest and mountain-dwelling sages of India. The germ of Enlightenment which had been borne, like a winged seed from distant fields, from worlds in space and time infinitely remote from ours — this very germ of Enlightenment found growth and development in the north-eastern corner of India. This very germ of Enlightenment found its full expression in the experience of the man, Gautama Buddha. The fountainhead of all Buddhism is this experience which is called ' Enlightenment '. With this experience of Enlightenment, the Buddha began His Teaching not with any dogmatic beliefs or mysteries, but with a valid, universal experience, which He gave to the world as universal truth. Therefore, the real definition of Buddhism is NOBLE TRUTH. Remember that the Buddha did not teach from theories. He always taught from a practical standpoint based on His understanding, His Enlightenment, and His realisation of the Truth.

Buddhism began with the Truth embodied over 2500 years ago in the person of Gautama, the Buddha. When the Buddha introduced His teachings, His intention was not to develop the concept of self in man's mind and create more ambition for eternal life and sense pleasure. Rather, His intention was to point out the futility of the worldly life and to show the correct, practical Path to salvation that He discovered.

The original Teachings of the Buddha disclosed the true nature of life and the world. However, a distinction must be made between the Buddha's original Teaching (often called the Dhamma or the Buddha Word) and the religion that developed based on His Teachings.

The Teachings of the Buddha not only started a religion, but inspired the blossoming of a whole civilisation. These Teachings became a great civilizing force that moved through the history of many a culture and nation. Indeed, Buddhism has become one of the greatest civilisations that the world has ever known. It has a wonderful history of achievement in the fields of literature, art, philosophy, psychology, ethics, architecture and culture. In the course of centuries, countless social educational institutions were established in the various nations that were dedicated to the Buddha's Teaching. The history of Buddhism was written in golden letters of brotherhood and goodwill. The religious beliefs and practices turned into a rational, scientific and practical religious way of life for spiritual development from the day the Buddha preached His Teaching and realised the real purpose and meaning of a life and a religion.

## Impact of Buddhism on Civilization

Today Buddhism remains as a great civilizing force in the modern world. As a civilizing force, Buddhism awakens the self-respect and feeling of self-responsibility of countless people and stirs up the energy of many a nation. It fosters spiritual progress by appealing to man's own thinking powers. It promotes in people the sense of tolerance by remaining free from religious and national narrowness and fanaticism. It tames the wild and refines the citizens to be clear and sober in mind. In short, Buddhism produces the feeling of self-reliance by teaching that the whole destiny of man lies in his own hand, and that he himself possesses the faculty of developing his own energy and insight in order to reach the highest goal.

For over two thousand years, Buddhism has satisfied the spiritual needs of nearly one-third of mankind. Today the appeal of Buddhism is as strong as ever. The Teachings of the Buddha remain among the richest spiritual resources of mankind because they lift the horizon of human effort to a higher level beyond a mere dedication to man's insatiable needs and appetites. Owing to its breadth of perspective, the Buddha's vision of life has a tendency to attract intellectuals who have exhausted their own (and others') minds. However, the fruit of the Buddha's vision is something more than intellectual gymnastics or solace for the intellectually effete.

Another appeal that Buddhism has is that it is realistic and offers a realistic view of life and of the world. It does not entice people into living in a fool's paradise, nor does it frighten and agonize people with all kinds of imaginary fears and guilt-feelings. Buddhism tells us exactly and objectively what we are and what the world around us is, and shows us the way to perfect freedom, peace, tranquility and happiness.

If humanity today is to be saved from reacting against the moral standards taught by religions, Buddhism is a most effective vehicle. Buddhism is the religion of humanity, whose founder was a man who sought no divine revelation or intervention in the formulation of His Teachings. In an age when man is overwhelmed by his success in the control of the material universe, man might like to look back and take stock of the achievements he has made in controlling the most difficult of all phenomena: his own self. It is in this quest that the modern man will find in Buddhism an answer to his numerous problems and doubts.

Today, Buddhism appeals to the West because it has no dogmas, and it satisfies both the reason and the heart alike. It insists on self-reliance coupled with tolerance for others. It embraces modern scientific discoveries if they are for constructive purposes. Buddhism points to man alone as the creator of his present life and as the sole designer of his own destiny. Such is the nature of Buddhism.

The Buddha's message of peace and compassion radiated in all directions and the millions who came under its influence adopted it very readily as a new way of religious life.

**Buddhist Contribution to Mankind**

Buddhism as a religion has served man's hopes and aspirations well; it has fostered within the social organism a commendable way of life and a communal spirit marked by endeavours towards peace and contentment. It has been in the forefront of human welfare.

Even in politics it was registered on many occasions as a significant break-through in fair treatment, democratic procedures and regard for basic, moral values. Buddhism has given a distinct flavour to the cultures of the Orient. Buddhism has supplied fine and ethical basic attitudes amongst the people who adopted it in one form or another.

Indeed, the immense potential of Buddhism has not been realised at all by most people who have adopted it only to a limited extent. The personal and general potential has been overshadowed by the actual contributions of Buddhism to art and literature. But the greatest potential of Buddhism lies in its rationalism which needs no revivals of any sort. (Reason, though often overruled to everyone's regret, is something that belongs to man, to civilized man, no matter how obscured it may be by the claims of other facets of human nature such as emotions.) If there is a renewal of and rededication to fundamental values in Buddhism, it is not through uncertain or occasional revelations or through gearing it to the dictates of secular or supernatural authority. Buddhism carries the seeds of self-renewal within itself.

The Buddha's contribution to the social and spiritual progress of mankind was so remarkable that His message which spread to several countries in Asia won the love and affection of the people with a devotion that was unprecedented.

# The Ultimate Truth

*The Ultimate Truth can be found in the Teaching of the Buddha.*

BUDDHISM recognises two kinds of Truth. The apparent conventional truth and the real or ultimate Truth. The ultimate Truth can be realized only through meditation, and not theorizing or speculating.

The Buddha's Teaching is the Ultimate Truth of the world. Buddhism, however, is not a revealed or an organised religion. It is the first example of the purely scientific approach applied to questions concerning the ultimate nature of existence. This timeless Teaching was discovered by the Buddha Himself without the help of any divine agency. This same teaching is strong enough to face any challenge without changing the basic principles of the doctrine. Any religion that is forced to change or adjust its original Teachings to suit the modern world, is a religion that has no firm foundation and no ultimate truth in it. Buddhism can maintain the Truth of the original Teaching of the Master even under the difficult conditions prevailing in the modern world. The Buddha did not introduce certain personal or worldly practices which have no connection with morality or religious observances. To the Buddha, such practices have no religious value. We must make the distinction between what the Buddha taught and what people preach and practise in the name of Buddhism.

Every religion consists of not only the teachings of the founder of that religion but also the rites and ceremonies which have grown up around the basic core of the teachings. These rituals and ceremonies have their origins in the cultural practices of the people who accepted the religion. Usually the founders of the great religions do not lay down precise rules about the rituals to be observed. But religious leaders who come after them formalize the religion and set up exacting codes of behaviour which the followers are not allowed to deviate from.

Even the religion which we call ' Buddhism ' is very different in its external practices from what the Buddha and His early followers carried out. Centuries of cultural and environmental influence have made Burmese, Thai, Chinese, Tibetan, Sri Lankan and Japanese Buddhism different. But these practices are not in conflict, because the Buddha taught that while the Truth remains absolute, the physical manifestation of this truth can differ according to the way of life of those who profess it.

A few hundred years after His passing away, the disciples of the Buddha organized a religion around the Teachings of the Master. While organising the religion, they incorporated, among other concepts and beliefs, various types of miracles, mysticism, fortune-telling, charms, talismans, mantras, prayers and many rites and rituals that were not found in the original Teaching. When these extraneous religious beliefs and practices were introduced, many people neglected to develop the most important practices found in the original Teaching: self-discipline, self-restraint, cultivation of morality and spiritual development. Instead of practising the original Teaching, they gave more of their attention and effort to self-protection from evil spirits and sought after prosperity or good luck. Gradually, people began to lose interest in the original Teachings and became more interested in discovering ways and means of getting rid of the so-called misfortunes or bad influences of stars, black magic, and sickness. In this manner, through time the religious practices and beliefs degenerated, being confined to worldly pursuits. Even today, many people believe that they can get rid of their difficulties through the influence of external powers. People still cling to this belief: hence they neglect to cultivate the strength of their will-power, intelligence, understanding and other related human qualities. In other words, people started to abuse their human intelligence by following those beliefs and practices in the name of Buddhism. They also polluted the purity of the Buddha's message.

Thus the modern religion we see in many countries is the product of normal human beings living in a country and adjusting to various social and cultural environments. However, Buddhism as a religion did not begin as a superworldly system that came down from heaven. Rather it was born and evolved through a long historical process. In its process of evolution, many people slowly moved away from the original Teachings of the founder and started different new schools or sects. All the other existing religions also face the same situation.

One should not come to a hasty conclusion either by judging the validity of a religion or by condemning the religion simply by observing what people perform through their blind faith in the name of that religion. To understand the real nature of a religion one must study and investigate the original Teachings of the founder of that religion.

In the face of the profusion of ideas and practices which were later developments, it is useful for us to return to the positive and timeless Dhamma taught by the Buddha. Whatever people believe and practise in the name of Buddhism the basic Teachings of the Buddha still exist in the original Buddhist texts.

# Two Main Schools of Buddhism

*The real followers of the Buddha can practise this religion without adhering to any school or sect.*

A few hundred years after the Buddha's passing away, there arose eighteen different schools or sects all of which claimed to represent the original Teachings of the Buddha. The differences between these schools were basically due to various interpretations of the Teachings of the Buddha. Over a period of time, these schools gradually merged into two main schools: Theravada and Mahayana. Today, a majority of the followers of Buddhism are divided into these two schools.

Basically Mahayana Buddhism grew out of the Buddha's teaching that each individual carries within himself the potential for Buddhahood. Theravadins say that this potential can be realised through individual effort. Mahayanists, on the other hand, believe that they can seek salvation through the intervention of other superior beings called Bodhisattas. According to them, Bodhisattas are future Buddhas who, out of compassion for their fellow human beings, have delayed their own attainment of Buddhahood until they have helped others towards liberation. In spite of this basic difference, however, it must be stressed that doctrinally there is absolutely no disagreement concerning the Dhamma as contained in the sacred Tripitaka texts. Because Buddhists have been encouraged by the Master to carefully inquire after the truth, they have been free to interpret the scriptures according to their understanding. But above all, both Mahayana and Theravada are one in their reverence for the Buddha.

---

*For a short, excellent exposition on this topic, read Dr. W. Rahula, ' Theravada and Mahayana Buddhism ' published by The Buddhist Missionary Society.*

The areas of agreement between the two schools are as follows:

1. Both accept Sakyamuni Buddha as the Teacher.
2. The Four Noble Truths are exactly the same in both schools.
3. The Eightfold Path is exactly the same in both schools.
4. The *Pattica-Samuppada* or teaching on Dependent Origination is the same in both schools.
5. Both reject the idea of a supreme being who created and governed this world.
6. Both accept *Anicca, Dukkha, Anatta* and *Sila, Samadhi, Panna* without any difference.

Some people are of the view that Theravada is selfish because it teaches that people should seek their own salvation. But how can a selfish person gain Enlightenment? Both schools accept the three *Yana* or *Bodhi* and consider the Bodhisatta Ideal as the highest. The Mahayana has created many mystical Bodhisattas, while the Theravada believes that a Bodhisatta is a man amongst us who devotes his entire life for the attainment of perfection, and ultimely becomes a fully Enlightened Buddha for the well-being and happiness of the world.

The terms Hinayana (Small Vehicle) and Mahayana (Great Vehicle) are not known in the Theravada Pali literature. They are not found in the Pali Canon *(Tripitaka)* or in the Commentaries on the *Tripitaka.*

Theravada Buddhists follow orthodox religious traditions that had prevailed in India two thousand five hundred years ago. They perform their religious services in the Pali language. They also expect to attain the final goal *(Nibbana)* by becoming a Supreme Enlightened Buddha, Paceka Buddha, or an Arahant (the highest stage of sainthood). The majority of them prefer the Arahantahood. Buddhists in Sri Lanka, Burma, and Thailand belong to this school. Mahayanists have changed the old religious customs. Their practices are in accordance with the customs and traditions of the countries where they live. Mahayanists perform their religious services in their mother tongue. They expect to attain the final goal *(Nibbana)* by becoming Buddhas. Hence, they honour both the Buddha and Bodhisatta (one who is destined to be a Buddha) with the same respect. Buddhists in China, Japan and Korea belong to this school. Most of those in Tibet and Mongolia follow another school of Buddhism which is known as Vajrayana. Buddhist scholars believe that this school inclines more towards the Mahayana sect.

It is universally accepted by scholars that the terms *Hinayana* and *Mahayana* are later invention. Historically speaking, the *Theravada* already existed long before these terms came into being. That *Theravada,* considered to be the original teaching of the Buddha, was introduced to Sri Lanka and established there in the 3rd century B.C., during the time of Emperor Asoka of India. At that time there was nothing called *Mahayana.* *Mahayana* as such appeared much later, about the beginning of the Christian Era. Buddhism that went to Sri Lanka, with its Tripitaka and Commentaries, in the 3rd Century B.C., remained there intact as *Theravada,* and did not come into the scene of the *Hinayana — Mahayana* dispute that developed later in India. It seems therefore not legitimate to include *Theravada* in either of these two categories. However, after the inauguration of the World Fellowship of Buddhists in 1950, well-informed people, both in the East and in the West, use the term *Theravada,* and not the term *Hinayana,* with reference to Buddhism prevalent in South-east Asian countries. There are still outmoded people who use the term *Hinayana.* In fact, the *Samdhi Nirmorcana* Sutra (a Mahayana Sutra) clearly says that the *Sravakayana — Theravada* and the *Mahayana* constitute one *Yana* (ekayana) and that they are not two different and distinct ' vehicles '. Although different schools of Buddhism held different opinions on the teaching of the Buddha, they never had any violence or blod shed for more than two thousands years. This is the uniqueness of Buddhist tolerance.

# 5

## BASIC DOCTRINES

### Tri-Pitaka (or Tipitaka)

*Tripitaka is the collection of the teachings of the Buddha over 45 years in the Pali language, and it consists of Sutta — conventional teaching, Vinaya — disciplinary code, and Abhidhamma — moral psychology.*

THE Tripitaka was compiled and arranged in its present form by those Arahants who had immediate contact with the Master Himself.

The Buddha has passed away, but the sublime Dhamma which He unreservedly bequeathed to humanity still exists in its pristine purity.

Although the Master has left no written records of His Teachings, His distinguished disciples preserved them by committing to memory and transmitting them orally from generation to generation.

Immediately after the final passing away of the Buddha, 500 distinguished Arahants held a convention known as the First Buddhist Council to rehearse the Doctrine taught by the Buddha. Venerable Ananda, the faithful attendant of the Buddha who had the special privilege of hearing all the discourses the Buddha ever uttered, recited the Dhamma, whilst the Venerable Upali recited the Vinaya, the rules of conduct for the Sangha.

One hundred years after the First Buddhist Council, during King Kalasoka, some disciples saw the need to change certain minor rules. The orthodox monks said that nothing should be changed while the others insisted on modifying some disciplinary rules *(Vinaya)*. Finally, the formation of different schools of Buddhism germinated after this council. And in the Second Council, only matters pertaining to the Vinaya were discussed and no controversy about the Dhamma was reported.

In the 3rd Century B.C. during the time of Emperor Asoka, the Third Council was held to discuss the differences of opinion held by the Sangha community. At this Council the differences were not confined to the Vinaya but were also connected with the Dhamma. At the end of this Council, the President of the Council, Ven. Moggaliputta Tissa, compiled a book called *Kathavatthu* refuting the heretical, false views and theories held by some disciples. The teaching approved and accepted by this Council was known as *Theravada*. The *Abhidhamma Pitaka* was discussed and included at this Council. The Council which was held in Sri Lanka in 80 B.C. is known as the 4th Council under the patronage of the pious King Vattagamini Abbaya. It was at this time in Sri Lanka that the *Tripitaka* was first committed to writing.

The *Tripitaka* consists of three sections of the Buddha's Teachings. They are the Discipline *(Vinaya Pitaka),* the Discourse *(Sutta Pitaka),* and Ultimate Doctrine *(Abhidhamma Pitaka).*

The *Vinaya Pitaka* mainly deals with the rules and regulations of the Order of monks *(Bhikkhus)* and nuns *(Bhikkhunis)*. It describes in detail the gradual development of the *Sasana (Dispensation)*. It also gives an account of the life and ministry of the Buddha. Indirectly it reveals some useful information about ancient history, Indian customs, arts, sciences, etc.

For nearly twenty-years since His Enlightenment, the Buddha did not lay down rules for the control of the Sangha. Later, as the occasion arose, the Buddha promulgated rules for the future discipline of the Sangha.

This Pitaka consists of the five following books:—

1. *Parajika Pali*          (Major Offences)
2. *Pacittiya Pali*         (Minor Offences)
3. *Mahavagga Pali*         (Greater Section)
4. *Cullavagga Pali*        (Smaller Section)
5. *Parivara Pali*          (Epitome of the Vinaya)

**Sutta Pitaka**

The Sutta Pitaka consists chiefly of discourses delivered by the Buddha Himself on various occasions. There are also a few discourses delivered by some of His distinguished disciples, such as the Venerables Sariputta, Ananda, Moggallana, etc., included in it. It is like a book of prescriptions, as the sermons embodied therein were expounded to suit the different occasions and the temperaments of various persons. There may be seemingly contradictory statements, but they should not be misconstrued as they were opportunely uttered by the Buddha to suit a particular purpose.

This *Pitaka* is divided into five *Nikayas* or collections, viz:—

1. *Digha Nikaya* (Collection of Long Discourses)
2. *Majjhima Nikaya* (Collection of Middle-length Discourses)
3. *Samyutta Nikaya* (Collection of Kindred Sayings)

4. *Anguttara Nikaya* (Collection of Discourses arranged in accordance with number)
5. *Khuddaka Nikaya* (Smaller Collection)

The fifth is subdivided into fifteen books:—

1. *Khuddaka Patha* (Shorter Texts)
2. *Dhammapada* (The Way of Truth)
3. *Udana* (Heartfelt sayings or Paeons of Joy)
4. *Iti Vuttaka* (' Thus said ' Discourses)
5. *Sutta Nipata* (Collected Discourses)
6. *Vimana Vatthu* (Stories of Celestial Mansions)
7. *Peta Vatthu* (Stories of Petas)
8. *Theragatha* (Psalms of the Brethren)
9. *Therigatha* (Psalms of the Sisters)
10. *Jataka* (Birth Stories)
11. *Niddesa* (Expositions)
12. *Patisambhida* (Analytical Knowledge)
13. *Apadana* (Lives of Saints)
14. *Buddhavamsa* (The History of Buddha)
15. *Cariya Pitaka* (Modes of Conduct)

## Abhidhamma Pitaka

The *Abhidhamma* is, to a deep thinker, the most important and interesting, as it contains the profound philosophy of the Buddha's teaching in contrast to the illuminating but simpler discourses in the Sutta Pitaka.

In the Sutta Pitaka one often finds references to individual, being, etc., but in the Abhidhamma, instead of such conventional terms, we meet with ultimate terms, such as aggregates, mind, matter, etc.

In the Sutta is found the *Vohara Desana* (Conventional Teaching), whilst in the Abhidhamma is found the *Paramattha Desana* (Ultimate Doctrine).

In the Abhidhamma everything is analysed and explained in detail, and as such it is called *analytical doctrine (Vibhajja Vada)*.

Four ultimate things *(Paramattha)* are enumerated in the Abhidhamma. They are *Citta,* (Consciousness), *Cetasika* (Mental concomitants), *Rupa* (Matter) and *Nibbana.*

The so-called being is microscopically analysed and its component parts are minutely described. Finally the ultimate goal and the method to achieve it is explained with all necessary details.

The Abhidhamma Pitaka is composed of the following works:—

1. *Dhamma-Sangani* (Enumeration of Phenomena)
2. *Vibhanga* (The Book of the Treatises)
3. *Katha Vatthu* (Point of Controversy)
4. *Puggala Pannatti* (Description of Individuals)
5. *Dhatu Katha* (Discussion with reference to Elements)
6. *Yamaka* (The Book of Pairs)
7. *Patthana* (The Book of Relations)

According to another classification, mentioned by the Buddha Himself, the whole Teaching is ninefold, namely — 1. *Sutta,* 2. *Geyya,* 3. *Veyyakarama,* 4. *Gatha,* 5. *Udana,* 6. *Itivuttaka,* 7. *Jataka,* 8. *Abbhutadhamma,* 9. *Vedalla.*

1. *Sutta* — These are the short, medium, and long discourses expounded by the Buddha on various occasions, such as *Mangala Sutta* (Discourse on Blessings), *Ratana Sutta* (The Jewel Discourse) *Metta Sutta* (Discourse on Goodwill), etc.
    According to the Commentary the whole Vinaya Pitaka is also included in this division.

2. *Geyya* — These are discourses mixed with *Gathas* or verses, such as the *Sagathavagga* of the *Samyutta Nikaya.*

3. *Veyyakarana* — Lit. exposition. The whole Abhidhamma Pitaka, discourses without verses, and everything that is not included in the remaining eight divisions belong to this class.

4. *Gatha* — These include verses found in the *Dhammapada* (Way of Truth), *Theragatha* (Psalms of the Brethren), *Therigatha* (Psalms of the Sisters), and those isolated verses which are not classed amongst the *Sutta*.

5. *Udana* — These are the 'Paeans of Joy' found in the *Udana,* one of the divisions of the *Khuddaka Nikaya.*

6. *Itivuttaka* — These are the 112 discourses which commence with the phrase — 'Thus the Blessed One has said'. *Itivuttaka* is one of the fifteen books that comprise the *Khuddaka Nikaya.*

7. *Jataka* — These are the 547 birth-stories related by the Buddha in connection with His previous births.

8. *Abbhutadhamma* — These are the few discourses that deal with wonderful and marvellous things, as for example the *Acchariya-Abbhutadhamma Sutta* of the *Majjhima Nikaya* (No. 123).

9. *Vedalla* — These are the pleasurable discourses, such as *Chulla Vedalla, Maha Vedalla* (M.N. Nos 43, 44), *Samma Ditthi Sutta* (M.N. No. 9), etc. In some of these discourses, the answers given to certain questions were put with a feeling of joy.

# What is Abhidhamma?

*Abhidhamma is the analytical doctrine of mental faculties and elements.*

THE *Abhidhamma Pitaka* contains the profound moral psychology and philosophy of the Buddha's teaching, in contrast to the simpler discourses in the *Sutta Pitaka.*

The knowledge gained from the *sutta* can certainly help us in overcoming our difficulties, as well as in developing our moral conduct and training the mind. Having such knowledge will enable one to lead a life which is peaceful, respectable, harmless and noble. By listening to the discourses, we develop understanding of the Dhamma and can mould our daily lives accordingly. The concepts behind certain words and terms used in the *Sutta Pitaka* are, however, subject to changes and should be interpreted within the context of the social environment prevailing at the Buddha's time. The concepts used in the *sutta* are like the conventional words and terms lay people use to express scientific subjects. While concepts in the *sutta* are to be understood in the conventional sense, those used in the *Abhidhamma* must be understood in the ultimate sense. The concepts expressed in the *Abhidhamma* are like the precise scientific words and terms used by scientists to prevent misinterpretations.

It is only in the *Abhidhamma* that explanations are given on how and at which mental beats a person can create good and bad *karmic* thoughts, according to his desires and other mental states. Clear explanations of the nature of the different mental faculties and precise analytical interpretations of the elements can be found in this important collection of discourses.

Understanding the Dhamma through the knowledge gained from the *sutta* is like the knowledge acquired from studying the prescriptions for different types of sicknesses. Such knowledge when applied can certainly help to cure certain types of sicknesses. On the other hand, a qualified physician, with his precise knowledge, can diagnose a wider range of sicknesses and discover their causes. This specialized knowledge puts him in a better position to prescribe more effective remedies. Similarly, a person who has studied the *Abhidhamma* can better understand the nature of the mind and analyse the mental attitudes which cause a human being to commit mistakes and develop the will to avoid evil.

The *Abhidhamma* teaches that the egoistic beliefs and other concepts such as ' *I* ', ' *you* ', ' *man* ' and ' *the world* ', which we use in daily conversation, do not adequately describe the *real* nature of existence. The conventional concepts do not reflect the fleeting nature of pleasures, uncertainties, impermanence of every component thing, and the conflict among the elements and energies intrinsic in all animate or inanimate things. The *Abhidhamma* doctrine gives a clear exposition of the ultimate nature of man and brings the analysis of the human condition further than other studies known to man.

The *Abhidhamma* deals with realities existing in the ultimate sense, or *paramattha dhamma* in Pali. There are four such realities:

1. *Citta,* mind or consciousness, defined as ' that which knows or experiences ' an object. *Citta* occurs as distinct momentary states of consciousness.

2. *Cetasika,* the mental factors that arise and occur along with the *citta.*

3. *Rupa,* physical phenomenon or material form.

4. *Nibbana,* the unconditioned state of bliss which is the final goal.

*Citta,* the *cetasika,* and *rupa* are conditioned realities. They arise because of conditions, and will disappear when the conditions sustaining them cease to continue to do so. They are impermanent states. *Nibbana,* on the other hand, is an unconditioned reality. It does not arise and, therefore, does not fall away. These four realities can be experienced regardless of the names we may choose to give them. Other than these realities, everything — be it within ourselves or without, whether in the past, present or future, whether coarse or subtle, low or lofty, far or near — is a concept and not an ultimate reality.

*Citta, cetisaka,* and *Nibbana* are also called *nama. Nibbana* is an unconditioned *nama.* The two conditioned *nama,* that is, *cita* and *cetasika,* together with *rupa* (form), make up psychophysical organisms, including human beings. Both mind and matter, or *nama-rupa,* are analysed in *Abhidhamma* as though under a microscope. Events connected with the process of birth and death are explained in detail. The *Abhidhamma* clarifies intricate points of the Dhamma and enables the arising of an understanding of reality, thereby setting forth in clear terms the Path of Emancipation. The realization we gain from the *Abhidhamma* with regard to our lives and the world is not in a conventional sense, but absolute reality.

The clear exposition of thought processes in *Abhidhamma* cannot be found in any other psychological treatise either in the east or west. Consciousness is defined, while thoughts are analysed and classified mainly from an ethical standpoint. The composition of each type of consciousness is set forth in detail. The fact that consciousness flows like a stream, a view propounded by psychologists like William James, becomes extremely clear to one who understands the *Abhidhamma*. In addition, a student of *Abhidhamma* can fully comprehend the *Anatta* (No-soul) doctrine, which is important both from a philosophical and ethical standpoint.

The *Abhidhamma* explains the process of rebirth in various planes after the occurrence of death without anything to pass from one life to another. This explanation provides support to the doctrine of *Kamma* and Rebirth. It also gives a wealth of details about the mind, as well as the units of mental and material forces, properties of matter, sources of matter, relationship of mind and matter.

In the *Abhidhammattha Sangaha,* a manual of *Abhidhamma,* there is a brief exposition of the ' Law of Dependent Origination ', followed by a descriptive account of the Causal Relations which finds no parallel in any other study of the human condition anywhere else in the world. Because of its analytics and profound expositions, the *Abhidhamma* is not a subject of fleeting interest designed for the superficial reader.

To what extent can we compare modern psychology with the analysis provided in the *Abhidhamma?* Modern psychology, limited as it is, comes within the scope of *Abhidhamma* in so far as it deals with the mind — with thoughts, thought processes, and mental states. The difference lies in the fact that *Abhidhamma* does not accept the concept of a psyche or a soul.

The analysis of the nature of the mind given in the *Abhidhamma* is not available through any other source. Even modern psychologists are very much in the dark with regards to subjects like mental impulses or mental beats *(Javana Citta)* as discussed in the *Abhidhamma*. Dr. Graham Howe, an eminent Harley Street psychologist, wrote in his book, the *Invisible Anatomy:*

' In the course of their work many psychologists have found, as the pioneer work of C.G. Jung has shown, that we are near to [the] Buddha. To read a little Buddhism is to realise that the Buddhists knew two thousand five hundred years ago far more about our modern problems of psychology than they have yet been given credit for. They studied these problems long ago, and found the answers too. We are now rediscovering the Ancient Wisdom of the East. '

Some scholars assert that the *Abhidhamma* is not the teaching of the Buddha, but it grew out of the commentaries on the basic teachings of the Buddha. These commentaries are said to be the work of great scholar monks. Tradition, however, attributes the nucleus of the *Abhidhamma* to the Buddha Himself.

Commentators state that the Buddha, as a mark of gratitude to His mother who was born as a deva in a celestial plane, preached the *Abhidhamma* to His mother together with other devas continuously for three months. The principal topics *(matika)* of the advanced teaching, such as moral states *(kusala dhamma)* and immoral states *(akusala dhamma),* were then repeated by the Buddha to Venerable Sariputta Thera, who subsequently elaborated them and later compiled them into six books.

From ancient times there were controversies as to whether the *Abhidhamma* was really taught by the Buddha. While this discussion may be interesting for academic purposes, what is important is for us to experience and understand the realities described in the *Abhidhamma*. One will realize for oneself that such profound and consistently verifiable truths can only emanate from a supremely enlightened source — from a Buddha. Much of what is contained in the *Abhidhamma* is also found in the *Sutta Pitaka,* and such sermons had never been heard until they were first uttered by the Buddha. Therefore, those who claim that the Buddha was not the source of the *Abhidhamma* would have to say the same thing about the *Sutta.* Such a statement, of course, cannot be supported by evidence.

According to the Theravada tradition, the essence, fundamentals and framework of the *Abhidhamma* are ascribed to the Buddha, although the tabulations and classifications may have been the work of later disciples. What is important is the essence. It is this that we would try to experience for ourselves. The Buddha Himself clearly took this stand of using the knowledge of the *Abhidhamma* to clarify many existing psychological, metaphysical and philosophical problems. Mere intellectual quibbling about whether the Buddha taught the *Abhidhamma* or not will not help us to understand reality.

The question is also raised whether the *Abhidhamma* is essential for Dhamma practice. The answer to this will depend on the individual who undertakes the practice. People vary in their levels of understanding, their temperaments and spiritual development. Ideally, all the different spiritual faculties should be harmonized, but some people are quite contented with devotional practices based on faith, while others are keen on developing penetrative insight. The *Abhidhamma* is most useful to those who want to understand the Dhamma in greater depth and detail. It aids the development of insight into the three characteristics of existence — impermanence, unsatisfactoriness, and non-self. It is useful not only for the periods devoted to formal meditation, but also during the rest of the day when we are engaged in various mundane chores. We derive great benefit from the study of the

*Abhidhamma* when we experience absolute reality. In addition, a comprehensive knowledge of the *Abhidhamma* is useful for those engaged in teaching and explaining the Dhamma. In fact the real meaning of the most important Buddhist terminologies such as *Dhamma, Kamma, Samsara, Sankhara, Paticca Samuppada* and *Nibbana* cannot be understood without a knowledge of *Abhidhamma.*

# Mind and Matter *(Nama-Rupa)*

*' What is mind? No matter. What is matter? Never mind. '*

ACCORDING to Buddhism, life is a combination of mind *(nama)* and matter *(rupa)*. Mind consists of the combination of sensations, perceptions, volitional activities and consciousness. Matter consists of the combination of the four elements of solidity, fluidity, motion and heat.

Life is the co-existence of mind and matter. Decay is the lack of co-ordination of mind and matter. Death is the separation of mind and matter. Rebirth is the recombination of mind and matter. After the passing away of the physical body *(matter)*, the mental forces *(mind)* recombine and assume a new combination in a different material form and condition another existence.

The relation of mind to matter is like the relation of a battery to an engine of a motor car. The battery helps to start the engine. The engine helps to charge the battery. The combination helps to run the motor car. In the same manner, matter helps the mind to function and the mind helps to set matter in motion.

Buddhism teaches that life is not the property of matter alone, and that the life-process continues or flows as a result of cause and effect. The mental and material elements that compose sentient beings from amoeba to elephant and also to man, existed previously in other forms.

Although some people hold the view that life originates in matter alone, the greatest scientists have accepted that mind precedes matter in order for life to originate. In Buddhism, this concept is called 'relinking consciousness'.

Each of us, in the ultimate sense, is mind and matter, a compound of mental and material phenomena, and nothing more. Apart from these realities that go to form the *nama-rupa* compound, there is no self, or soul. The mind part of the compound is what experiences an object. The matter part does not experience anything. When the body is injured, it is not the body that feels the pain, but the mental side. When we are hungry it is not the stomach that feels the hunger but again the mind. However, mind cannot eat the food to ease the hunger. The mind and its factors, makes the body digest the food. Thus neither the *nama* nor the *rupa* has any efficient power of its own. One is dependent on the other; one supports the other. Both mind and matter arise because of conditions and perish immediately, and this is happening every moment of our lives. By studying and experiencing these realities we will get insight into: (1) what we truly are; (2) what we find around us; (3) how and why we react to what is within and around us; and (4) what we should aspire to reach as a spiritual goal.

To gain insight into the nature of the psycho-physical life is to realise that life is an illusion, a mirage or a bubble, a mere process of becoming and dissolving, or arising and passing away. Whatever exists, arises from causes and conditions.

# Four Noble Truths

*Why are we here? Why are we not happy with our lives? What is the cause of our unsatisfactoriness? How can we see the end of unsatisfactoriness and experience eternal peace?*

THE Buddha's Teaching is based on the Four Noble Truths. To realise these Truths is to realise and penetrate into the true nature of existence, including the full knowledge of oneself. When we recognise that all phenomenal things are transitory, are subject to suffering and are void of any essential reality, we will be convinced that true and enduring happiness cannot be found in material possessions and worldly achievement, that true happiness must be sought only through mental purity and the cultivation of wisdom.

The Four Noble Truths are a very important aspect of the teaching of the Buddha. The Buddha has said that it is because we fail to understand the Four Noble Truths that we have continued to go round in the cycle of birth and death. In the very first sermon of the Buddha, the *Dhammachakka Sutta,* which He gave to the five monks at the Deer Park in Sarnath was on the Four Noble Truths and the Eightfold Path. What are the Four Noble Truths? They are as follows:

The Noble Truth of *Dukkha*
The Noble Truth of the Cause of *Dukkha*
The Noble Truth of the End of *Dukkha*
The Noble Truth of the path leading to the End of *Dukkha*

There are many ways of understanding the Pali word ' *Dukkha* '. It has generally been translated as ' suffering ' or ' unsatisfactoriness ', but this term as used in the Four Noble Truths has a deeper and wider meaning. *Dukkha* contains not only the ordinary meaning of suffering, but also includes deeper ideas such as imperfection, pain, impermanence, disharmony, discomfort, irritation, or awareness of incompleteness and insufficiency. By all means, *Dukkha* includes physical and mental suffering: birth, decay, disease, death, to be united with the unpleasant, to be separated from the pleasant, not to get what one desires. However, many people do not realise that even during the moments of joy and happiness, there is *Dukkha* because these moments are all impermanent states and will pass away when conditions change. Therefore, the truth of *Dukkha* encompasses the whole of existence, in our happiness and sorrow, in every aspect of our lives. As long as we live, we are very profoundly subjected to this truth.

Some people may have the impression that viewing life in terms of *Dukkha* is a rather pessimistic way of looking at life. This is not a pessimistic but a realistic way of looking at life. If one is suffering from a disease and refuses to recognise the fact that one is ill, and as a result of which refuses to seek for treatment, we will not consider such a mental attitude as being optimistic, but merely as being foolish. Therefore, by being both optimistic or pessimistic, one does not really understand the nature of life, and is therefore unable to tackle life's problems in the right perspective. The Four Noble Truths begin with the recognition of *Dukkha* and then proceed to analyse its cause and find its cure. Had the Buddha stopped at the Truth of *Dukkha,* then one may say Buddhism has identified the problem but has not given the cure; if such is the case, then the human situation is hopeless. However, not only is the Truth of *Dukkha* recognised, the Buddha proceeded to analyse its cause and the way to cure it. How can Buddhism be considered to be pessimistic if the cure to the problem is known? In fact, it is a teaching which is filled with hope.

In addition, even though *Dukkha* is a noble truth, it does not mean that there is no happiness, enjoyment and pleasure in life. There is, and the Buddha has taught various methods with which we can gain more happiness in our daily life. However, in the final analysis, the fact remains that the pleasure or happiness which we experience in life is impermanent. We may enjoy a happy situation, or the good company of someone we love, or we enjoy youth and health. Sooner or later, when these states change we experience suffering. Therefore, while there is every reason to feel glad when one experiences happiness, one should not cling to these happy states or be side-tracked and forget about working one's way to complete Liberation.

If we wish to cure ourselves from suffering, we must first identify its cause. According to the Buddha, craving or desire (*tanha* or *raga*) is the cause of suffering. This is the Second Noble Truth. People crave for pleasant experiences, crave for material things, crave for eternal life, and when disappointed, crave for eternal death. They are not only attached to sensual pleasures, wealth and power, but also to ideas, views, opinions, concepts, beliefs. And craving is linked to ignorance, that is, not seeing things as they really are, or failing to understand the reality of experience and life. Under the delusion of Self and not realising *Anatta* (non-Self), a person clings to things which are impermanent, changeable, perishable. The failure to satisfy one's desires through these things causes disappointments and suffering.

### The Danger of Selfish Desire

Craving is a fire which burns in all beings: every activity is motivated by desire. They range from the simple physical desire of animals to the complex and often artificially stimulated desires of the civilised man. To satisfy desire, animals prey upon one another, and human beings fight, kill, cheat, lie and perform various forms of unwholesome deeds. Craving is a powerful mental force present in all forms of life, and is the chief cause of the ills in life. It is this craving that leads to repeated births in the cycle of existence.

Once we have realised the cause of suffering, we are in the position to put an end to suffering. So, how do we put an end to suffering? Eliminate it at its root by the removal of craving in the mind. This is the Third Noble Truth. The state where craving ceases is known as *Nibbana*. The word *Nibbana* is composed of ' *ni* ' and ' *vana* ', meaning the departure from or end of craving. This is a state which is free from suffering and rounds of rebirth. This is a state which is not subjected to the laws of birth, decay and death. This state is so sublime that no human language can express it. *Nibbana* is Unborn, Unoriginated, Uncreated, Unformed. If there were not this Unborn, this

Unoriginated, this Uncreated, this Unformed, then escape from the conditioned world is not possible.

*Nibbana* is beyond logic and reasoning. We may engage in highly speculative discussions regarding *Nibbana* or ultimate reality, but this is not the way to really understand it. To understand and realise the truth of *Nibbana,* it is necessary for us to walk the Eightfold Path, and to train and purify ourselves with diligence and patience. Through spiritual development and maturity, we will be able to realise the Third Noble Truth.

The Noble Eightfold Path is the Fourth Noble Truth which leads to *Nibbana.* It is a way of life consisting of eight factors. By walking on this Path, it will be possible for us to see an end to suffering. Because Buddhism is a logical and consistent teaching embracing every aspect of life, this noble Path also serves as the finest possible code for leading a happy life. Its practice brings benefits to oneself and others, and it is not a Path to be practised by those who call themselves Buddhists alone, but by each and every understanding person, irrespective of his religious beliefs.

# The Noble Eightfold Path — The Middle Way

*This is the Path for leading a religious life without going to extremes.*

AN outstanding aspect of the Buddha's Teaching is the adoption of the Eightfold Path as a noble way of life. Another name for the Eightfold Path is the Middle Path. The Buddha advised His followers to follow this Path so as to avoid the extremes of sensual pleasures and self-mortification. The Middle Path is a righteous way of life which does not advocate the acceptance of decrees given by someone outside oneself. A person practises the Middle Path, the guide for moral conduct, not out of fear of any supernatural agency, but out of the intrinsic value in following such an action. He chooses this self-imposed discipline for a definite end in view: self-purification.

The Middle Path is a planned course of inward culture and progress. A person can make real progress in righteousness and insight by following this Path, and not by engaging in external worship and prayers. According to the Buddha, anyone who lives in accordance with the Dhamma will be guided and protected by that very Law. When a person lives according to Dhamma, he will also be living in harmony with the universal law.

Every Buddhist is encouraged to mould his life according to the Noble Eightfold Path as taught by the Buddha. He who adjusts his life according to this noble way of living will be free from miseries and calamities both in this life-time and hereafter. He will also be able to develop his mind by restraining from evil and observing morality.

The Eightfold Path can be compared to a road map. Just as a traveller will need a map to lead him to his destination, we all need the Eightfold Path which shows us how to attain Nibbana, the final goal of human life. To attain the final goal, there are three aspects of the Eightfold Path to be developed by the devotee. He has to develop *Sila* (Morality), *Samadhi* (Mental Culture) and *Panna* (Wisdom). While the three must be developed simultaneously, the intensity with which any one area is to be practised varies according to a person's own spiritual development. A devotee must first develop his morality, that is, his actions should bring good to other living beings. He does this by faithfully adhering to the precepts of abstaining from killing, slandering, stealing, becoming intoxicated or being lustful. As he develops his morality, his mind will become more easily controlled, enabling him to develop his powers of concentration. Finally, with the development of concentration, wisdom will arise

## Gradual Development

With His infinite wisdom, the Buddha knew that not all humans have the same ability to reach spiritual maturity at once. So He expounded the Noble Eightfold Path for the gradual development of the spiritual way of life in a practical way. He knew that not all people can become perfect in one lifetime. He said that *Sila, Samadhi,* and *Panna,* must and can be developed over many lifetimes with diligent effort. This Path finally leads to the attainment of ultimate peace where there is no more unsatisfactoriness.

**Righteous Life**

The Eightfold Path consists of the following eight factors:

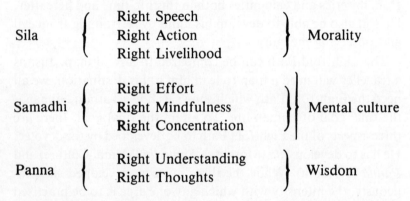

| Sila | { | Right Speech<br>Right Action<br>Right Livelihood | } | Morality |
| Samadhi | { | Right Effort<br>Right Mindfulness<br>Right Concentration | } | Mental culture |
| Panna | { | Right Understanding<br>Right Thoughts | } | Wisdom |

What is *Right Understanding?* It is explained as having the knowledge of the Four Noble Truths. In other words, it is the understanding of things as they really are. Right Understanding also means that one understands the nature of what are wholesome *kamma* (merits) and unwholesome *kamma* (demerits)*, and how they may be performed with the body, speech and mind. By understanding *kamma,* a person will learn to avoid evil and do good, thereby creating favourable outcomes in his life. When a person has Right Understanding, he also understands

---

*\*Merits and demerits are elaborated in Chapter 8.*

the Three Characteristics of Life (that all compounded things are transient, subject to suffering, and without a Self) and understands the Law of Dependent Origination. A person with complete Right Understanding is one who is free from ignorance, and by the nature of that enlightenment removes the roots of evil from his mind and becomes liberated. A lofty aim of a practising Buddhist is to cultivate Wisdom and gain Right Understanding about himself, life and all phenomena.

When a person has Right Understanding, he or she develops *Right Thought* as well. This factor is sometimes known as ' Right Resolution ', ' Right Aspirations ' and ' Right Ideas '. It refers to the mental state which eliminates wrong ideas or notions and promotes the other moral factors to be directed to Nibbana. This factor serves a double purpose of eliminating evil thoughts and developing pure thoughts. Right Thought is important because it is one's thoughts which either purify or defile a person.

There are three aspects to Right Thought. First, a person should maintain an attitude of detachment from worldly pleasures rather than being selfishly attached to them. He should be selfless in his thoughts and think of the welfare of others. Second, he should maintain loving-kindness, goodwill and benevolence in his mind, which is opposed to hatred, ill-will or aversion. Third, he should act with thoughts of harmlessness or compassion to all beings, which is opposed to cruelty and lack of consideration for others. As a person progresses along the spiritual path, his thoughts will become increasingly benevolent, harmless, selfless, and filled with love and compassion.

Right Understanding and Right Thought, which are Wisdom factors, will lead to good, moral conduct. There are three factors under moral conduct: Right Speech, Right Action and Right Livelihood. *Right Speech* involves respect for truth and respect for the welfare for others. It means to avoid lying, to avoid back biting or slander, to avoid harsh speech, and to avoid idle talk. We have often underestimated the power of speech and tend to use little control over our speech faculty. But we have all been hurt by someone's words at some time of our life, and similarly we have been encouraged by the words of another. It is said that a harsh word can wound more deeply than weapons, whereas a gentle word can change the heart and mind of the most hardened criminal. So to develop a harmonious society, we should control, cultivate and use our speech positively. We speak words which are truthful, bring harmony, kind and meaningful. The Buddha once said 'pleasant speech is sweet as honey, truthful speech is beautiful like a flower, and wrong speech is unwholesome like filth'.

The next factor under good, moral conduct is *Right Action*. Right Action entails respect for life, respect for property, and respect for personal relationships. It corresponds to the first three of the Five Precepts to be practised by every Buddhist, that is, abstinence from killing, stealing, and sexual misconduct. Life is dear to all, and all tremble at punishment, all fear death and value life. Hence, we should abstain from taking a life which we ourselves cannot give and we should not harm other sentient beings. Respect for property means that we should not take what is not given, by stealing, cheating, or force. Respect for personal relationships means that we should not commit adultery and avoid sexual misconduct, which is important for maintaining the love and trust of those we love as well as making our society a better place to live in.

*Right Livelihood* is a factor under moral conduct which refers to how we earn our living in society. It is an extension of the two other factors of Right Speech and Right Action which refer to the respect for truth, life, property and personal relationships. Right Livelihood means that we should earn a living without violating these principles of a moral conduct. Buddhists are discouraged from being engaged in the following five kinds of livelihood: trading in human beings, trading in weapons, trading in flesh, trading in intoxicating drinks and drugs, and trading in poison. Some people may say that they have to do such a business for their living and, therefore, it is not wrong for them to do so. But this argument is entirely baseless. If it were valid, then thieves, murderers, gangsters, thugs, smugglers and swindlers can also just as easily say that they are also doing such unrighteous acts only for their living and, therefore, there is nothing wrong with their way of life.

Some people believe that fishing and hunting animals for pleasure and slaughtering animals for food are not against the Buddhist precepts. This is another misconception that arises owing to a lack of knowledge in Dhamma. All these are not decent actions and bring suffering to other beings. But in all these actions, the one who is harmed most of all is the one who performs these unwholesome actions. Maintaining a life through wrong means is not in accordance with the Buddha's teaching. The Buddha once said, ' Though one should live a hundred years immorally and unrestrained, yet it would indeed be better to live one day virtuously and meditatively. ' (*Dhammapada* 103) It is better to die as a cultured and respected person than to live as a wicked person.

The remaining three factors of the Noble Eightfold Path are factors for the development of wisdom through the purification of the mind. They are Right Effort, Right Mindfulness, and Right Concentration. These factors, when practised, enable a person to strengthen and gain control over the mind, thereby ensuring that his actions will continue to be good and that his mind is being prepared to realise the Truth, which will open the door to Freedom, to Enlightenment.

*Right Effort* means that we cultivate a positive attitude and have enthusiasm in the things we do, whether in our career, in our study, or in our practice of the Dhamma. With such a sustained enthusiasm and cheerful determination, we can succeed in the things we do. There are four aspects of Right Effort, two of which refer to evil and the other two to good. First, is the effort to reject evil that has already arisen; and second, the effort to prevent the arising of evil. Third, is the effort to develop unarisen good, and fourth, the effort to maintain the good which has arisen. By applying Right Effort in our lives, we can reduce and eventually eliminate the number of unwholesome mental states and increase and firmly establish wholesome thoughts as a natural part of our mind.

Right Effort is closely associated with *Right Mindfulness.* The practice of mindfulness is important in Buddhism. The Buddha said that mindfulness is the one way to achieve the end of suffering. Mindfulness can be developed by being constantly aware of four particular aspects. These are the application of mindfulness with regard to the body (body postures, breathing and so forth), feelings (whether pleasant, unpleasant or neutral); mind (whether the mind is greedy or not, angry, dispersed or deluded or not); and mind objects (whether there are mental hindrances to concentration, the Four Noble Truths, and so on). Mindfulness is essential even in our daily life in which we act in full awareness of our actions, feelings and thoughts as well as that of our environment. The mind should always be clear and attentive rather than distracted and clouded.

Whereas Right Mindfulness is directing our attention to our body, feelings, mind, or mental object or being sensitive to others, in other words, putting our attention to where we choose to, *Right Concentration* is the sustained application of that attention on the object without the mind being distracted. Concentration is the practice of developing one-pointedness of the mind on one single object, either physical or mental. The mind is totally absorbed in the object without distractions, wavering, anxiety or drowsiness. Through practice under an experienced teacher, Right Concentration brings two benefits. Firstly, it leads to mental and physical well-being, comfort, joy, calm, tranquility. Secondly, it turns the mind into an instrument capable of seeing things as they truly are, and prepares the mind to attain wisdom.

The Noble Eightfold Path is the fourth important truth taught by the Buddha. As a competent spiritual physician, the Buddha has identified a disease that afflicts all forms of life, and this is *Dukkha* or unsatisfactoriness. He then diagnosed the cause of the unsatisfactoriness to be selfish greed and craving. He discovered that there is a cure for the disease, *Nibbana,* the state where all unsatisfactoriness ceases. And the prescription is the Noble Eightfold Path. When a competent doctor treats a patient for a serious illness, his prescription is not only for physical treatment, but it is also psychological. The Noble Eightfold Path, the path leading to the end of suffering, is an integrated therapy designed to cure the disease of *samsara* through the cultivation of moral speech and action, the development of the mind, and the complete transformation of one's level of understanding and quality of thought. It shows the way to gain spiritual maturity and be released completely from suffering.

# Everything is Changeable

*What exists is changeable and what is not changeable does not exist.*

LOOKING at life, we notice how it changes and how it continually moves between extremes and contrasts. We notice rise and fall, success and failure, loss and gain; we experience honour and contempt, praise and blame; and we feel how our hearts respond to all that happiness and sorrow, delight and despair, disappointment and satisfaction, fear and hope. These mighty waves of emotion carry us up, fling us down, and no sooner we find some rest, then we are carried by the power of a new wave again. How can we expect a footing on the crest of the waves? Where shall we erect the building of our life in the midst of this ever-restless ocean of existence?

This is a world where any little joy that is allotted to beings is secured only after many disappointments, failures and defeats. This is a world where scanty joy grows amidst sickness, desperation and death. This is a world where beings who a short while ago were connected with us by sympathetic joy are at the next moment in want of our compassion. Such a world as this needs equanimity. This is the nature of the world where we live with our intimate friends and the next day they become our enemies to harm us.

The Buddha described the world as an unending flux of becoming. All is changeable, continuous transformation, ceaseless mutation, and a moving stream. Everything exists from moment to moment. Everything is a recurring rotation of coming into being and then passing out of existence. Everything is moving from birth to death. Life is a continuous movement of change towards death. The matter or material forms in which life does or does not express itself, are also a continuous movement or change towards decay. This teaching of the impermanent nature of everything is one of the main pivots of Buddhism. Nothing on earth partakes of the character of absolute reality. That there will be no death of what is born is impossible. Whatever is subject to origination is subject also to destruction. Change is the very constituent of reality.

In accepting the law of impermanency or change, the Buddha denies the existence of eternal substances. Matter and spirit are false abstractions that, in reality, are only changing factors *(Dhamma)* which are connected and which arise in functional dependence on each other.

Today, scientists have accepted the law of change that was discovered by the Buddha. Scientists postulate that there is nothing substantial, solid and tangible in the world. Everything is a vortex of energy, never remaining the same for two consecutive moments. The whole wide world is caught up in this whirl and vortex of change. One of the theories postulated by scientists is the prospect of the ultimate coldness following upon the death or destruction of the sun. Buddhists are not dismayed by this prospect. The Buddha taught that universes or world cycles arise and pass away in endless succession, just as the lives of individuals do. Our world will most certainly come to an end. It has happened before with previous worlds and it will happen again.

' The world is a passing phenomenon. We all belong to the world of time. Every written word, every carved stone, every painted picture, the structure of civilisation, every generation of man, vanishes away like the leaves and flowers of forgotten summers. What exists is changeable and what is not changeable does not exist. '

Thus all gods and human beings and animals and material forms — everything in this universe — is subject to the law of impermanency. Buddhism teaches us:

> ' The body like a lump of foam:
> The feelings like a water bubble;
> Perception like a mirage;
> Volitional activities like a plantain tree;
> And Consciousness like jugglery. ' *(Samyutta Nikaya)*

# What is Kamma?

*Kamma is an impersonal, natural law that operates in accordance with our actions. It is a law in itself and does not have any law-giver. Kamma operates in its own field without the intervention of an external, independent, ruling agent.*

KAMMA or *karma* can be put in the simple language of the child: do good and good will come to you, now, and hereafter. Do bad and bad will come to you, now, and hereafter.

In the language of the harvest, *kamma* can be explained in this way: if you sow good seeds, you will reap a good harvest. If you sow bad seeds, you will reap a bad harvest.

In the language of science, *kamma* is called the law of cause and effect: every cause has an effect. Another name for this is the law of moral causation. Moral causation works in the moral realm just as the physical law of action and reaction works in the physical realm.

In the *Dhammapada, kamma* is explained in this manner: the mind is the chief *(forerunner)* of all good and bad states. If you speak or act with a good or bad mind, then happiness or unhappiness follows you just as the wheel follows the hoof of the ox or like your shadow which never leaves you.

*Kamma* is simply action. Within animate organisms there is a power or force which is given different names such as instinctive tendencies, consciousness, etc. This innate propensity forces every conscious being to move. He moves mentally or physically. His motion is action. The repetition of actions is habit and habit becomes his character. In Buddhism, this process is called *kamma*.

In its ultimate sense, *kamma* means both good and bad, mental action or volition. ' *Kamma* is volition, ' says the Buddha. Thus *kamma* is not an entity but a process, action, energy and force. Some interpret this force as 'action-influence.' It is our own doings reacting on ourself. The pain and happiness man experiences are the results of his own deeds, words and thoughts reacting on themselves. Our deeds, words and thoughts produce our prosperity and failure, our happiness and misery.

*Kamma* is an impersonal, natural law that operates strictly in accordance with our actions. It is a law in itself and does not have any lawgiver. *Kamma* operates in its own field without the intervention of an external, independent ruling agency. Since there is no hidden agent directing or administering rewards and punishments, Buddhists do not rely on prayer to some supernatural forces to influence karmic results. According to the Buddha, *kamma* is neither predestination nor some sort of determinism imposed on us by some mysterious, unknown powers or forces to which we must helplessly submit ourselves.

Buddhists believe that man will reap what he has sown; we are the result of what we were, and we will be the result of what we are. In other words, man is not one who will absolutely remain to be what he was, and he will not continue to remain as what he is. This simply means that *kamma* is not complete determinism. The Buddha pointed out that if everything is determined, then there would be no free will and no moral or spiritual life. We would merely be the slaves of our past. On the other hand, if everything is undetermined, then there can be no cultivation of moral and spiritual growth. Therefore, the Buddha accepted neither strict determinism nor strict undeterminism.

**Misconceptions regarding *Kamma***

The misinterpretations or irrational views on *kamma* are stated in the *Anguttara Nikaya* which suggests that the wise will investigate and abandon the following views:-

1.  the belief that everything is a result of acts in previous lives;
2.  the belief that all is the result of creation by a Supreme Ruler; and
3.  the belief that everything arises without reason or cause.

If a person becomes a murderer, a thief, or an adulterer, and, if his actions are due to past actions, or caused by the creation of a Supreme Ruler, or if that happened by mere chance, then this person would not be held responsible for his evil action.

Yet another misconception about *kamma* is that it operates only for certain people according to their faiths. But the fate of a man in his next life does not in the least depend on what particular religion he chooses. Whatever may be his religion, man's fate depends entirely on his deeds by body, speech and thought. It does not matter what religious label he himself holds, he is bound to be in a happy world in his next life so long as he does good deeds and leads an unblemished life. He is bound to be born to lead a wretched life if he commits evil and harbours wicked thoughts in his mind. Therefore, Buddhists do not proclaim that they are the only blessed people who can go to heaven after their death. Whatever the religion he professes, man's kammic thought alone determines his own destiny both in this life and in the next. The teaching of kamma does not indicate a post-mortem justice. The Buddha did not teach this law of *kamma* to protect the rich and to comfort the poor by promising illusory happiness in an after life.

According to Buddhism *kamma* explains the inequalities that exist among mankind. These inequalities are due not only to heredity, environment and nature but also to *kamma* or the results of our own actions. Indeed *kamma* is one of the factors which are responsible for the success and the failure of our life.

Since *kamma* is an invisible force, we cannot see it working with our physical eyes. To understand how *kamma* works, we can compare it to seeds: the results of *kamma* are stored in the subconscious mind in the same way as the leaves, flowers, fruits and trunk of a tree are stored in its seed. Under favourable conditions, the fruits of *kamma* will be produced just as with moisture and light, the leaves and trunk of a tree will sprout from its tiny seed.

The working of *kamma* can also be compared to a bank account: a person who is virtuous, charitable and benevolent in his present life is like a person who is adding to his good *kamma*. This accrued good *kamma* can be used by him to ensure a trouble-free life. But he must replace what he takes or else one day his account will be exhausted and he will be bankrupt. Then whom will he be able to blame for his miserable state? He can blame neither others nor fate. He alone is responsible. Thus a good Buddhist cannot be an escapist. He has to face life as it is and not run away from it. The kammic force cannot be controlled by inactivity. Vigorous activity for good is indispensable for one's own happiness. Escapism is the resort of the weak, and an escapist cannot escape the effects of the kammic law.

The Buddha says, ' There is no place to hide in order to escape from kammic results. ' *(Dhammapada 127)*

## Our Own Experience

To understand the law of *kamma* is to realise that we ourselves are responsible for our own happiness and our own misery. We are the architects of our *kamma*. Buddhism explains that man has every possibility to mould his own *kamma* and thereby influence the direction of his life. On the other hand, a man is not a complete prisoner of his own actions; he is not a slave of his *kamma*. Nor is man a mere machine that automatically releases instinctive forces that enslave him. Nor is man a mere product of nature. Man has within himself the strength and the ability to change his *kamma*. His mind is mightier than his *kamma* and so the law of *kamma* can be made to serve him. Man does not have to give up his hope and effort in order to surrender himself to his own kammic force. To off-set the reaction of his bad *kamma* that he has accumulated previously, he has to do more meritorious deeds and to purify his mind rather than by praying, worshipping, performing rites or torturing his physical body in order to overcome his kammic effects. Therefore, man can overcome the effect of his evil deeds if he acts wisely by leading a noble life.

Man must use the material with which he is endowed to promote his ideal. The cards in the game of life are within us. We do not select them. They are traced to our past *kamma;* but we can call as we please, do what suits us and as we play, we either gain or lose.

*Kamma* is equated to the action of men. This action also creates some karmic results. But each and every action carried out without any purposeful intention, cannot become a *Kusala-Kamma* (skilful action) or *Akusala-Kamma* (unskilful action). That is why the Buddha interprets *kamma* as volitional activities. That means, whatever good and bad deeds we commit ourselves without any purposeful intention, are not strong enough to be carried forward to our next life. However, ignorance of the nature of the good and bad effect of the *kamma* is not an excuse to justify or avoid the karmic results if they were committed intentionally. A small child or an ignorant man may commit many evil deeds. Since they commit such deeds with intention to harm or injure, it is difficult to say that they are free from the karmic results. If that child touches a burning iron-rod the heat element does not spare the child without burning his fingers. The karmic energy also works exactly in the same manner. Karmic energy is unbiased; it is like energy of gravity.

The radical transformations in the characters of Angulimala and Asoka illustrate man's potential to gain control over his kammic force.

Angulimala was a highway robber who murdered more than a thousand of his fellow men. Can we judge him by his external actions? For within his lifetime, he became an Arahanta and thus redeemed his past misdeeds.

Asoka, the Indian Emperor, killed thousands and thousands to fight his wars and to expand his empire. Yet after winning the battle, he completely reformed himself and changed his career to such an extent that today, ' Amidst the tens of thousands of names of monarchs that crowd the columns of history, their majesties and royal highnesses and the like, the name of Asoka shines and shines almost alone, as a star, ' says a well-known world historian H.G. Wells.

**Other Factors Which Support *Kamma***

Although Buddhism says that man can eventually control his kammic force, it does not state that everything is due to *kamma*. Buddhism does not ignore the role played by other forces of nature. According to Buddhism there are five orders or processes

of natural laws *(niyama)* which operate in the physical and mental
worlds:

1. seasonal laws *(utu niyama)* physical inorganic order e.g.,
   seasonal phenomena of winds and rains, etc.
2. the biological laws *(bija niyama)* relating to seasonal
   changes etc.,
3. the kammic law *(kamma niyama)* relating to moral
   causation or the order of act and result,
4. natural phenomena *(Dhamma niyama)* relating to electrical
   forces, movement of tides etc., and
5. psychological laws *(citta niyama)* which govern the
   processes of consciousness.

Thus *kamma* is considered only as one of the five natural laws
that account for the diversity in this world.

**Can *Kamma* Be Changed?**

*Kamma* is often influenced by circumstances: beneficient and
malevolent forces act to counter and to support this self-operating
law. These other forces that either aid or hinder this *kamma* are
birth, time or conditions, appearances, and effort.

A favourable birth *(gati sampatti)* or an unfavourable birth
*(vipatti)* can develop or hinder the fruition of *kamma*. For
instance, if a person is born to a noble family or in a state of
happiness, his fortunate birth will provide an easy opportunity
for his good *kamma* to operate. An unintelligent person who,
by some good *kamma*, is born in a royal family, will, on account
of his noble parentage be honoured by the people. If the same
person were to have a less fortunate birth, he would not be
similarly treated.

Good appearance *(upadhi sampatti)* and poor appearance
*(upadhi vipatti)* are two other factors that hinder or favour the
working of *kamma*. If by some good *kamma*, a person obtains
a good birth, but is born deformed by some bad *kamma*, then
he will not be able to fully enjoy the beneficial results of his good
*kamma*. Even a legitimate heir to a throne may not perhaps be

raised to that high position if he happens to be physically or mentally deformed. Beauty, on the other hand, will be an asset to the possessor. A good-looking son of poor parents may attract the attention of others and may be able to distinguish himself through their influence. Also, we can find cases of people from poor, obscure family backgrounds who rise to fame and popularity as film actors or actresses or beauty queens.

Time and occasion are other factors that influence the working of *kamma*. In the time of famine or during the time of war, all people without exception are forced to suffer the same fate. Here the unfavourable conditions open up possibilities for evil *kamma* to operate. The favourable conditions, on the other hand, will prevent the operation of bad *kamma*.

Effort or intelligence is perhaps the most important of all the factors that affect the working of *kamma*. Without effort, both worldly and spiritual progress is impossible. If a person makes no effort to cure himself of a disease or to save himself from his difficulties, or to strive with diligence for his progress, then his evil *kamma* will find a suitable opportunity to produce its due effects. However, if he endeavours to surmount his difficulties, his good *kamma* will come to help him. When shipwrecked in a deep sea, the *Bodhisatta* during one of his previous births, made an effort to save himself and his old mother, while the others prayed to the gods and left their fate in the hands of these gods. The result was that the *Boddhisatta* escaped while the others were drowned.

Thus the working of *kamma* is aided or obstructed by birth, beauty and ugliness, time and personal effort or intelligence. However, man can overcome immediate karmic effects by adopting certain methods. Yet, he is not free from such karmic effects if he remains within this *Samsara* — cycle of birth and death. Whenever opportunities arise the same karmic effects that he overcame, can affect him again. This is the uncertainty of worldly life. Even the Buddha and Arahantas were affected by certain *kammas,* although they were in their final birth.

The time factor is another important aspect of the karmic energy for people to experience the good and bad effects. People experience certain karmic effects only within this lifetime while certain karmic effects become effective immediately hereafter in the next birth. And certain other karmic effects follow the doers as long as they remain in this wheel of existence until they stop their rebirth after attaining *Nibbana*. The main reason for this difference is owing to mental impulsion *(Javana Citta)* of the people at the time when a thought arises in the mind to do good or bad.

**Impartial Energy**

Those who do not believe that there is an energy known as *kamma* should understand that this karmic energy is not a by-product of any particular religion although Hinduism, Buddhism and Jainism acknowledge and explain the nature of this energy. This is an existing universal law which has no religious label. All those who violate this law, have to face the consequences irrespective of their religious beliefs, and those who live in accordance with this law experience peace and happiness in their life. Therefore, this karmic law is unbiased to each and every person, whether they believe it or not; whether, they have a religion or not. It is like any other existing universal law. Please remember that *kamma* is not the exclusive property of Buddhism.

If we understand *kamma* as a force or a form of energy, then we can discern no beginning. To ask where is the beginning of *kamma* is like asking where is the beginning of electricity. *Kamma* like electricity does not begin. It comes into being under certain conditions. Conventionally we say that the origin of *kamma* is volition but this is as much conventional as saying that the origin of a river is a mountain top.

Like the waves of the ocean that flow into one another, one unit of consciousness flows into another and this merging of one thought consciousness into another is called the working of *kamma*. In short, every living being, according to Buddhism, is an electric current of life that operates on the automatic switch of *kamma*.

*Kamma* being a form of energy is not found anywhere in this fleeting consciousness or body. Just as mangoes are not stored anywhere in the mango tree but, dependent on certain conditions, they spring into being, so does *kamma*. *Kamma* is like wind or fire. It is not stored up anywhere in the Universe but comes into being under certain conditions.

# Rebirth

*Unsatisfied desire for existence and sensual pleasures is the cause of rebirth.*

BUDDHISTS regard the doctrine of rebirth not as a mere theory but as a verifiable fact. The belief in rebirth forms a fundamental tenet of Buddhism. However, the belief in rebirth is not confined to Buddhists; it is also found in other countries, in other religions, and even among free thinkers. Pythagoras could remember his previous birth. Plato could remember a number of his previous lives. According to Plato, man can be reborn only up to ten times. Plato also believed in the possibility of rebirth in the animal kingdom. Among the ancient people in Egypt and China, a common belief was that only well-known personalities like emperors and kings have rebirths. A well-known Christian authority named Origen, who lived in 185-254 A.D., believed in rebirth. According to him, there is no eternal suffering in a hell. Gorana Bruno, who lived in the sixteenth century, believed that the soul of every man and animal transmigrates from one being to another. In 1788, a wellknown philosopher, Kant, criticized eternal punishment. Kant also believed in the possibility of rebirth

---

*To get further information on this subject, read ' Do You Believe In Rebirth? ' by the same author and the book '31 planes of existence' by Egerton Baptist.*

in other celestial bodies. Schopenhauer (1788-1860), another great philosopher, said that where the will to live existed there must be of necessity life. The will to live manifests itself successively in ever new forms. The Buddha explained this 'will to exist' as the craving for existence.

It is possible but not very easy for us to actually verify our past lives. The nature of mind is such that it does not allow most people the recollection of their previous lives. Our minds are overpowered by the five hindrances: sensual desire, ill-will, sloth, restlessness and doubt. Because of these hindrances, our vision is earth-bound and hence we cannot visualise rebirths. Just as a mirror does not reflect an image when it is covered with dirt, so the mind does not allow most people the recollection of previous lives. We cannot see the stars during daytime, not because they are not there in the sky, but because they are outshone by the sunlight. Similarly, we cannot remember our past lives because our mind at present is always over-burdened with many thoughts in the present, day-to-day events and mundane circumstances.

A consideration of the shortness of our life-span on earth will help us to reflect on rebirth. If we consider life and its ultimate meaning and goal, and all the varied experience possible for man, we must conclude that in a single life there is not enough time for man to carry out all that is intended by nature, to say nothing about what man himself desires to do. The scale of experience is enormous. There is a vast range of powers latent in man which we see and can even develop if the opportunity is presented to us. This is especially true today if special investigation is made. We find ourselves with high aspirations but with no time to attain them. Meanwhile, the great troop of passions and desires, selfish motives and ambitions, make war within us and with others. These forces pursue each other to the time of our death. All these forces must be tried, conquered, subdued and used. One life is just not enough for all this. To say that we must have but one life here with such possibilities put before us and impossible to develop is to make the universe and life a huge and cruel joke.

The Buddhist doctrine of rebirth should be differentiated from the teachings of transmigration and reincarnation of other religions. Buddhism denies the existence of a permanent, god-created soul or an unchanging entity that transmigrates from one life to another.

Just as relative identity is made possible by causal continuity without a Self or Soul, so death can issue in rebirth without a transmigrating Soul. In a single life, each thought-moment flashes in and out of being, giving rise to its successor with its perishing. Strictly speaking, this momentary rise and fall of every thought is a birth and death. Thus even in a single life we undergo countless births and deaths every second. But because the mental process continues with the support of a single physical body, we regard the mind-body continuum as constituting a single life.

What we ordinarily mean by death is the cessation of the body's vital functions. When the physical body loses its vitality it can. no longer support the current of consciousness, the mental side of the process. But as long as there is a clinging to life, a desire to go on existing, the current of consciousness does not come to a stop with the body's loss of life. Rather, when death takes place, when the body dies away, the mental current, driven by the thirst for more existence, will spring up again with the support of a new physical body, one which has just come into being through the meeting of sperm and egg. Thus, rebirth takes place immediately after death. The stream of memory may be interrupted and the sense of identity transferred to the new situation, but the entire accumulation of experience and disposition has been transmitted to the newborn being, and the cycle of becoming begins to revolve for still another term.

For Buddhism, therefore, death does not spell either the entrance to eternal life or complete annihilation. It is, rather, the portal to a new rebirth which will be followed by more growth, decay, and then till another death.

At the last moment, no renewed physical functioning occurs in a dying man's mind. This is just like a motorist releasing the accelerator before stopping, so that no more pulling power is given to the engine. Similarly, no more material qualities of *Kamma* arise.

Buddhists do not maintain that the present life is the only life between two eternities of misery and happiness; nor do they believe angels will carry them to heaven and leave them there for all eternity. They believe that this present life is only one of the indefinite numbers of states of being and that this earthly life is but one episode among many others. They believe that all beings will be reborn somewhere for a limited period of time as long as their good and bad *Kamma* remains in the subconscious mind in the form of mental energy. The interpretation of the subconscious mind in the Buddhist context should not be confused with that given by modern psychologists since the concepts are not exactly synonymous.

What is the cause of rebirth? The Buddha taught that ignorance produces desires. Unsatisfied desire is the cause of rebirth. When all unsatisfied desire is extinguished, then rebirth ceases. To stop rebirth is to extinguish all desires. To extinguish desire, it is necessary to destroy ignorance. When ignorance is destroyed, the worthlessness of every such rebirth, is perceived, as well as the paramount need to adopt a course of life by which the desire for such repeated births can be abolished.

Ignorance also begets the illusive and illogical idea that there is only one existence for man, and the other illusion that this one life is followed by states of eternal pleasure or torment.

The Buddha taught that ignorance can be dispelled and sorrow removed by realisation of the Four Noble Truths, and not through any other source. To disperse all ignorance, one must persevere in the practice of an all-embracing altruism in conduct, intelligence and wisdom. One must also destroy all desire for the lower, personal pleasures and selfish desire.

How does rebirth take place? When this physical body is no more capable of functioning, energies do not die with it, but continue to take some other shape or form, which we call another life. The kammic force manifesting itself in the form of a human being can also manifest itself in the form of an animal. This can happen if man has no chance to develop his positive kammic forces. This force, called craving, desire, volition, thirst to live, does not end with the non-functioning of the body but continues to manifest itself in another form, producing re-existence which is called rebirth.

Today, there are people in various countries who have spontaneously developed memory of their past births. The experiences of these people have been well-documented in newspapers and periodicals. Some of these people never accepted that there was such a thing as rebirth until memory fragments of their previous lives came to them. Much of the information they revealed about their past lives has been investigated and found to be valid.

Through hypnotism, some people have managed to reveal information of previous lives. Certain hypnotic states that penetrate into the subconscious mind make the recalling of past lives possible.

Rebirth or becoming again and again is a natural occurrence not created by any particular religion or god. Belief in rebirth or disbelief does not make any difference to the process of rebirth or avoiding rebirth. Rebirth takes place as long as craving for existence and craving for sensual pleasures or attachment exist in the mind. Those strong mental forces prevail in each and every living being in this universe. Those who hope and pray that they be not born again must understand that their wishes will not materialise until they make earnest efforts to eradicate their craving and attachment. Having seen and experienced the uncertainty and unsatisfactoriness of life under worldly conditions, wise people try to rid themselves of these repeated births and deaths by following the correct path. Those who cannot reduce their craving and attachment must be prepared to face all unsatisfactory and uncertain situations associated with rebirth and becoming again and again.

**Is Rebirth Simultaneous?**

Another difficult thing to understand about rebirth is whether the occurrence of rebirth is simultaneous or not. This is a controversial issue even amongst prominent Buddhist scholars. According to Abhidhamma, rebirth (conception) takes place immediately after the death of a being without any intermediate state. At the same time, some others believe that a person, after his death, would evolve into a spirit form for a certain number of days before rebirth takes place. Another interpretation regarding the same belief is that it is not the spirit, but the deceased person's consciousness or mental energy remaining in space, supported by his own mental energies of craving and attachment. However, sooner or later rebirth must take place. The spirits *(petas),* who are beings born in spirit forms, are unfortunate living beings and their lives in the spirit form is not permanent. It is also a form of rebirth which is temporary.

Another concept that many people cannot understand is that in the process of rebirth a man can be reborn as an animal and an animal can be reborn as a man. The animal nature of the man's mind and the animal way of life adopted by him can condition him to be born as an animal. The condition and behaviour of the mind is responsible for the next existence. On the other hand, a person who is born in animal form, owing to certain mental abuses during a previous birth, could be reborn as a human being, if that animal has not committed any serious evil acts. It is a well-known fact that some animals are very intelligent and understanding. This is a clear evidence to prove that they are tending towards the human life. A person who is born as an animal can again be born as a human being when the bad *kamma* which conditioned his birth as an animal is expended and the good *kamma* which was stored becomes dominant.

**Dying Moment**

In the dying man's consciousness, there are three types of consciousness *(Vinnana)* functioning at the moment of death:

rebirth-linking consciousness *(patisandhi-citta),* the current of passive consciousness or the current of life-continuum *(bhavanga)* and consciousness disconnecting the present life *(cuti-citta).* At the last moment of a man's present life the *(patisandhi-citta)* or rebirth-linking consciousness arises, having the three signs as its objects. The *patisandhi-citta* remains in the course of cognition for five faint thought-moments *Javana* and then sinks down into *bhavanga.* At the end of *bhavanga* the *cuti-citta* arises, disconnecting the present life and sinks down into *bhavanga.* At this very moment comes the end of the present life. At the end of that *bhavanga* another *patisandhi-citta* rises up in the next life and from this very moment the new life begins. This is the process of death and rebirth according to Buddhism, and only in Buddhism is the process of these natural phenomena found explained in minute detail.

A Buddhist faces death not as a crisis in life but as a normal event, for he knows that whoever is born must suffer, ' decay ', and ultimately die. Or, as someone so aptly puts it, ' Everyone is born with the certificate of death at his birth. ' If we could all look at death in such an intelligent and rational way, we would not cling to life so tenaciously.

' *Ayamantima jati'natthidani punabbhavo* '

This is my final birth and there is no more rebirth for me.

*(Dhamma Cakka Sutta)*

# Nibbana

*Nibbana is the highest bliss, a supramundane state of eternal happiness. The happiness of Nibbana cannot be experienced by indulging the senses but by calming them.*

NIBBANA is the final goal of Buddhism. What is *Nibbana* then? It is not easy to know what *Nibbana* really is; it is easier to know what *Nibbana* is not.

*Nibbana* is not nothingness or extinction. Would the Buddha leave His family and kingdom and preach for 45 years — all for nothingness?

*Nibbana* is not a paradise. Several centuries after the Buddha, some of the Buddhist sects began to introduce *Nibbana* as a paradise. Their purpose of equating *Nibbana* with a heavenly world was to convince the 'less-intellectually-gifted' and to attract them to the teachings of the sect. Striving for *Nibbana* came to mean looking for a nice place where everything is beautiful and where everyone is eternally happy. This might be a very comfortable folktale, but it is not the *Nibbana* that the Buddha experienced and introduced. During His time the Buddha did not deny the idea of paradise as it was presented in the early Indian religions. But the Buddha knew that this paradise was within *Samsara* and the final liberation was beyond it. The Buddha could see that the Path to *Nibbana* led beyond the heavens.

If *Nibbana* is not a place, where is *Nibbana* then? *Nibbana* exists just as fire exists. However, there is no storage place for fire or for *Nibbana* . But when you rub pieces of wood together, then the friction and heat are the proper conditions for fire to arise. Likewise, when the nature in man's mind is such that he is free from all defilements, then Nibbanic bliss will appear.

You can experience *Nibbana*. Until you experience the supreme state of Nibbanic bliss, you can only speculate as to what it really is. For those who insist on the theory, the texts offer some help. The texts suggest that *Nibbana* is a supra-mundane state of unalloyed happiness.

By itself, *Nibbana* is quite unexplainable and quite undefinable. As darkness can be explained only by its opposite, light, and as calm can only be explained by its opposite, motion, so likewise *Nibbana,* as a state equated to the extinction of all suffering can be explained by its opposite — the suffering that is being endured in *Samsara.* As darkness prevails wherever there is no light, as calm prevails wherever there is no motion, so likewise *Nibbana* is everywhere where suffering and change and impurity do not prevail.

A sufferer who scratches his sores can experience a temporary relief. This temporary relief will aggravate the wounds and cause the disease to be enhanced. The joy of the final cure can hardly be compared to the fleeting relief obtained from the scratching. Likewise, satisfying the craving for sense-desires brings only temporary gratification or happiness which prolongs the stay in *Samsara*. The cure for the samsaric disease is *Nibbana. Nibbana* is an end of the cravings which cause all the sufferings of birth, old age, disease, death, grief, lamentation and despair. The joy of Nibbanic cure can hardly be compared to the temporary Samsaric pleasure gained through fulfilling the sense desires.

It is dangerous to speculate on what *Nibbana* is; it is better to know how to prepare the conditions necessary for *Nibbana,* how to attain the inner peace and clarity of vision that leads to *Nibbana.* Follow the Buddha's advice: put His Teachings into practice. Get rid of all your defilements which are rooted in greed, hatred, and delusion. Purify yourself of all desires and realise absolute selflessness. Lead a life of right moral conduct and constantly practise meditation. By active exertion, free yourself from all selfishness and illusion. Then, *Nibbana* is gained and experienced.

**Nibbana and Samsara**

A well-known Mahayana Buddhist scholar, Nagarjuna, says that *Samsara* and *Nibbana* are one. This interpretation can easily be misunderstood by others. However to state that the concept of *Samsara* and *Nibbana* are the same is to say that there is no difference in voidness of component things and the unconditioned state of *Nibbana*. In accordance with the Pali Tipitaka, *Samsara* is described as the unbroken continuation of the five aggregates, four elements and twelve bases or sources of mental processes whereas *Nibbana* is described as the extinction of those relative physical and mental sources.

However, it is admitted that those who gain Nibbanic bliss, can experience it during their existence in *Samsara*. In any case, after their death, the link with those elements will be eliminated, for the simple reason that *Nibbana* is unconditioned, not relative or interdependent. If there is to be anything at all after *Nibbana,* it would have to be 'Absolute Truth'.

You must learn to be detached from all worldly things. If there is any attachment to anyone or to anything or if there is any aversion to anyone or anything, you will never attain *Nibbana,* for *Nibbana* is beyond all opposites of attachment and aversion, likes and dislikes.

When that ultimate state is attained, you will fully understand this worldly life for which you now crave. This world will cease to be an object of your desire. You will realise the sorrow and impermanence and impersonality of all that lives and that does not live. By depending on teachers or holy books without using your own effort in the right manner, it is difficult to gain realisation of *Nibbana.* Your dreams will vanish. No castles will be built in the air. The tempest will be ended. Life's struggles will be over. Nature's processes will have ceased. All your worries, miseries, responsibilities, disturbances, burdens, physical and mental ailments and emotions will vanish after attaining this most blissful state of *Nibbana.*

To say that *Nibbana* is nothingness simply because one cannot perceive it with the five senses, is as illogical as to say that light does not exist simply because the blind do not see it.

*Nibbana* is attainable in this present life. Buddhism does not state that its ultimate goal could be reached only in life beyond. When *Nibbana* is realised in this life with the body remaining it is called *Sopadisesa Nibbana.* When an Arahant attains *Pari Nibbana,* after the dissolution of the body, without any reminder of physical existence, it is called *Anupadisesa Nibbana.*

# Law of Dependent Origination

*' No God, no Brahma can be found*
*No matter of this wheel of life*
*Just bare phenomena roll*
*Depend on conditions all. ' (Visuddhi Magga)*

THE Law of Dependent Origination is one of the most important teachings of the Buddha, and it is also very profound. The Buddha has often expressed His experience of Enlightenment in one of two ways, either in terms of having understood the Four Noble Truths, or in terms of having understood the nature of the dependent origination. However, more people have heard about the Four Noble Truths and can discuss it than the Law of Dependent Origination, which is just as important.

Although the actual insight into dependent origination arises with spiritual maturity, it is still possible for us to understand the principle involved. The basis of dependent origination is that life or the world is built on a set of relations, in which the arising and cessation of factors depend on some other factors which condition them. This principle can be given in a short formula of four lines:

> *When this is, that is*
> *This arising, that arises*
> *When this is not, that is not*
> *This ceasing, that ceases.*

On this principle of interdependence and relativity rests the arising, continuity and cessation of existence. This principle is known as the Law of Dependent Origination or in Pali, *Paticcasamuppada*. This law emphasises an important principle that all

---

*Read an excellent exposition of the Law of Dependent Origination in Egerton C. Baptist's book, The Buddha: His Birth, Life and Teachings.*

phenomena in this universe are relative, conditioned states and do not arise independently of supportive conditions. A phenomenon arises because of a combination of conditions which are present to support its arising. And the phenomenon will cease when the conditions and components supporting its arising change and no longer sustain it. The presence of these supportive conditions, in turn, depend on other factors for their arising, sustenance and disappearance.

The Law of Dependent Origination is a realistic way of understanding the universe and is the Buddhist equivalent of Einstein's Theory of Relativity. The fact that everything is nothing more than a set of relations is consistent with the modern scientific view of the material world. Since everything is conditioned, relative, and interdependent, there is nothing in this world which could be regarded as a permanent entity, variously regarded as an ego or an eternal soul, which many people believe in.

The phenomenal world is built on a set of relations, but is this the way we would normally understand the world to be? We create fictions of its permanency in our minds because of our desires. It is almost natural for human beings to cling to what they consider as beautiful or desirable, and to reject what is ugly or undesirable. Being subjected to the forces of greed and hatred, they are misled by delusion, clouded by the illusion of the permanency of the object they cling to or reject. Therefore, it is hard for us to realise that the world is like a bubble or mirage, and is not the kind of reality we believe it to be. We do not realise that it is unreal in actuality. It is like a ball of fire, which when whirled around rapidly, can for a time, create the illusion of a circle.

The fundamental principle at work in dependent origination is that of cause and effect. In dependent origination, what actually takes place in the causal process is described in detail. To illustrate the nature of dependent origination of the things around us, let us consider an oil lamp. The flame in an oil lamp burns dependent upon the oil and the wick. When the oil and the wick are present, the flame in an oil lamp burns. If either of these is absent, the flame will cease to burn. This example illustrates the principle of dependent origination with respect to a flame in an oil lamp. Or in an example of a plant, it is dependent upon the seed, earth, moisture, air and sunlight for the plant to grow. All these phenomena arise dependent upon a number of causal factors, and not independently. This is the principle of dependent origination.

In the Dhamma, we are interested to know how the principle of dependent origination is applied to the problem of suffering and rebirth. The issue is how dependent origination can explain why we are still going round in Samsara, or explain the problem of suffering and how we can be free from suffering. It is not meant to be a description of the origin or evolution of the universe. Therefore, one must not be mistaken into assuming that ignorance, the first factor mentioned in the dependent origination, is the first cause. Since everything arises because of some preceeding causes, there can be no first cause.

According to the Law of Dependent Origination, there are twelve factors which account for the continuity of existence birth after birth. The factors are as follows:

1. Through ignorance are conditioned volitional actions or *kamma*-formations.
2. Through volitional actions is conditioned consciousness.
3. Through consciousness are conditioned mental and physical phenomena.
4. Through mental and physical phenomena are conditioned the six faculties (i.e., five physical sense-organs and mind).
5. Through the six faculties is conditioned (sensorial and mental) contact.
6. Through (sensorial and mental) contact is conditioned sensation.
7. Through sensation is conditioned desire, ' thirst '.

8. Through desire (' thirst ') is conditioned clinging.
9. Through clinging is conditioned the process of becoming.
10. Through the process of becoming is conditioned birth.
11. Through birth are conditioned decay, death, sorrow, lamentation, pain, grief and despair.

This is how life arises, exists and continues, and how suffering arises. These factors may be understood as sequentially spanning over a period of three life-times: the past life, the present life, and the future life. In the dependent origination, ignorance and mental formation belong to the past life, and represent the conditions that are responsible for the occurrence of this life. The following factors, namely, consciousness, mental and physical phenomena, the six senses, contact, sensation, desire, clinging and becoming, are factors involved in the present life. The last two factors, birth and decay and death, belong to the future life.

In this law, the first factor of Ignorance gives rise to Volitional Activities (or *kamma*). Ignorance means not knowing or understanding the true nature of our existence. Through Ignorance, good or evil deeds are performed which will lead a person to be reborn. Rebirth can occur in various planes of existence: the human world, the celestial or higher planes, or even suffering planes depending of the quality of a person's *kamma*. When a person dies, his Volitional Activities will condition the arising of Consciousness, in this case to mean the re-linking Consciousness which arises as the first spark of a new life in the process of re-becoming.

Once the re-linking Consciousness has taken place, life starts once again. Dependent on the Consciousness, there arise Mind and Matter, that is, a new ' being ' is born. Because there are Mind and Matter, there arise the six Sense-organs (the sixth sense is the mind itself). With the arising of the Sense-organs, there arises Contact. Contact with what? Contact with sights, sounds, smells, tastes, tactile objects, and mental objects.

These sights, sounds, smells, tastes, tactile objects, and mental objects can be beautiful, pleasing and enticing. On the other hand, they can be ugly and distasteful. Therefore, dependent on Contact arises Sensations: feelings that are pleasant, unpleasant or neutral. Because of these feelings, the laws of attraction (greed) and repulsion (aversion) are now set in motion. Beings are naturally attracted to pleasant objects and repelled by unpleasant objects. As a result of Sensation, Desire arises. A person desires and thirsts for forms that are beautiful and enticing; sounds that are beautiful and enticing; tastes, smells, touch, and objects which the mind regards as beautiful and enticing. From these Desires, he develops very strong Clinging to the beautiful object (or strongly rejects the repulsive object). Now because of this Clinging and attachment, the next life is conditioned and there arises Becoming. In other words, the processes of Becoming are set in motion by Clinging.

The next link in this chain of Dependent Origination is that Becoming conditions the arising of Birth. And finally, dependent on Birth arise Decay and Death, followed by Sorrow, Lamentation, Pain, Grief and Despair.

The process can be ceased if the formula is taken in the reverse order: Through the complete cessation of ignorance (through the cultivation of Insight), volitional activities or *kamma*-formations cease; through the cessation of volitional activities, consciousness ceases; ... through the cessation of birth, the other factors of decay, death, sorrow, etc., cease. Therefore, one can be free from the rounds of rebirth through the eradication of ignorance.

To re-iterate what was mentioned earlier, this doctrine of Dependent Origination merely explains the processes of Birth and Death, and is not a theory of the evolution of the world. It deals with the Cause of Re-birth and Suffering, but in no way attempts to show the absolute Origin of Life. Ignorance in Dependent Origination is the ignorance of the Four Noble Truths. It is very important for us to understand the Four Noble Truths because it is the ignorance of these Truths that has trapped us all in the endless cycle of birth and death.

According to the Buddha, while He was speaking to Ananda: It is by their not being able to comprehend the Dependent Origination, that people are entangled like a ball of cotton, and not being able to see the Truth, are always afflicted by Sorrow, — born often into conditions that are dismal and dreary, where confusion and prolonged suffering prevail. And, they do not know how to disentangle themselves to get out.

# Eternalism and Nihilism

*The Buddha rejected both extremes of eternalism and nihilism.*

To develop Right View or Perfect View, we must first be aware of two views which are considered imperfect or wrong.

The first view is eternalism. This doctrine or belief is concerned with eternal life or with eternal things. Before the Buddha's time, it was taught that there is an abiding entity which could exist forever, and that man can live the eternal life by preserving the eternal soul in order to be in union with Supreme Being. In Buddhism, this teaching is called *sassata ditthi* — the view of eternalists. Such views still exist even in the modern world owing to man's craving for eternity.

Why did the Buddha deny the teaching of eternalism? Because when we understand the things of this world as they truly are, we cannot find anything which is permanent or which exists forever. Things change and continue to do so according to the changing conditions on which they depend. When we analyse things into their elements or into reality, we cannot find any abiding entity, any everlasting thing. This is why the eternalist view is considered wrong or false.

The second false view is nihilism or the view held by the nihilists who claim that there is no life after death. This view belongs to a materialistic philosophy which refuses to accept knowledge of mental conditionality. To subscribe to a philosophy of materialism is to understand life only partially. Nihilism ignores the side of life which is concerned with mental conditionality. If one claims that after the passing away or ceasing of a life, it does not come to be again, the continuity of mental conditions is denied. To understand life, we must consider all conditions, both mental and material. When we understand mental and material conditions, we cannot say that there is no life after death and that there is no further becoming after passing away. This nihilist view of existence is considered false because it is based on incomplete understanding of reality. That is why nihilism was also rejected by the Buddha. The teaching of *kamma* is enough to prove that the Buddha did not teach annihilation after death; Buddhism accepts ' survival ' not in the sense of an eternal soul, but in the sense of a renewed becoming.

Throughout the Buddha's long period of teaching the Dhamma to His followers, He actively discouraged speculative arguments. During the 5th century B.C. India was a veritable hive of intellectual activity where scholars, yogis, philosophers, kings and even ordinary householders were constantly engaged in the philosophical arguments pertaining to human existence. Some of these were either ridiculously trivial or totally irrelevant. Some people wasted valuable time arguing at great length about all manner of subjects. They were far more concerned about proving their powers in mental gymnastics than seeking genuine solutions to the problems that beset humanity. (In the 18th century Jonathan Swift satirized a similar pastime in England when he showed the Lilliputians in ' *Gulliver's Travels* ' waging a war to decide whether an egg should be broken on its sharp end or its broad end).

The Buddha also refused to get involved in speculations regarding the universe. He stated very clearly that the problem facing mankind is not in his past or his future but in the immediate present. Knowledge about Eternalism or Nihilism can in no way help man to break the present fetters which bind him to existence and which are the source of all his feelings of discontent which arise from his inability to completely satisfy his cravings. The Buddha stated that before one can begin to tread the path which leads to Nibbana one must have Right View. Only when one knows clearly what one is seeking will one be able to attain it.

# Can the First Cause be Known?

*It is rather difficult for us to understand how the world came into existence without a first cause. But it is very much more difficult to understand how that first cause came into existence at the beginning.*

ACCORDING to the Buddha, it is inconceivable to find a first cause for life or anything else. For in common experience, the cause becomes the effect and the effect becomes the cause. In the circle of cause and effect, a first cause is incomprehensible. With regard to the origin of life, the Buddha declares, ' Without cognizable end is this recurrent wandering in *Samsara* (cycle of birth and death). Beings arc obstructed by ignorance and fettered by craving. A first beginning of these beings is not to be perceived. ' *(Anamatagga Samyutta* in *Samyutta Nikaya.)* This life-stream flows on *ad infinitum,* as long as it is fed by the muddy waters of ignorance and craving. When these two are cut off, only then does the life-stream cease to flow, only then does rebirth come to an end.

It is difficult to conceive an end of space. It is difficult to conceive an eternal duration of what we call time. But it is more difficult to conceive time when there is no time. Likewise it is rather difficult for us to understand how this world came into existence with a first cause. And it is more difficult to understand how that first cause came into existence at the beginning. For if the first cause can exist though uncreated, there is no reason why the other phenomena of the universe must not exist without having also been created.

As to the question how all beings came into existence without a first cause, the Buddhist's reply is that there is no answer because the question itself is merely a product of man's limited comprehension. If we can understand the nature of time and relativity, we must see that there could not have been any beginning. It can only be pointed out that all the usual answers to the question are fundamentally defective. If it is assumed that for a thing to exist, it must have had a creator who existed before it, it follows logically that the creator himself must have had a creator, and so on back to infinity. On the other hand, if the creator could exist without a prior cause in the form of another creator, the whole argument falls to the ground. The theory of a creator does not solve any problems, it only complicates the existing ones.

Thus Buddhism does not pay much attention to theories and beliefs about the origin of the world. Whether the world was created by a god or it came into existence by itself makes little difference to Buddhists. Whether the world is finite or infinite also makes little difference to Buddhists. Instead of following this line of theoretical speculations, the Buddha advises people to work hard to find their own salvation.

Scientists have discovered many causes which are responsible for the existence of life, plants, planets, elements and other energies. But it is impossible for anyone to find out any particular first cause for their existence. If they go on searching for the first cause of any existing life or thing, they point certain causes as the main cause but that never becomes the first cause. In the process of searching for the first cause one after the other, they will come back to the place where they were. This is because, cause becomes the effect and the next moment that effect becomes the cause to produce another effect. That is what the Buddha says, ' It is incomprehensible and the universe is beginningless. '

# Is There an Eternal Soul?

*Belief in an eternal soul is a misconception of the human consciousness.*

## Soul-Theories

WITH regard to the soul theory, there are three kinds of teachers in the world:

The first teacher teaches the existence of an eternal ego-entity that outlasts death: He is the eternalist.

The second teacher teaches a temporary ego-entity which becomes annihilated at death: He is the materialist.

The third teacher teaches neither an eternal nor a temporary ego-entity: He is the Buddha.

The Buddha teaches that what we call ego, self, soul, personality, etc., are merely conventional terms that do not refer to any real, independent entity. According to Buddhism there is no reason to believe that there is an eternal soul that comes from heaven or that is created by itself and that will transmigrate or proceed straight away either to heaven or hell after death. Buddhists cannot accept that there is anything either in this world or any other world that is eternal or unchangeable. We only cling to ourselves and hope to find something immortal. We are like children who wish to clasp a rainbow. To children, a rainbow is something vivid and real; but the grown-ups know that it is merely an illusion caused by certain rays of light and drops of water. The light is only a series of waves or undulations that have no more reality than the rainbow itself.

Man has done well without discovering the soul. He shows no signs of fatigue or degeneration for not having encountered any soul. No man has produced anything to promote mankind by postulating a soul and its imaginary working. Searching for a soul in man is like searching for something in a dark empty room.

But the poor man will never realise that what he is searching for is not in the room. It is very difficult to make such a person understand the futility of his search.

Those who believe in the existence of a soul are not in a position to explain what and where it is. The Buddha's advice is not to waste our time over this unnecessary speculation and devote our time to strive for our salvation. When we have attained perfection then we will be able to realise whether there is a soul or not. A wandering ascetic named Vacchagotta asked the Buddha whether there was an *Atman* (self) or not. The story is as follows:

> Vacchagotta comes to the Buddha and asks:
> 'Venerable Gotama, is there an *Atman*?'
> The Buddha is silent.
> 'Then Venerable Gotama, is there no *Atman*?'
> Again the Buddha is silent.
> Vacchagotta gets up and goes away.

After the ascetic has left, Ananda asks the Buddha why He did not answer Vacchagotta's question. The Buddha explains His position:

' Ananda, when asked by Vacchagotta, the Wanderer: ' Is there a Self? ', if I had answered: ' There is a Self ', then, Ananda, that would be siding with those recluses and brahmanas who hold the eternalist theory *(sassata-vada).* '

' And Ananda, when asked by the Wanderer: ' Is there no Self? ', if I had answered: ' There is no Self ', then that would be siding with those recluses and brahmanas who hold the annihilationist theory *(uccedavada)* '.

' Again, Ananda, when asked by Vacchagotta: ' Is there a Self? ', if I had answered: ' There is a Self ', would that be in accordance with my knowledge that all dhammas are without Self? '

' Surely not, Sir. '

' And again, Ananda, when asked by the Wanderer: ' Is there no Self? ', if I had answered: ' There is no Self ', then that would have created a greater confusion in the already confused Vacchagotta. For he would have thought: Formerly indeed I had an *Atman* (Self), but now I haven't got one.' *(Samyutta Nikaya)*

The Buddha regarded soul-speculation as useless and illusory. He once said, ' Only through ignorance and delusion do men indulge in the dream that their souls are separate and self-existing entities. Their heart still clings to Self. They are anxious about heaven and they seek the pleasure of Self in heaven. Thus they cannot see the bliss of righteousness and the immortality of truth. ' Selfish ideas appear in man's mind due to his conception of Self and craving for existence.

## Anatta: The Teaching of No-Soul

The Buddha countered all soul-theory and soul-speculation with His *Anatta* doctrine. *Anatta* is translated under various labels: No-Soul, No-Self, egolessless, and soullessness.

To understand the *Anatta* doctrine, one must understand that the eternal soul theory — ' I have a soul ' — and the material theory — ' I have no soul ' — are both obstacles to self-realisation or salvation. They arise from the misconception ' *I AM*'. Hence, to understand the *Anatta* doctrine, one must not cling to any opinion or views on soul-theory; rather, one must try to see things objectively as they are and without any mental projections. One must learn to see the so-called 'I' or Soul or Self for what it really is: merely a combination of changing forces. This requires some analytical explanation.

The Buddha taught that what we conceive as something eternal within us, is merely a combination of physical and mental aggregates or forces *(pancakkhandha),* made up of body or matter *(rupakkhandha),* sensation *(vedanakkhandha),* perception *(sannakkhandha),* mental formations *(samkharakkhandha)* and consciousness *(vinnanakkhandha).* These forces are working together in a flux of momentary change; they are never the same for two consecutive moments. They are the component forces of the psycho-physical life. When the Buddha analyzed the psycho-physical life, He found only these five aggregates or forces. He did not find any eternal soul. However, many people still have the misconception that the soul is the consciousness. The Buddha declared in unequivocal terms that consciousness depends on matter, sensation, perception and mental formations and that it cannot exist independently of them.

The Buddha said, ' The body, O monks, is not the Self. Sensation is not the Self. Perception is not the Self. The mental constructions are not the Self. And neither is consciousness the Self. Perceiving this, O monks, the disciple sets no value on the body, or on sensation, or on perception, or on mental constructions, or on consciousness. Setting no value on them, he becomes free of passions and he is liberated. The knowledge of liberation arises there within him. And then he knows that he has done what has to be done, that he has lived the holy life, that he is no longer becoming this or that, that his rebirth is destroyed. ' *(Anatta-Lakkhana Sutta)*

The *Anatta* doctrine of the Buddha is over 2500 years old. Today the thought current of the modern scientific world is flowing towards the Buddha's Teaching of *Anatta* or No-Soul. In the eyes of the modern scientists, man is merely a bundle of ever-changing sensations. Modern physicists say that the apparently solid universe is not, in reality, composed of solid substance at all, but actually a flux of energy. The modern physicist sees the whole universe as a process of transformation of various forces of which man is a mere part. The Buddha was the first to realize this.

A prominent author, W.S. Wily, once said, ' The existence of the immortal in man is becoming increasingly discredited under the influence of the dominant schools of modern thought. ' The belief in the immortality of the soul is a dogma that is contradicted by the most solid, empirical truth.

The mere belief in an immortal soul, or the conviction that something in us survives death, does not make us immortal unless we know what it is that survives and that we are capable of identifying ourselves with it. Most human beings choose death instead of immortality by identifying themselves with that which is perishable and impermanent by clinging stubbornly to the body or the momentary elements of the present personality, which they mistake for the soul or the essential form of life.

About those researches of modern scientists who are now more inclined to assert that the so-called ' Soul ' is no more than a bundle of sensations, emotions, sentiments, all relating to the physical experiences, Prof. James says that the term ' Soul ' is a mere figure of speech to which no reality corresponds.

It is the same *Anatta* doctrine of the Buddha that was introduced in the *Mahayana* school of Buddhism as *Sunyata* or voidness. Although this concept was elaborated by a great *Mahayana* scholar, *Nagarjuna,* by giving various interpretations, there is no extraordinary concept in *Sunyata* far different from the Buddha's original doctrine of *Anatta.*

The belief in Soul or Self and the Creator God, is so strongly rooted in the minds of many people that they cannot imagine why the Buddha did not accept these two issues which are indispensable to many religions. In fact some people got a shock or became nervous and tried to show their emotion when they heard that the Buddha rejected these two concepts. That is the main reason why to many unbiased scholars and psychologists Buddhism stands unique when compared to all the other religions. At the same time, some other scholars who appreciate the various other aspects of Buddhism thought that Buddhism would be enriched by deliberately re-interpreting the Buddha word ' *Atta* ' in order to introduce the concept of Soul and Self into Buddhism. The Buddha was aware of this unsatisfactoriness of man and the conceptual upheaval regarding this belief.

All conditioned things are impermanent,
All conditioned things are *Dukka*—Suffering,
All conditioned or unconditioned things *(dhamma)*
are soulless or selfless. *(Dhammapada 277, 278, 279)*

There is a parable in our Buddhist texts with regard to the belief in an eternal soul. A man, who mistook a moving rope for a snake, became terrified by that fear in his mind. Upon discovery that it was only a piece of rope, his fear subsided and his mind became peaceful. The belief in an eternal soul is equated to the rope — man's imagination.

# 6

## BUDDHISM *VIS-A-VIS* OTHER APPROACHES

### Is Buddhism Similar to Other Contemporary Teachings in India?

*The Dhamma realised by the Buddha was unheard before.*

THE Buddha said in His first sermon, the *Dhammacakka Sutta,* that the Dhamma which He preached was unheard of before. Knowledge of the Dhamma which arose was clear to His vision, to His knowledge, to His wisdom, to His penetration, and to His Enlightenment.

Some people claim that the Buddha did not preach a new doctrine but merely reformed the old teaching which was existing in India. However, the Buddha was no mere reformer of Hinduism as some protagonists of this ancient creed make Him out to be. The Buddha's way of life and doctrine were substantially different from the way of life and the religious beliefs people had in India. The Buddha lived, taught and died as a non-Vedic and non-Brahmanic religious Teacher. Nowhere did the Buddha acknowledge His indebtedness to the existing religious beliefs and practices. The Buddha considered Himself as initiating a rational religious method, as opening a new path. In fact He had revolutionised the religious way of life in a dignified manner.

That was the main reason why many other religious groups could not agree with Him. He was condemned, criticised and insulted by the most noted teachers and sects of the Vedic-Brahmanic tradition. It was with the intention of destroying or absorbing the Buddha and His Teaching, that the Brahmans of the pre-Christian era went so far as to accept the Buddha as an *Avatara* or incarnation of their God. Yet some others despised Him as a *vasalaka,* a *mundaka,* a *samanaka,* a *nastika* and *sudra.* (These words were used in India during the Buddha's time to insult a religious man).

There is no doubt that the Buddha reformed certain customs, religious duties, rites and ethics and ways of living. The greatness of His character was like a pin-point that pricked the balloon of false beliefs and practices so that they could burst and reveal their emptiness.

But as far as the fundamental, philosophical and psychological teachings are concerned, it is groundless to say that the Buddha had copied ideas from any existing religion at that time. For instance, the idea of the Four Noble Truths, the Eightfold Path and Nibbana, were not known before His coming. Although the belief in *kamma* and rebirth was very common, the Buddha gave quite logical and reasonable explanations to this belief and introduced it as natural law of cause and effect. Despite all these the Buddha did not ridicule any sincere existing religious belief or practice. He appreciated the value in many where He found Truth and He even gave a better explanation of their beliefs. That is why He once said that the Truth must be respected wherever it is. However, He was never afraid to speak out against hypocrisy and falsehood.

# Is Buddhism a Theory or a Philosophy?

*The enlightenment of the Buddha is not a product of mere intellect.*

DURING the time of the Buddha there were many learned men in India who pursued knowledge simply for its own sake. These people were full of theoretical knowledge. Indeed, some of them went from city to city challenging anyone to a debate and their greatest thrill was to defeat an opponent in such verbal combats. But the Buddha said that such people were no nearer to the realization of the truth because in spite of their cleverness and knowledge they did not have true wisdom to overcome greed, hatred and delusion. In fact, these people were often proud and arrogant. Their egoistic concepts disturbed the religious atmosphere.

According to the Buddha, one must first seek to understand one's own mind. This was to be done through concentration which gives one a profound inner wisdom or realization. And this insight is to be gained not by philosophical argument or worldly knowledge but by the silent realization of the illusion of the self.

Buddhism is a righteous way of life for the peace and happiness of every living being. It is a method to get rid of miseries and to find liberation. The Teachings of the Buddha are not limited to one nation or race. It is neither a creed nor a mere faith. It is a Teaching for the entire universe. It is a Teaching for all time. Its objectives are selfless service, good-will, peace, salvation and deliverance from suffering.

Salvation in Buddhism is an individual affair. You have to save yourself just as you have to eat, drink and sleep by yourself. The advice rendered by the Buddha points the Way to liberation; but His advice was never intended to be taken as a theory or philosophy. When He was questioned as to what theory He propounded, the Buddha replied that He preached no theories and whatever He did preach was a result of His own experience. Thus His Teaching does not offer any theory. Theory cannot bring one nearer to spiritual perfection. Theories are the very fetters that bind the mind and impede spiritual progress. The Buddha said, 'Wise men give no credence to passing theories. They are past believing everything they see and hear.'

Theories are products of the intellect and the Buddha understood the limitations of the human intellect. He taught that enlightenment is not a product of mere intellect. One cannot achieve emancipation by taking an intellectual course. This statement may seem irrational but it is true. Intellectuals tend to spend too much of their valuable time in study, critical analysis and debate. They usually have little or no time for practice.

A great thinker (philosopher, scientist, metaphysician, etc.) can also turn out to be an intelligent fool. He may be an intellectual giant endowed with the power to perceive ideas quickly and to express thoughts clearly. But if he pays no attention to his actions and their consequences, and if he is only bent on fulfilling his own longings and inclinations at any cost then, according to the Buddha, he is an intellectual fool, a man of inferior intelligence. Such a person will indeed hinder his own spiritual progress.

The Buddha's Teaching contains practical wisdom that cannot be limited to theory or to philosophy because philosophy deals mainly with knowledge but it is not concerned with translating the knowledge into day-to-day practices.

Buddhism lays special emphasis on practice and realization. The philosopher sees the miseries and disappointments of life but, unlike the Buddha, he offers no practical solution to overcome our frustrations which are part of the unsatisfactory nature of life. The philosopher merely pushes his thoughts to dead ends. Philosophy is useful because it has enriched our intellectual imagination and diminished dogmatic assurance which closes the mind to further progress. To that extent, Buddhism values philosophy, but it has failed to quench spiritual thirst.

Remember that the chief aim of a Buddhist is to attain purity and enlightenment. Enlightenment vanquishes ignorance which is the root of birth and death. However, this vanquishing of ignorance cannot be achieved except by the exercise of one's confidence. All other attempts — especially mere intellectual attempts are not very effective. This is why the Buddha concluded: ' These [metaphysical] questions are not calculated to profit; they are not concerned with the Dhamma; they do not lead to right conduct, or to detachment, or to purification from lusts, or to quietude, or to a calm heart, or to real knowledge, or to higher insight, or to Nibbana. ' *(Malunkyaputta Sutta — Majjhima Nikaya).* In place of metaphysical speculation, the Buddha was more concerned with teaching a practical understanding of the Four Noble Truths that He discovered: what Suffering is; what the origin of Suffering is; what the cessation of Suffering is; how to overcome Suffering and realize final Salvation. These Truths are all practical matters to be fully understood and realised by anyone who really experiences emancipation.

Enlightenment is the dispelling of ignorance; it is the ideal of the Buddhist life. We can now clearly see that enlightenment is not an act of the intellect. Mere speculation has something alien to it and does not come so intimately into contact with life. This is why the Buddha placed great emphasis on personal experience. Meditation is a practical scientific system to verify the Truth that comes through personal experience. Through meditation, the will tries to transcend the condition it has put on itself, and this is the awakening of consciousness. Metaphysics merely ties us down in a tangled and matted mass of thoughts and words.

# Is Buddhism Pessimistic?

*Buddhism is neither pessimistic nor optimistic but a realistic religion.*

SOME critics argue that Buddhism is morbid, cynical, hovering on the dark and shadowy side of life, an enemy of harmless pleasures, and an unfeeling trampler on the innocent joys of life. They see Buddhism as being pessimistic, as fostering an attitude of hopelessness towards life, as encouraging a vague, general feeling that pain and evil predominate in human affairs. These critics base their views on the First Noble Truth that all conditioned things are in a state of suffering. They seem to have forgotten that not only had the Buddha taught the cause and end of Suffering, but he had taught the way to *end* Suffering. In any case, is there any religious teacher who praised this worldly life and advised us to cling to it?

If the founder of this religion, the Buddha, was such a pessimist, one would expect His personality to be portrayed on more severe lines than has been done. The Buddha image is the personification of Peace, Serenity, Hope and Goodwill. The magnetic and radiant smile of the Buddha which is said to be inscrutable and enigmatic, is the epitome of His doctrine. To the worried and the frustrated, His smile of Enlightenment and hope is an unfailing tonic and soothing balm.

The Buddha radiated His love and compassion in all directions. Such a person can hardly be a pessimist. And when the sword-happy kings and princes listened to Him, they realised that the only true conquest is the conquest of the Self and the best way to win the hearts of the people was to teach them to appreciate the Dhamma — Truth.

The Buddha cultivated His sense of humour to such a high degree that His bitter opponents were disarmed with the greatest ease. Often they could not help laughing at themselves. The Buddha had a wonderful tonic; He cleaned their systems of dangerous toxins and they became enthusiastic thereafter to follow in His footsteps. In His sermons, dialogues and discussions, He maintained that poise and dignity which won for Him the respect and affection of the people. How can such a person be a pessimist?

The Buddha never expected His followers to be constantly brooding over the suffering of life and leading a miserable and unhappy existence. He taught the fact of suffering only so that He could show people how to overcome this suffering and move in the direction of happiness. To become an Enlightened person, one must have joy, one of the factors that the Buddha recommended us to cultivate. Joy is hardly pessimistic.

There are two Buddhists texts called the *Theragatha* and *Therigatha* which are full of the joyful utterances of the Buddha's disciples, both male and female, who found peace and happiness in life through His Teaching. The king of Kosala once told the Buddha that unlike many a disciple of other religious systems who looked haggard, coarse, pale, emaciated and unprepossessing, His disciples were 'joyful and elated, jubilant and exultant, enjoying the spiritual life, serene, peaceful and living with a gazelle's mind, light-hearted.' The king added that he believed that this healthy disposition was due to the fact that 'these Venerable Ones had certainly realized the great and full significance of the Blessed One's Teachings' *(Majjhima Nikaya).*

When asked why His disciples, who lived a simple and quiet life with only one meal a day, were so radiant, the Buddha replied: 'They do not repent the past, nor do they brood over the future. They live in the present. Therefore they are radiant. By brooding over the future and repenting the past, fools dry up like green reeds cut down [in the sun]' *(Samyutta Nikaya).*

As a religion, Buddhism preaches the unsatisfactory nature of everything in this world. Yet one cannot simply categorize Buddhism as a pessimistic religion, because it also teaches us how to get rid of this unhappiness. According to the Buddha, even the worst sinner, after paying for what he has done, can attain salvation. Buddhism offers every human being the hope of attaining his salvation one day. Other religions, however, take it for granted that some people will be bad forever and have an eternal hell waiting for them. In that respect, such religions are more pessimistic. Buddhists deny such a belief.

Buddhism is neither optimistic nor pessimistic. It does not encourage man to look at the world through his changing feelings of optimism and pessimism. Rather, Buddhism encourages us to be realistic: we must learn to see things as they truly are.

# Is Buddhism Atheistic?

*Atheism is associated with a materialistic doctrine that knows nothing higher than this world.*

THE Buddha has condemned godlessness by which He meant the denial of worship and renunciation, the denial of moral and social obligations, and the denial of a religious life. He recognized most emphatically the existence of moral and spiritual values. He acclaimed the supremacy of the moral law. Only in one sense can Buddhism be described as atheistic, namely, in so far as it denies the existence of an eternal omnipotent God or God-head who is the creator and ordainer of the world. The word 'atheism', however, frequently carries a number of disparaging overtones or implications which are in no way applicable to the Buddha's Teaching. Those who use the word 'atheism', often associate it with a materialistic doctrine that knows nothing higher than this world of the senses and the slight happiness it can bestow. Buddhism advocates nothing of that sort.

There is no justification for branding Buddhists as atheists, nihilists, pagans, heathens or communists just because they do not believe in a Creator God. The Buddhist concept of God is different from that of other religions. Differences in belief do not justify name-calling and slanderous words.

Buddhism agrees with other religions that true and lasting happiness cannot be found in this material world. The Buddha adds that true and lasting happiness cannot be found on the higher or supramundane plane of existence to which the name of heavenly or divine world is given. While the spiritual values advocated by Buddhism are orientated to a state transcending the world with the attainment of Nibbana, they do not make a separation between the 'beyond' and the 'here and now'. They have firm roots in the world itself, for they aim at the highest realisation in this present existence.

PART THREE

# LEADING A BUDDHIST LIFE

# 7

# MORAL FOUNDATION FOR MANKIND

## What is the Purpose of Life?

*Man is the highest fruit on the tree of evolution. It is for man to realise his position in nature and understand the true meaning of his life.*

To know the purpose of life, you will first have to study the subject through your experience and insight. Then, you will discover for yourself the true meaning of life. Guidelines can be given, but you must create the necessary conditions for the arising of realisation yourself.

There are several prerequisites to the discovery of the purpose of life. First, you must understand the nature of man and the nature of life. Next, you keep your mind calm and peaceful through the adoption of a religion. When these conditions are met, the answer you seek will come like the gentle rain from the sky.

## Understanding the nature of man

Man may be clever enough to land on the moon and discover wondrous things in the universe, but he has yet to delve into the inner workings of his own mind. He has yet to learn how his mind can be developed to its fullest potential so that its true nature can be realised.

As yet, man is still wrapped in ignorance. He does not know who he really is or what is expected of him. As a result, he misinterprets everything and acts on that misinterpretation. Is it not conceivable that our entire civilisation is built on this misinterpretation? The failure to understand his existence leads him to assume a false identity of a bloated, self-seeking egoist, and to pretend to be what he is not or is unable to be.

Man must make an effort to overcome ignorance to arrive at realisation and Enlightenment. All great men are born as human beings from the womb, but they worked their way up to greatness. Realisation and Enlightenment cannot be poured into the human heart like water into a tank. Even the Buddha had to cultivate His mind to realise the real nature of man.

Man can be enlightened — a Buddha — if he wakes up from the ' dream ' that is created by his own ignorant mind, and becomes fully awakened. He must realise that what he is today is the result of an untold number of repetitions in thoughts and actions. He is not ready-made: he is continually in the process of becoming, always changing. And it is in this characteristic of change that his future lies, because it means that it is possible for him to mould his character and destiny through the choice of his actions, speech and thoughts. Indeed, he becomes the thoughts and actions that he chooses to perform.  Man is the

highest fruit on the tree of evolution. It is for man to realise his
position in nature and to understand the true meaning of his life.

## Understanding the nature of life

Most people dislike facing the true facts of life and prefer to
lull themselves into a false sense of security by sweet dreaming
and imagining. They mistake the shadow for the substance. They
fail to realise that life is uncertain, but that death is certain. One
way of understanding life is to face and understand death which
is nothing more than a temporary end to a temporary existence.
But many people do not like even to hear of the word ' death '.
They forget that death will come, whether they like it or not.
Recollections on death with the right mental attitude can give
a person courage and calmness as well as an insight into the nature
of existence.

Besides understanding death, we need a better understanding
of our life. We are living a life that does not always proceed as
smoothly as we would like it to. Very often, we face problems
and difficulties. We should not be afraid of them because the
penetration into the very nature of these problems and difficulties
can provide us with a deeper insight into life. The worldly
happiness in wealth, luxury, respectable positions in life which
most people seek is an illusion. The fact that the sale of sleeping
pills and tranquillizers, admissions to mental hospitals and suicide
rates have increased in relation to modern material progress is
enough testimony that we have to go beyond worldly, material
pleasure to seek for real happiness.

## The need for a religion

To understand the real purpose of life, it is advisable for a
person to choose and follow an ethical-moral system that restrains
a person from evil deeds, encourages him to do good, and enables
him to purify his mind. For simplicity, we shall call this system
' religion '

Religion is the expression of the striving man: it is his greatest power, leading him onwards to self-realisation. It has the power to transform one with negative characteristics into someone with positive qualities. It turns the ignoble, noble; the selfish, unselfish; the proud, humble; the haughty, forbearing; the greedy, benevolent; the cruel, kind; the subjective, objective. Every religion, represents, however imperfectly, a reaching upwards to a higher level of being. From the earliest times, religion has been the source of man's artistic and cultural inspiration. Although many forms of religion had come into being in the course of history, only to pass away and be forgotten, each one in its time had contributed something towards the sum of human progress. Christianity helped to civilise the West, and the weakening of its influence has marked a downward trend of the Occidental spirit. Buddhism, which civilised the greater part of the East long before, is still a vital force, and in this age of scientific knowledge is likely to extend and to strengthen its influence. It does not, at any point, come into conflict with modern knowledge, but embraces and transcends all of it in a way that no other system of thought has ever done before or is ever likely to do. Western man seeks to conquer the universe for material ends. Buddhism and Eastern philosophy strive to attain harmony with nature or spiritual satisfaction.

Religion teaches a person how to calm down the senses and make the heart and mind peaceful. The secret of calming down the senses is to eliminate desire which is the root of our disturbances. It is very important for us to have contentment. The more people crave for their property, the more they have to suffer. Property does not give happiness to man. Most of the rich people in the world today are suffering from numerous physical and mental problems. With all the money they have, they cannot buy a solution to their problems. Yet, the poorest men who have learnt to have contentment may enjoy their lives far more than the richest people do. As one rhyme goes:

> *' Some have too much and yet do crave*
> *I have little and seek no more;*
> *They are but poor though much more they have*
> *And I am rich with little store.*
> *They poor, I rich; they beg, I give;*
> *They lack, I have; they pine, I live. '*

## Searching for a purpose in life

The aim in life varies among individuals. An artist may aim to paint masterpieces that will live long after he is gone. A scientist may want to discover some laws, formulate a new theory, or invent a new machine. A politician may wish to become a prime minister or a president. A young executive may aim to be a managing director of a multinational company. However, when you ask the artist, scientist, politician and the young executive why they aim such, they will reply that these achievements will give them a purpose in life and make them happy. Everyone aims for happiness in life, yet experience shows time and again that its attainment is so elusive.

## Realisation

Once we realise the nature of life (characterised by unsatisfactoriness, change, and egolessness) as well as the nature of man's greed and the means of getting them satisfied, we can then understand the reason why the happiness so desperately sought by many people is so elusive like catching a moonbeam in their hands. They try to gain happiness through accumulation. When they are not successful in accumulating wealth, gaining position, power and honour, and deriving pleasure from sense satisfaction, they pine and suffer, envying others who are successful in doing so. However, even if they are ' successful ' in getting these things, they suffer as well because they now fear losing what they have gained, or their desires have now increased for more wealth, higher position, more power, and greater pleasure. Their desires can never seem to be completely satiated. This is why an understanding of life is important so that we do not waste too much time doing the impossible.

It is here that the adoption of a religion becomes important, since it encourages contentment and urges a person to look beyond the demands of his flesh and ego. In a religion like Buddhism, a person is reminded that he is the heir of his karma and the master of his destiny. In order to gain greater happiness, he must be prepared to forego short-term pleasures. If a person does not believe in life after death, even then it is enough for him to lead a good, noble life on earth, enjoying a life of peace and happiness here and now, as well as performing actions which are for the benefit and happiness of others. Leading such a positive and wholesome life on earth and creating happiness for oneself and others is much better than a selfish life of trying to satisfy one's ego and greed.

If, however, a person believes in life after death, then according to the Law of Karma, rebirth will take place according to the quality of his deeds. A person who has done many good deeds may be born in favourable conditions where he enjoys wealth and success, beauty and strength, good health, and meets good spiritual friends and teachers. Wholesome deeds can also lead to rebirth in the heavens and other sublime states, while unwholesome deeds lead to rebirth in suffering states. When a person understands the Law of Karma, he will then make the effort to refrain from performing bad actions, and to try to cultivate the good. By so acting, he gains benefits not only in this life, but in many other lives to come.

When a person understands the nature of man, then some important realisations arise. He realises that unlike a rock or stone, a human being possesses the innate potential to grow in wisdom, compassion, and awareness — and be transformed by this self-development and growth. He also understands that it is not easy to be born as a human being, especially one who has the chance to listen to the Dhamma. In addition, he is fully aware that his life is impermanent, and he should, therefore, strive to practise the Dhamma while he is still in a position to do so. He realises that the practice of Dhamma is a life-long educative process which enables him to release his true potentials trapped within his mind by ignorance and greed.

Based on these realisations and understanding, he will then try to be more aware of what and how he thinks, speaks and acts. He will consider if his thoughts, speech and actions are beneficial, done out of compassion and have good effects for himself as well as others. He will realise the true value of walking the road that leads to complete self transformation, which is known to Buddhists as the Noble Eightfold Path. This Path can help a person to develop his moral strength *(sila)* through the restraint of negative actions and the cultivation of positive qualities conducive for personal, mental and spiritual growth. In addition, it contains many techniques which a person can apply to purify his thoughts, expand the possibilities of the mind, and bring about a complete change towards a wholesome personality. This practice of mental culture *(bhavana)* can widen and deepen the mind towards all human experience, as well as the nature and characteristics of phenomena, life and the universe. In short, this leads to the cultivation of wisdom *(panna)*. As his wisdom grows, so will his love, compassion, kindness, and joy. He will have greater awareness to all forms of life and better understanding of his own thoughts, feelings, and motivations.

In the process of self-transformation, a person will no longer aspire for a divine birth as his ultimate goal in life. He will then set his goal much higher, and model himself after the Buddha who has reached the summit of human perfection and attained the ineffable state we call Enlightenment or *Nibbana*. It is here that a man develops a deep confidence in the Triple Gem and adopts the Buddha as his *spiritual ideal*. He will strive to eradicate greed, develop wisdom and compassion, and to be completely liberated from the bounds of *Samsara*.

# Buddhism for Man in Society

*This religion can be practised either in society or in seclusion.*

THERE are some who believe that Buddhism is so lofty and sublime a system that it cannot be practised by ordinary men and women in the workaday world. These same people think that one has to retire to a monastery or to some quiet place if one desires to be a true Buddhist.

This is a sad misconception that comes from a lack of understanding of the Buddha. People jump to such conclusions after casually reading or hearing something about Buddhism. Some people form their impression of Buddhism after reading articles or books that give only a partial or lopsided view of Buddhism. The authors of such articles and books have only a limited understanding of the Buddha's Teaching. His Teaching is not meant only for monks in monastries. The Teaching is also for ordinary men and women living at home with their families. The Noble Eightfold Path is the Buddhist way of life that is intended for all people. This way of life is offered to all mankind without any distinction.

The vast majority of people in the world cannot become monks or retire into caves or forests. However noble and pure Buddhism may be, it would be useless to the masses if they could not follow it in their daily life in the modern world. But if you understand the spirit of Buddhism correctly, you can surely follow and practise it while living the life of an ordinary man.

There may be some who find it easier and more convenient to accept Buddhism by living in a remote place; in other words, by cutting themselves off from the society of others. Yet, other people may find that this kind of retirement dulls and depresses their whole being both physically and mentally, and that it may therefore not be conducive to the development of their spiritual and intellectual life.

True renunciation does not mean running away physically from the world. Sariputta, the chief disciple of the Buddha, said that one man might live in a forest devoting himself to ascetic practices, but might be full of impure thoughts and 'defilements'. Another might live in a village or a town, practising no ascetic discipline, but his mind might be pure, and free from 'defilements'. ' Of these two, ' said Sariputta, ' the one who lives a pure life in the village or town is definitely far superior to, and greater than, the one who lives in the forest. ' *(Majjhima Nikaya)*

The common belief that to follow the Buddha's Teaching one has to retire from a normal family life is a misconception. It is really an unconscious defence against practising it. There are numerous references in Buddhist literature to men and women living ordinary, normal family lives who successfully practised what the Buddha taught and realized *Nibbana.* Vacchagotta the Wanderer, once asked the Buddha straightforwardly whether there were laymen and women leading the family life who followed His Teaching successfully and attained the high spiritual states. The Buddha categorically stated that there were many laymen and women leading the family life who had followed His Teaching successfully and attained the high spiritual states.

It may be agreeable for certain people to live a retired life in a quiet place away from noise and disturbances. But it is certainly more praiseworthy and courageous to practise Buddhism living among fellow beings, helping them and offering service to them. It may perhaps be useful in some cases for a man to live in retirement for a time in order to improve his mind and character, as a preliminary to moral, spiritual and intellectual training, to be strong enough to come out later and help others. But if a man lives all his life in solitude, thinking only of his own happiness and salvation, without caring for his fellowmen, this surely is not in keeping with the Buddha's Teaching which is based on love compassion and service to others.

One might now ask, ' If a man can follow Buddhism while living the life of an ordinary man, why was the Sangha, the Order of Monks, established by the Buddha? ' The Order provides opportunity for those who are willing to devote their lives not only to their own spiritual and intellectual development, but also to the service of others. An ordinary layman with a family cannot be expected to devote his whole life to the service of others, whereas a Monk, who has no family responsibilities or any other worldly ties, is in a position to devote his life 'for the good of the many'. *(Dr. Walpola Rahula)*

And what is this ' good ' that many can benefit from? The monk cannot give material comfort to a layman, but he can provide spiritual guidance to those who are troubled by worldly, family emotional problems and so on. The monk devotes his life to the pursuit of knowledge of the Dhamma as taught by the Buddha. He explains the Teaching in simplified form to the untutored layman. And if the layman is well educated, he is there to discuss the deeper aspects of the teaching so that both can gain intellectually from the discussion.

In Buddhist countries, monks are largely responsible for the education of the young. As a result of their contribution, Buddhist countries have populations which are literate and well-versed in spiritual values. Monks also comfort those who are bereaved and emotionally upset by explaining how all mankind is subject to similar disturbances.

In turn, the layman is expected to look after the material well-being of the monk who does not gain income to provide himself with food, shelter, medicine and clothing. In common Buddhist practice, it is considered meritorious for a layman to contribute to the health of a monk because by so doing he makes it possible for the monk to continue to minister to the spiritual needs of the people and for his mental purity.

# The Buddhist Way of Life for Householders

*The Buddha considered economic welfare as a requisite for human happiness, but moral and spiritual development for a happy, peaceful and contented life.*

A man named Dighajanu once visited the Buddha and said, ' Venerable Sir, we are ordinary laymen, leading a family life with wife and children. Would the Blessed One teach us some doctrines which will be conducive to our happiness in this world and hereafter? '

The Buddha told him that there are four things which are conducive to a man's happiness in this world. First: he should be skilled, efficient, earnest, and energetic in whatever profession he is engaged, and he should know it well *(utthana-sampada)*; second: he should protect his income, which he has thus earned righteously, with the sweat of his brow *(arakkha-sampada)*; third; he should have good friends *(kalyana-mitta)* who are faithful, learned, virtuous, liberal and intelligent, who will help him along the right path away from evil; fourth: he should spend reasonably, in proportion to his income, neither too much nor too little, i.e., he should not hoard wealth avariciously nor should he be extravagant — in other words he should live within his means *(sama-jivikata)*.

Then the Buddha expounds the four virtues conducive to a layman's happiness hereafter: (1) *Saddha:* he should have faith and confidence in moral, spiritual and intellectual values; (2) *Sila:* he should abstain from destroying and harming life, from stealing and cheating, from adultery, from falsehood, and from intoxicating drinks; (3) *Caga:* he should practise charity, generosity, without attachment and craving for his wealth; (4) *Panna:* he should develop wisdom which leads to the complete destruction of suffering, to the realisation of *Nibbana*.

---

*Abstract from the book ' What the Buddha Taught ' by Ven. Dr. W. Rahula.*

Sometimes the Buddha even went into details about saving money and spending it, as, for instance, when he told the young man *Sigala* that he should spend one fourth of his income on his daily expenses, invest half in his business and put aside one fourth for any emergency.

Once the Buddha told *Anathapindika,* the great banker, one of His most devoted lay disciples who founded for Him the celebrated Jetavana monastery at Savatthi, that a layman who leads an ordinary family life has four kinds of happiness. The first happiness is to enjoy economic security or sufficient wealth acquired by just and righteous means *(atthi-sukha);* the second is spending that wealth liberally on himself, his family, his friends and relatives, and on meritorious deeds *(bhoga-sukha);* the third to be free from debts *(anana-sukha);* the fourth happiness is to live a faultless, and a pure life without committing evil in thought, word or deed *(anavajja-sukha).*

It must be noted here that first three are economic and material happiness which is 'not worth part' of the spiritual happiness arising out of a faultless and good life.

From the few examples given above, one can see that the Buddha considered economic welfare as a requisite for human happiness, but that He did not recognize progress as real and true if it was only material, devoid of a spiritual and moral foundation. While encouraging material progress, Buddhism always lays great stress on the development of the moral and spiritual character for a happy, peaceful and contented society.

Many people think that to be a good Buddhist one must have absolutely nothing to do with the materialistic life. This is not correct. What the Buddha teaches is that while we can enjoy material comforts without going to extremes, we must also conscientiously develop the spiritual aspects of our lives. While we can enjoy sensual pleasures as laymen, we should never be unduly attached to them to the extent that they hinder our spiritual progress. Buddhism emphasizes the need for a man to follow the Middle Path.

# 8

# BUDDHIST MORALITY
# AND PRACTICE

## Buddhist Ethics

*Man-made moral laws and customs do not form Buddhist Ethics.*

THE world today is in a state of turmoil; valuable ethics are being upturned. The forces of materialistic scepticism have turned their dissecting blades on the traditional concepts of what are considered humane qualities. Yet, any person who has a concern for culture and civilisation will concern himself with practical, ethical issues. For ethics has to do with human conduct. It is concerned with our relationship with ourselves and with our fellow-men.

The need for ethics arises from the fact that man is not perfect by nature: he has to train himself to be good. Thus morality becomes the most important aspect of living.

Buddhist ethics are not arbitary standards invented by man for his own utilitarian purpose. Nor are they arbitrarily imposed from without. Man-made laws and social customs do not form the basis of Buddhist ethics. For example, the styles of dress that are suitable for one climate, period or civilisation may be considered indecent in another; but this is entirely a matter of social custom and does not in any way involve ethical considerations. Yet the artificialities of social conventions are continually confused with ethical principles that are valid and unchanging.

Buddhist ethics finds its foundation not on the changing social customs but rather on the unchanging laws of nature. Buddhist ethical values are intrinsically a part of nature, and the unchanging law of cause and effect *(kamma)*. The simple fact that Buddhist ethics are rooted in natural law makes its principles both useful and acceptable to the modern world. The fact that the Buddhist ethical code was formulated over 2,500 years ago does not detract from its timeless character.

Morality in Buddhism is essentially practical in that it is only a means leading to the final goal of ultimate happiness. On the Buddhist path to Emancipation, each individual is considered responsible for his own fortunes and misfortunes. Each individual is expected to work his own deliverance by his understanding and effort. Buddhist salvation is the result of one's own moral development and can neither be imposed nor granted to one by some external agent. The Buddha's mission was to enlighten men as to the nature of existence and to advise them how best to act for their own happiness and for the benefit of others. Consequently, Buddhist ethics are not founded on any commandments which men are compelled to follow. The Buddha advised men on the conditions which were most wholesome and conducive to long-term benefit for self and others. Rather than addressing sinners with such words as ' shameful ', ' wicked ', ' wretched ',

' unworthy ', and ' blasphemous ' He would merely say, ' You are foolish in acting in such a way since this will bring sorrow upon yourselves and others'.

The theory of Buddhist ethics finds its practical expression in the various precepts. These precepts or disciplines are nothing but general guides to show the direction in which the Buddhist ought to turn to on his way to final salvation. Although many of these precepts are expressed in a negative form, we must not think that Buddhist morality, consists of abstaining from evil without the complement of doing good.

The morality found in all the precepts can be summarized in three simple principles — ' To avoid evil; to do good, to purify the mind. ' This is the advice given by all the Buddhas.

*(Dhammapada, 183)*

In Buddhism, the distinction between what is good and what is bad is very simple: all actions that have their roots in *greed, hatred, and delusion* that spring from selfishness foster the harmful delusion of selfhood. These actions are demeritorious or unskilful or bad. They are called *Akusala Kamma.* All those actions which are *rooted in the virtues of generosity, love and wisdom,* are meritorious — *Kusala Kamma.* The criteria of good and bad apply whether the actions are of thought, word or deed.

## Buddhist ethics are based on intention or volition

' KAMMA is volition, ' says the Buddha. Actions themselves are considered as neither good nor bad but ' only the intention and thought makes them so. ' Yet Buddhist ethics does not maintain that a person may commit what are conventionally regarded as ' sins ' provided that he does so with the best of intentions. Had this been its position, Buddhism would have confined itself to questions of psychology and left the uninteresting task of drawing up lists of ethical ruled and framing codes of conducts to less emancipated teachings. The connection between thoughts and deeds, between mental and material action is an extension of thought. It is not possible to commit murder with a good heart because taking of life is simply the outward expression of a state of mind dominated by hate or greed. Deeds are condensations of thoughts just as rain is a condensation of vapour. Deeds proclaim from the rooftops of action only what has already been committed in the silent and secret chambers of the heart.

A person who commits an immoral act thereby declares that he is not free from unwholesome states of mind. Also, a person who has a purified and radiant mind, who has a mind empty of all defiled thoughts and feelings, is incapable of committing immoral actions.

Buddhist ethics also recognizes the objectivity of moral values. In other words, the kammic consequences of actions occur in accordance with natural kammic law, regardless of the attitude of the individual or regardless of social attitudes toward the act. For example, drunkeness has kammic consequences; it is evil since it promotes one's own unhappiness as well as the unhappiness of others. The kammic effects of drunkeness exist despite what the drunkard or his society may think about the habit of drinking. The prevailing opinions and attitudes do not in the least detract from the fact that drunkeness is objectively evil. The consequences — psychological, social, and kammic — make actions moral or immoral — regardless of the mental attitudes of those judging the act. Thus while ethical relativism is recognized, it is not considered as undermining the objectivity of values.

# What is Vinaya?

*Vinaya is the disciplinary code for self training laid down by the Buddha for monks and nuns to observe. Vinaya plays a pivotal role in their monastic way of life.*

THE Buddha did not formulate the code of discipline in a single exercise. However, He instituted certain rules as and when the need arose. *Vinaya Pitaka* and its commentary contain many significant stories about how and why certain rules were laid down by the Buddha. According to the Buddha the best form of Vinaya was to discipline the mind, words and action. The early disciples of the Buddha were highly developed spiritually and they had little need for a set of rules to be imposed upon them. However, as the monastic order (the Sangha) grew in numbers, it attracted many others, some of whom were not so highly developed spiritually. There arose some problems regarding their conduct and way of life such as taking part in lay activities for their livelihood and yielding to temptation for sense pleasure. Owing to this situation, the Buddha had to lay down guidelines for the monks and nuns to follow so that they could distinguish the difference between the life of monks and laymen. The holy order of the monks and the nuns was a well-established religious order when compared with other existing ascetic practices at that time.

The Buddha prescribed all the necessary guidance to maintain the holy order in every aspect of life. When the Buddha passed away, these rules were collated so that the Order could be organised around them. The code of conduct prescribed by the Buddha can be divided into two broad areas. These are Universal Moral Codes, *Lokavajja,* most of which are applicable to all members of the Order and lay people alike for leading a religious life. Certain other disciplinary codes or rules which can be instituted to meet the existing cultural and social constraints of the country at any one time are called *Pannatti Vajja.* In the first category are the Universal Laws which restricted all immoral and harmful evil deeds. The second category of rules applied almost directly to the monks and nuns in the observance of manners, traditions, duties, customs and etiquette. Breaking of moral codes pertaining to the *Lokavajja* create bad reputation as well as bad kamma, whereas violation of disciplinary codes based on social conditions do not necessarily create bad kamma. However, they are subject to criticism as violation in any form pollute the purity and dignity of the holy Order. These rules were largely based on the socio-cultural situation or way of life prevailing in India 25 centuries ago. According to the *Maha Parinibbana Sutta,* the Buddha had proclaimed that some ' minor ' rules could be altered or amended to accommodate changes due to time and environment, provided they do not encourage immoral or harmful behaviour. In fact, during the Buddha's time itself, certain minor rules were amended by the monks with His permission. The Buddha also advocated that sick monks and nuns be exempted from certain Vinaya rules. However, once the rules had been enumerated by the disciples in the First Council, convened three months after the passing away of the Buddha, it was decided that all the rules should be maintained in toto because no one was certain as to which of the rules should be altered. Finally, the disciples decided to uphold all the precepts prescribed by the Buddha. As time went on however, the rules became fossilized and some orthodox disciples insisted that the rules should be followed strictly to the letter rather than in the spirit. It was precisely to prevent rigid adherence to mere rules of this kind that the Buddha did not appoint a successor to take over after Him. He had said that the understanding of the Dhamma and upholding of the Dhamma as the master should be enough to help one lead a holy life. Another reason why the early disciples did not agree to change any of the precepts was that there was no reason or occasion for them to do so within such a short period of time after the passing away of the Buddha. This was because, at that time, most of those who had renounced their worldly life had done so with sincerity and conviction. However, when the social conditions started to change and when Buddhism spread to many other parts of India and other countries, the decision made by the disciples not to change any precepts in the First Council became a very big problem because some of the rules could not be adapted to meet the political and economic changes under varying circumstances.

## Development of Sangha Community

The Sangha community, in the course of time, evolved themselves into several sects, many of whom, while adhering to some major precepts as laid down by the Buddha, had, however, tended to ignore some of the minor rules. The Theravada sect appeared to be more orthodox, while the Mahayana and some other sects tended to be more liberal in their outlook and religious observances. The Theravada sect tried to observe the Vinaya to the very letter despite of changing circumstances and environment. Minor changes of the precepts had, however, taken place from time to time, but were not officially recognised even amongst the members of the Theravada sect. For instance, we can look at the rule regarding the partaking of food after the stipulated time of the day. The Theravada sect has not openly acknowledged the fact that certain variations could be allowed under special circumstances. Whilst members of other schools adapt themselves to the wearing of robes with appropriate colour and pattern, the Theravada sect has continued to adhere to the use of the original robes that were traditionally prescribed despite the changed social and climatic conditions. Many of practices of the monkhood are clearly understood only by those who are born into traditional Buddhist cultures.

At the other extreme, there are some monks who insist on observing the very letter of the Vinaya code rather than in its spirit, even though such action would embarrass the people around them. For example, more and more Buddhist monks are being invited to western countries where the culture of the people and the climatic conditions are so vastly different from that in Asia, but which could be regarded as strange and exotic elsewhere. Here again the monk must apply his common sense and try not to make a mockery of himself in the eyes of the people. The important rule to be observed is that no immoral, cruel, harmful and indecent acts are created and that the sensivities of others are respected. If the monks can lead their lives as honest, kind, harmless and understanding human beings by maintaining their human dignity and disciplines, then such qualities will be appreciated in any part of the world. Maintaining the so-called traditions and customs of their respective countries of origin have little to do with the essence of the Dhamma as taught by the Buddha.

Then, there is another problem. Many people, especially those in the West who have accepted the Buddhist way of life, having read the Vinaya rules in the texts, think that the monks must follow all the rules in toto in any part of the world, in exactly the same manner as they were recorded in the texts. We must remember that some of these rules which were practiced in Indian society 25 centuries ago are irrelevant even in Asia today. It must be clearly borne in mind that the Buddha instituted the rules only for the members of the Sangha community who lived in India, in fact in the region where He lived. Those monks never had any experience of the way of life in another country. Their main concern was with the spiritual development with the minimum of disruption and annoyance to the society where they lived. But if they lived today, they may experience many other new problems, if they strictly observe all the rules in a country where people cannot appreciate or understand them.

The disciplinary code for lay devotees show how a layman can live a virtuous and noble life without renouncing the worldly life. The Buddha's advice to lay people is contained in such discourses as the *Mangala, Parabhava, Sigalovada, Vasala* and *Vygghapajja* and many other discourses.

Many Vinaya rules apply only to those who have renounced the worldly life. Of course a layman may follow some of the rules if they help him to develop greater spirituality.

## Changing Society

When society changes, monks cannot remain as traditionalists without adapting to the changes, although they have renounced the worldly life. People who cannot understand this situation criticise the behaviour of certain monks because of those changes. However, when the monks want to amend even certain minor precepts, they would have to do it with the sanction of a recognised Sangha Council. Individual monks are not at liberty to change any Vinaya rules according to their whims and fancies. Such a Council of Sangha members can also impose certain sanction against monks who have committed serious violations of the disciplinary code and whose behaviour discredits the Sangha. The Buddha instituted the Council to help monks to prevent evil deeds and avoid temptation in a worldly life. The rules were guidelines rather than inviolable laws handed down by some divine authority.

In Asian countries particularly, monks are accorded great respect and reverence. Lay people respect them as teachers of the Dhamma and as men who have sacrificed the worldly life in order to lead a holy life. Monks devote themselves to the study and practice of the Dhamma and do not earn a living. Laymen, therefore, see to their material well-being while they in turn look to the monks for their spiritual needs.

As such, monks are expected to conduct themselves in such a way that will earn them the respect and reverence of the public. If, for example, a monk is seen in a disreputable place, he will be criticized even if he is not involved in any immoral action. Therefore, it is the duty of the monks to avoid certain uncongenial surroundings so as to maintain the dignity of the holy Order.

If a monk does not respect the feelings of his lay devotees and behaves according to what he alone thinks is right, then the lay devotees are not bound to look after his needs. There are many instances recorded in the Buddhist Texts that even during the Buddha's time, lay devotees had refused to look after arrogant, quarrelsome or irresponsible monks. Monks can be criticized for doing certain worldly things which only lay people are at liberty to do.

## Dhamma and Vinaya

Many people have not yet realised that the Dhamma, the Truth expounded by the Buddha, is not changeable under any circumstances. Certain Vinaya rules are also included into the same category and they are not subject to change under any circumstances. But some other Vinaya rules are subject to change so as to prevent certain undue inconveniences. Dhamma and Vinaya are not the same. Some monks try to observe certain traditions rigidly as if they are important religious principles although others cannot find any religious significance or implication in their practices. At the same time some selfish and cunning persons may even try to maintain certain outward manifestations of purity, in order to mislead innocent devotees to regard them as pious and sincere monks. Many so-called Buddhist practices in Asian countries that monks and others follow are not necessarily religious precepts but traditional practices upheld by the people. On the other hand, certain manners introduced for monks to observe as disciplines truly maintain the dignity and serenity of the holy Order. Although religious traditions and customs can create a congenial atmosphere for spiritual development, some Vinaya rules need to be amended according to changing social conditions. If this is not done, monks will have to face numerous problems in the course of their survival and in their association with the public.

Some lay people criticize monks for handling money. It is difficult to carry out their religious activities and to be active in modern society without dealing with money. What a monk must do is to consider himself as unattached to the money or property as personal belongings. That is what the Buddha meant. Of course, there may be some who deliberately misinterpret the rules to suit their material gain. They will have to bear the consequences of their own inability to gain spiritual development.

However, those who choose to confine themselves to an isolated area for meditation for peace of mind, should be able to carry out their religious duties without hindrance from worldly things which can become burdensome. But they must first ensure that they have enough supporters to attend to their needs. While there can be such monks who wish to retire completely from society there must be enough monks in society to attend to the numerous religious needs of the general public. Otherwise, people may think that Buddhism cannot contribute very much in their day to day lives.

## Characteristic of a Monk

Among the salient characteristics of a monk are purity, voluntary poverty, humility, simplicity, selfless service, self-control, patience, compassion and harmlessness. He is expected to observe the four kinds of Higher Morality — namely:

| | | |
|---|---|---|
| *Patimokkha Sila* | — | The Fundamental Moral Code (major offences related to immoral, cruel, harmful and selfish activities). |
| *Indriyasamvara Sila* | — | Morality pertaining to sense-restraint. |
| *Ajivaparisuddhi Sila* | — | Morality pertaining to purity of livelihood. |
| *Paccayasannissita Sila* | — | Morality pertaining to the use of requisites pertaining to life. |

These four kinds of morality are collectively called *Sila-Visuddhi* (Purity of Virtue).

When a person enters the Order and receives his ordination he is called a *Samanera* — Novice Monk. He is bound to observe Ten *Samanera* Precepts with certain disciplinary codes for leading a monastic life until he receives his higher ordination — *Upasampada* — to become a Bhikkhu or fully fledged monk.

A *bhikkhu* or monk is bound to observe the above-mentioned four kinds of higher morality which comprise 227 rules apart from several other minor ones. The four major ones which deal with celibacy and abstinence from stealing, murder, and false claims to higher spirituality must strictly be observed. If he violates any one of these, a monk is regarded as a defeated person in the Sangha community. He will be deprived of certain religious rights by the Sangha community. In the case of other rules which he violates, he has to face many other consequences and make amends according to the gravity of the offence.

There are no vows for a *bhikkhu*. He becomes a *bhikkhu* of his own accord in order to lead a Holy Life for as long as he likes. There is therefore no need for him to feel trapped by a vow he made earlier and to be hypocritical because he alone can decide whether or not he wishes to obey the rules. He is at liberty to leave the Order at any time and can lead a lay Buddhist way of life when he wishes to do so.

# Ten Meritorious and Ten Evil Actions

*A fortunate or unfortunate life depends on individual merits and demerits.*

THE performance of good actions gives rise to merit *(punna)*, a quality which purifies and cleanses the mind. If the mind is unchecked, it has the tendency to be ruled by evil tendencies, leading one to perform bad deeds and getting into trouble. Merit purifies the mind of the evil tendencies of greed, hatred and delusion. The greedy mind encourages a person to desire, accumulate and hoard; the hating mind drags him to dislike and anger; and the deluded mind makes one become entangled in greed and hatred, thinking that these evil roots are right and worthy. Demeritorious deeds give rise to more suffering and reduce the opportunities for a person to know and practise the Dhamma.

Merit is important to help us along our journey through life. It is connected with what are good and beneficial to oneself and others, and can improve the quality of the mind. While the material wealth a person gathers can be lost by theft, flood, fire, confiscation, etc., the benefit of merits follows him from life to life and cannot be lost, although it can be exhausted if no attempts are made to perform more merits. A person will experience happiness here and now as well as hereafter through the performance of merit.

Merit is a great facilitator: It opens the doors of opportunity everywhere. A meritorious person will succeed in whatever venture he puts his effort into. If he wishes to do business, he will meet with the right contacts and friends. If he wishes to be a scholar, he will be awarded with scholarships and supported by academic mentors. If he wishes to progress in meditation, he will meet with a skillful meditation teacher who guides him through his spiritual development. His dreams will be realised through the grace of his treasury of merit. It is merit which enables a person to be reborn in the heavens, and provides him with the right conditions and support for his attainment of *Nibbana*.

There are several rich fields of merit (recipients of the deed) which give rise to bountiful results to the performer of the good deed. Just as some soil can yield a better harvest (say black fertile soil compared to stony soil), a good deed performed to some persons can give rise to more merits than to others. The rich fields of merits include the Sangha or holy people, mother, father and needy. Good deeds performed to these persons will manifest in many ways and be the fountainhead of many wondrous results.

The Buddha taught ten meritorious deeds for us to perform in order to gain a happy and peaceful life as well as to develop knowledge and understanding. The ten meritorious deeds are:

1. Charity
2. Morality
3. Mental culture

4. Reverence or respect
5. Service in helping others
6. Sharing merits with others
7. Rejoicing in the merits of others
8. Preaching and teaching the Dhamma
9. Listening to the Dhamma
10. Straightening one's views

The performance of these ten meritorious deeds will not only benefit oneself, but others as well, besides giving benefits to the recipients. Moral conduct benefits all beings with whom one comes into contact. Mental culture brings peace to others and inspires them to practise the Dhamma. Reverence gives rise to harmony in society, while service improves the lives of others. Sharing merits with others shows that one is concerned about others' welfare, while rejoicing in others' merits encourages others to perform more merits. Teaching and listening to the Dhamma are important factors for happiness for both the teacher and listener, while encouraging both to live in line with Dhamma. Straightening one's views enables a person to show to others the beauty of Dhamma. In the *Dhammapada,* the Buddha taught:

' Should a person perform good,
He should do it again and again;
He should find pleasure therein;
For blissful is the accumulation of good. '    — 118

' Think not lightly of good, saying,
'It will not come near to me' —
Even by the falling of drops a water-jar is filled.
Likewise the wise man, gathering little by little,
Fills himself with good. '    — 122

**Ten Evil Deeds**

There are ten demeritorious deeds from which Buddhists are advised to keep away. These deeds are rooted in greed, hatred and delusion, and will bring suffering to others but especially to oneself in this life and later lives. When a person understands the Law of Kamma and realises that bad deeds bring bad results, he will then practise Right Understanding and avoid performing these actions.

There are three bodily actions which are kammically unwholesome. They are: (1) Killing of living beings, (2) Stealing, and (3) Unlawful sexual intercourse. These bodily deeds correspond to the first three of the Five Precepts for people to follow.

The effects of killing to the performer of the deed are brevity of life, ill-health, constant grief due to the separation from the loved, and living in constant fear. The bad consequences of stealing are poverty, misery, disappointment, and a dependent livelihood. The bad consequences of sexual misconduct are having many enemies, always being hated, and union with undesirable wives and husbands.

Four verbal actions are kammically unwholesome, and they are as follows: (1) Lying, (2) Slander and tale-bearing, (3) Harsh speech, and (4) Frivolous and meaningless talk. Except for lying, the other unwholesome deeds performed by speech may be viewed as extensions of the Fourth Precept.

The bad consequences of lying to the one who performs the deed are being subject to abusive speech and vilification, untrustworthiness, and physical unpleasantness. The bad effect of slandering is losing one's friends without any sufficient cause. The results of harsh speech are being detested by others and having a harsh voice. The inevitable effects of frivolous talk are defective bodily organs and speech which no one believes.

The three other demeritorious deeds are performed by the mind, and they are as follows: (1) Covetousness, or eagerly desirous especially of things belonging to others, (2) Ill-will, and (3) Wrong views. These three deeds correspond to the three evil roots of greed, hatred and delusion. The non-observance of the Fifth

Precept of abstention from intoxicants can not only lead to the performance of these three demeritorious mental actions after the mind is intoxicated, but also the other demeritorious deeds performed by body and speech.

The undesirable result of covetousness is the non-fulfilment of one's wishes. The consequences of illwill are ugliness, manifold diseases, and having a detestable nature. Finally, the consequences of false view are having gross desires, lack of wisdom, being of dull wit, having chronic diseases and blameworthy ideas.

A person should always perform good actions and restrain himself from doing evil actions. If, however, a person has performed an evil action, it is necessary for him to realise where he has done wrong and make an effort not to repeat the mistake. This is the true meaning of repentence, and in this way only will a person progress along the noble path to salvation.

Praying for forgiveness is meaningless if, after the prayer is made, a person repeats the evil action again and again. Who is there to ' wash away a person's sins ' except he himself? This has to begin with *realisation,* the wonderful cleansing agent. First, he realises the nature of his deed and the extent of the harm incurred. Next, he realises that this deed is unwholesome, learns from it, and makes the resolution not to repeat it. Then, he performs many good deeds to the affected party as well as to others, as much as possible. In this way, he overcomes the effect of bad deed with a shower of good deeds.

No wrong doer, according to Buddhism, is beyond redemption or rehabilitation, especially with realisation and Right Effort. To be seduced into believing that a person can ' wash away ' his bad deeds through some other ' miraculous ' way is not only a mere superstition, but worse, it is also not useful particularly to the spiritual development of the person himself. It will only cause him to continue to remain ignorant and morally complacent. This misplaced belief can, in fact, do a person much more harm than the effects of the wrong deed he feared so much.

# Precepts

*By observing precepts, not only do you cultivate your moral strength, but you also perform the highest service to your fellow beings.*

EVERY country or society has its code of what are considered to be moral actions within its social context. These codes are often linked to the society's interest and its code of law. An action is considered right so long as it does not break the law and transgress public or individual sensitivities. These man-made codes are flexible and amended from time to time to suit changing circumstances. Important as they are to society, these man-made standards cannot serve as a reliable guide to some principles of morality which can be applied universally.

By contrast, Buddhist morality is not the invention of human minds. Neither is it based on tribal ethics which are gradually being replaced by humanistic codes. It is based on the universal law of cause and effect *(kamma),* and considers a ' good ' or ' bad ' action in terms of the manner it affects oneself and others. An action, even if it brings benefit to oneself, cannot be considered a good action if it causes physical and mental pain to another being.

Buddhist morality addresses a very common, yet crucial question: How can we judge if an action is good or bad? The answer, according to Buddhism, is a simple one. The quality of an action hinges on the intention or motivation *(cetana)* from which it originates. If a person performs an action out of greed, hatred, and delusion, his action is considered to be unwholesome. On the other hand, if he performs an action out of love, charity, and wisdom, his action is a wholesome one. Greed, Hatred and Delusion are known as the 'Three Evil Roots ', while love, charity

---

*For further details on the Eight Precepts, see ' Handbook of Buddhists ' by the same author.*

and wisdom as the ' Three Good Roots '. The word ' root ' refers
to the intention from which that action originates. Therefore,
no matter how a person tries to disguise the nature of his action,
the truth can be found by examining his thoughts which gave
rise to that action. And the mind is the source of all our speech
and action.

In Buddhism, a person's first duty is to cleanse himself of the
mental defilements of greed, hatred and ignorance. The reason
for doing this is not because of fear or desire to please some divine
beings. If this is so, a person is still lacking in wisdom. He is
only acting out of fear like the little child who is afraid of being
punished for being naughty. A Buddhist should act out of
understanding and wisdom. He performs wholesome deeds
because he realises that by so doing he develops his moral strength
which provides the foundation for spiritual growth, leading to
Liberation. In addition, he realises that his happiness and
suffering are self-created through the operation of the Law of
*Kamma.* To minimise the occurrence of troubles and problems
in his life, he makes the effort to refrain from doing evil. He
performs good actions because he knows that these will bring
him peace and happiness. Since everyone seeks happiness in life,
and since it is possible for him to provide the condition for
happiness, then there is every reason for him to do good and avoid
evil. Furthermore, the uprooting of these mental defilements, the
source of all anti-social acts, will bring great benefits to others
in society.

**Five Precepts**

Lay Buddhist morality is embodied in the Five Precepts, which
may be considered at two levels. First, it enables men to live
together in civilized communities with mutual trust and respect.
Second, it is the starting point for the spiritual journey towards
Liberation. Unlike commandments, which are supposedly divine
commands imposed on men, precepts are accepted voluntarily

by the person himself, especially when he realises the usefulness of adopting some training rules for disciplining his body, speech and mind. Understanding, rather than fear of punishment, is the reason for following the precepts. A good Buddhist should remind himself to follow the Five Precepts daily. They are as follows:
 ' I take the training rule to refrain from:

1. killing living creatures
2. taking what is not given
3. sexual misconduct
4. false speech
5. taking intoxicating drugs and liquor,

Besides understanding the Five Precepts merely as a set of rules of abstention, a Buddhist should remind himself that through the precepts he practices the Five Ennoblers as well. While the Five Precepts tells him *what not to do,* the Five Ennoblers tells him which *qualities to cultivate,* namely, loving kindness, renunciation, contentment, truthfulness, and mindfulness. When a person observes the First Precept of not killing, he controls his hatred and cultivates loving kindness. In the Second Precept, he controls his greed and cultivates his renunciation or non-attachment. He controls sensual lust and cultivates his contentment in the Third Precept. In the Fourth Precept, he abstains from false speech and cultivates truthfulness, while he abstains from unwholesome mental excitement and develops mindfulness through the Fifth Precept. Therefore, when a person understands the ennoblers, he will realise that the observance of the Five Precepts does not cause him to be withdrawn, self-critical and negative, but to be a positive personality filled with love and care as well as other qualities accruing to one who leads a moral life.

The precepts are the basic practice in Buddhism. The purpose is to eliminate crude passions that are expressed through thought, word and deed. The precepts are also an indispensable basis for people who wish to cultivate their minds. Without some basic moral code, the power of meditation can often be applied for some wrong and selfish motive.

**Eight Precepts**

In many Buddhist countries, it is customary among the devotees to observe the Eight Precepts on certain days of the month, such as the full moon and new moon days. These devotees will come to the temple early in the morning and spend twenty-four hours in the temple, observing the precepts. By observing the Eight Precepts, they cut themselves off from their daily life which is bombarded with material and sensual demands. The purpose of observing the Eight Precepts is to develop relaxation and tranquility, to train the mind, and to develop oneself spiritually.

During this period of observing the precepts, they spend their time reading religious books, listening to the Teachings of the Buddha, meditating, and also helping with the religious activities of the temple. The following morning, they change from Eight Precepts to the Five Precepts intended for daily observance, and return home to resume their normal life.

The Eight Precepts are to abstain from:
1. Killing;
2. Stealing;
3. Sexual acts;
4. Lying;
5. Liquor;
6. Taking food after the sun had crossed the zenith;
7. Dancing, singing, music, unseemly shows, the use of garlands, perfumes, unguents and things that tend to beautify and adorn the person, and
8. Using high and luxurious seats.

Some people find it hard to understand the significance of a few of these precepts. They think that Buddhists are against dancing, singing, music, the cinema, perfume, ornaments and luxurious things. There is no rule in Buddhism that states that every lay Buddhist must abstain from these things. The people who choose to abstain from these entertainments are devout Buddhists who observe these precepts only for a short period as a way of self discipline. The reason for keeping away from these entertainments and ornamentations is to calm down the senses even for a few hours and to train the mind so as not to be enslaved to sensual pleasures. These entertainments increase the passions of the mind and arouse emotions which hinder a person's spiritual development. By occasionally restraining himself from these entertainments, a person will make progress towards overcoming his weaknesses and exercise greater control over himself. However, Buddhists do not condemn these entertainments.

Observance of precepts (both the Five and Eight Precepts) when performed with an earnest mind is certainly a meritorious act. It brings great benefits to this life and the lives hereafter. Therefore, a person should try his best to observe the precepts with understanding and as often as he can.

# Loving-Kindness

*What is lacking in the world today is loving-kindness or goodwill.*

IN the world today, there is sufficient material wealth. There are very advanced intellectuals, brilliant writers, talented speakers, philosophers, psychologists, scientists, religious advisors, wonderful poets and powerful world leaders. In spite of these intellectuals, there is no real peace and security in the world today. Something must be lacking. What is lacking is loving-kindness or goodwill amongst mankind.

Material gain in itself can never bring lasting happiness and peace. Peace must first be established in man's own heart before he can bring peace to others and to the world at large. The real way to achieve peace is to follow the advice given by religious teachers.

In order to practise loving-kindness, one must first practise the Noble Principle of non-violence and must always be ready to overcome selfishness and to show the correct path to others. The fighting is not to be done with the physical body, because the wickedness of man is not in his body but in his mind. Non-violence is a more effective weapon to fight against evil than retaliation. The very nature of retaliation is to increase wickedness.

In order to practise loving-kindness, one must also be free from selfishness. Much of the love in this world of self centred, only a love of one is own self:

' Not out of love for the husband loved; but the husband is loved for love of self. Children are loved by the parents, not out of love for the children, but for love of self. The gods are loved, not out of love for the gods, but for love for self. Not out of love is anybody loved, but for love of self are loved. '

Man should learn how to practise selfless love to maintain real peace and his own salvation. Just as suicide kills physically, selfishness kills spiritual progress. Loving-kindness in Buddhism is neither emotional or selfish. It is loving-kindness that radiates through the purified mind after eradicating hatred, jealousy, cruelty, enmity and grudges. According to the Buddha, *Metta* — Loving-kindness is the most effective method to maintain purity of mind and to purify the mentally polluted atmosphere.

The word ' love ' is used to cover a very wide range of emotions human beings experience. Emphasis on the base animal lust of one sex for another has much debased the concept of a feeling of amity towards another being. According to Buddhism, there are many types of emotions, all of which come under the general term ' love ' First of all, there is selfish love and there is selfless love. One has selfish love when one is concerned only with the satisfaction to be derived for oneself without any consideration for the partner's needs or feelings. Jealousy is usually a symptom of selfish love. Selfless love, on the other hand, is felt when one

person surrenders his whole being for the good of another —
parents feel such love for their children. Usually human beings
feel a mixture of both selfless and selfish love in their relationships
with each other. For example, while parents make enormous
sacrifices for their children, they usually expect something in
return.

Another kind of love, but closely related to the above, is
brotherly love or the love between friends. In a sense, this kind
of love can also be considered selfish because the love is limited
to particular people and does not encompass others. In another
category we have sexual love, where partners are drawn towards
each other through physical attraction. It is the kind that is most
exploited by modern entertainment and it can cover anything from
uncomplicated teenage infatuations to the most complex of
relationships between adults.

On a scale far higher than these, is Universal Love or *Metta*.
This all-embracing love is the great virtue expressed by the
Buddha. Lord Buddha, for example, renounced His kingdom,
family and pleasures so that He could strive to find a way to
release mankind from an existence of suffering. In order to gain
His Enlightenment, He had to struggle for many countless lives.
A lesser being would have been disheartened, but not the Buddha-
elect. It is for this He is called ' The Compassionate One '. The
Buddha's boundless love extended not only to human beings but
all living creatures. It was not emotional or selfish, but a love
without frontiers, without discrimination. Unlike the other kinds
of love, Universal love can never end in disappointment or
frustration because it expects no reward. It creates more happiness
and satisfaction. One who cultivates universal love will also
cultivate sympathetic joy and equanimity and he will then have
attained to the sublime state.

In this book, *The Buddha's Ancient Path* Ven. Piyadassi says:

' Love is an active force. Every act of the loving one is done
with the stainless mind to help, to succour, to cheer, to make

the paths of others easier, smoother and more adapted to the conquest of sorrow, the winning of the highest bliss.

' The way to develop love is through thinking out the evils of hate, and the advantages of non-hate; through thinking out according to actuality, according to karma, that really there is none to hate, that hate is a foolish way of feeling which breeds more and more darkness, that obtructs right understanding. Hate restricts; love release. Hatred strangles; love enfranchises. Hatred brings remorse; love brings peace. Hatred agitates; love quietens, stills, calms. Hatred divides; love unites. Hatred hardens; love softens. Hatred hinders; love helps. And thus through a correct study and appreciation of the effects of hatred and the benefits of love, should one develop love. '

In *Metta Sutta,* the Buddha has expounded the nature of love in Buddhism. ' Just as a mother would protect her only child even at the risk of her own life, even so, let him cultivate a boundless heart towards all beings. Let his thoughts of boundless love pervade the whole world, above, below and across without any obstruction, without any hatred, without any enmity. '

# Real Charity

*You perform real charity if you can give freely without expecting anything in return.*

THE essence of true charity is to give something without expecting anything in return for the gift. If a person expects some material benefit to arise from his gift, he is only performing an act of bartering and not charity. A charitable person should not make other people feel indebted to him or use charity as a way of exercising control over them. He should not even expect others to be grateful, for most people are forgetful though not necessarily ungrateful. The act of true charity is wholesome, has no strings attached, and leaves both the giver and the recipient free.

The meritorious deed of charity is highly praised by every religion. Those who have enough to maintain themselves should think of others and extend their generosity to deserving cases. Among people who practise charity, there are some who give as a means of attracting others into their religion or creed. Such an act of giving which is performed with the ulterior motive of conversion cannot really be said to be true charity.

The Buddhist views charity as an act to reduce personal greed which is an unwholesome mental state which hinders spiritual progress. A person who is on his way to spiritual growth must try to reduce his own selfishness and his strong desire for acquiring more and more. He should reduce his strong attachment to possessions which, if he is not mindful, can enslave him to greed. What he owns or has should instead be used for the benefit and happiness of others: his loved ones as well as those who need his help.

When giving, a person should not perform charity as an act of his body alone, but with his heart and mind as well. There must be joy in every act of giving. A distinction can be made between giving as a normal act of generosity and *dana*. In the normal act of generosity a person gives out of compassion and kindness when he realises that someone else is in need of help, and he is in the position to offer the help. When a person performs *dana,* he gives as a means of cultivating charity as a virtue and of reducing his own selfishness and craving. He exercises wisdom when he recalls that *dana* is a very important quality to be practised by every Buddhist, and is the first perfection *(paramita)* practised by the Buddha in many of His previous births in search for Enlightenment. A person performs *dana* in appreciation of the great qualities and virtues of the Triple Gem.

There are many things which a person can give. He can give material things: food for the hungry, and money and clothes to the poor. He can also give his knowledge, skill, time, energy or effort to projects that can benefit others. He can provide a sympathetic ear and good counsel to a friend in trouble. He can restrain himself from killing other beings, and by so doing perform a gift of life to the helpless beings which would have otherwise been killed. He can also give a part of his body for the sake of others, such as donating his blood, eyes, kidney, etc. Some who seek to practise this virtue or are moved by great compassion or concern for others may also be prepared to sacrifice their own lives. In His previous births, the Bodhisatta had many a time given away parts of His body for the sake of others. He had also given up His life so that others might live, so great was His generosity and compassion.

But the greatest testimony to the Buddha's great compassion is His priceless gift to humanity — the Dhamma which can liberate all beings from suffering. To the Buddhist, the highest gift of all is the gift of Dhamma. This gift has great powers to change a life. When a person receives Dhamma with a pure mind and practises the Truth with earnestness, he cannot fail to change. He will experience greater happiness, peace and joy in his heart and mind. If he was once cruel, he becomes compassionate. If he was once revengeful, he becomes forgiving. Through Dhamma, the hateful becomes more compassionate, the greedy more generous, and the restless more serene. When a person has tasted Dhamma, not only will be experience happiness here and now, but also happiness in the lives hereafter as he journeys to *Nibbana*.

# The Buddhist Attitude to Animal Life

*If we believe that animals were created by someone for men, it would follow that men were also created for animals since some animals do eat human flesh.*

ANIMALS are said to be conscious only of the present. They live with no concern for the past or future. Likewise, little children seem to have no notion of the future. They also live in the present until their faculties of memory and imagination are developed.

Men possess the faculty of reasoning. The gap between man and animal widens only to the extent that man develops his reasoning faculty and acts accordingly. Buddhists accept that animals not only possess instinctive power but also, to a lesser degree, thinking power.

In some respects, animals are superior to men. Dogs have a kenner sense of hearing; insects have a keener sense of smell; hawks are speedier; eagles can see a greater distance. Undoubtedly, men are wiser; but men have so much to learn from the ants and bees. Much of the animal is still in us. But we also have much more: we have the potential of spiritual development.

Buddhism cannot accept that animals were created by someone for men; if animals were created for men then it could follow that men were also created for animals since there are some animals which eat human flesh.

Buddhists are encouraged to love all living beings and not to restrict their love only to human beings. They should practise loving kindness towards every living being. The Buddha's advice is that it is not right for us to take away the life of any living being since every living being has a right to exist. Animals also have fear and pain as do human beings. It is wrong to take away their lives. We should not misuse our intelligence and strength to destroy animals even though they may sometimes be a nuisance to us. Animals need our sympathy. Destroying them is not the only method to get rid of them. Every living being is contributing something to maintain this world. It is unfair for us to deprive their living rights.

In his Handbook of Reason, D. Runes says:

' We can hardly speak of morals in relation to creatures we systematically devour, mostly singed but sometimes raw. There are men and women who practise horse love, dog love, cat love. But these very same people would take a deer or a calf by its neck, slit its throat, drink the blood straight away or in a pudding, and bite off the flesh. And who is to say that a horse they cherish is nobler than a deer they feed on? Indeed, there are people who eat cats, dogs and horses but would use a cow only as a work animal. '

Some cry over a little bird or goldfish that expired; others travel long distances to catch fish on a nasty hook for food or mere pleasure or shooting birds for fun. Some go into deep jungle for hunting animals as a game while others spend a lot to keep the same animals at home as their pets.

Some keep frogs to foretell the weather; others cut off their legs and fry them. Some tenderly tend birds in gilded cages; others serve them for breakfast. It is all quite confusing. One thought stands out in a world where man clubs man for gain or sheer gore, there is hardly time to ponder over his morals in relation to animals.

Every religion advices us to love our fellow humans. Some even teach us to love them more if they belong to the same religion. But Buddhism is supreme in that it teaches us to show equal care and compassion for each and every creature in the universe. The destruction of any creature represents a disturbance of the Universal Order.

The Buddha was very clear in His teachings against any form of cruelty to any living being. One day the Buddha saw a man preparing to make a animal sacrifice. On being asked why he was going to kill innocent animals, the man replied that it was because it would please the gods. The Buddha then offered Himself as the sacrifice, saying that if the life of an animal would please the gods then the life of a human being, more valuable, would please the gods even more.

Man's cruelty towards animals is another expression of his uncontrolled greed. Today we destroy animals and deprive them of their natural rights so that we can expand our environments for our convenience. But we are already beginning to pay the price for this selfish and cruel act. Our environment is threatened and if we do not take stern measures for the survival of other creatures, our own existence on this earth may not be guaranteed.

It is true that the existence of certain creatures is a threat to human existence. But we never consider that humans are the greatest threat to every living being on this earth and in the air whereas the existence of other creatures is a threat only to certain living beings.

Since every creature contributes something for the maintanence of the planet and atmosphere, destroying them is not the solution to overcome our disturbances. We should take other measures to maintain the balance of nature.

# The Need for Tolerance Today

*'If a person foolishly does me wrong, I will return to him the protection of my boundless love. The more evil that comes from him the more good will go from me. I will always give off only the fragrance of goodness.' (Buddha)*

PEOPLE today are restless, weary filled with fear and discontentment. They are intoxicated with the desire to gain fame, wealth and power. They crave for gratification of the senses. People are passing their days in fear, suspicion and insecurity. In this time of turmoil and crisis, it becomes difficult for people to coexist peacefully with their fellowmen. There is therefore, a great need for tolerance in the world today so that peaceful co-existence among the people of the world can be possible.

The world has bled and suffered from the disease of dogmatism and of intolerance. The land of many countries today are soaked with the blood spilled on the altar of various political struggles, as the skies of earlier millenia were covered with the smoke of burning martyrs of various faiths. Whether in religion or politics people have been conscious of a mission to bring humanity to their way of life and have been aggresive towards other ways of life. Indeed, the intolerance of the crusading spirit has spoiled the records of religions.

Let us look back on this present century of highly publicized *' Progress '* — a century of gadgets and inventions. The array of new scientific and technical inventions is dazzling — telephones, electric motors, aeroplanes, radios, television, computers, space ships, satellites and electronic devices .... Yet in this same century the children of the earth who have developed all these inventions as the ultimate in progress, are the same people who have butchered millions of others by bayonets or bullets or gas. Amidst all the great ' progress ', where does the spirit of tolerance stand?

Today man is interested in exploring outer space. But he is totally unable to live as man-to-man in peace and harmony. Man will eventually desecrate the moon and other planets.

For the sake of material gain, modern man violates nature. His mental activities are so preoccupied with his pleasure that he is unable to discover the purpose of life. This unnatural behaviour of present mankind is the result of his wrong conception of human life and its ultimate aim. It is the cause of the frustration, fear, insecurity and intolerance of our present time.

In fact, today intolerance is still practised in the name of religion. People merely talk of religion and promise to provide short cuts to paradise, they are not interested in practising it. If Christians live by the Sermon on the Mount, if Buddhists follow the Noble Eightfold Path, if Muslims really follow the concept of Brotherhood and if the Hindus shape their life in oneness, definitely there will be peace and harmony in this world. Inspite of these invaluable Teachings of the great religious teachers, people have still not realised the value of tolerance. The intolerance that is practised in the name of religion is most disgraceful and deplorable.

The Buddha's advice is ' Let us live happily, not hating those who hate us. Among those who hate us, let us live free from hatred. Let us live happily and free from ailment. Let us live happily and be free from greed; among those who are greedy.'

*(Dhammapada 197,200)*

# Buddhist Funeral Rites

*A real Buddhist funeral is a simple, solemn and dignified religious service.*

## Religious Day

As practised in many Buddhist countries, a real Buddhist funeral is a simple, solemn and dignified ceremony. Unfortunately, some people have included many unnecessary, extraneous items and superstitious practices into the funeral rites. The extraneous items and practices vary according to the traditions and customs of the people. They were introduced in olden days by people who probably could not understand the nature of life, nature of death, and what life would be after death. When such ideas were incorporated into Buddhist practices, people tended to blame Buddhism for expensive funeral rites. If only the Buddhist public would approach proper persons who have studied the real Teachings of the Buddha and Buddhist tradition, they could receive advice on how to perform Buddhist funeral rites. It is most unfortunate that a bad impression has been created that Buddhism encourages people to waste their money and time on unnecessary practices. It must be clearly understood that Buddhism has nothing to do with such debased practices.

Buddhists are not very particular regarding the burial or cremation of a dead body. In many Buddhist countries, cremation is customary. For hygienic and economic reasons, it is advisable to cremate. Today, the population in the world is increasing and if we continue to have dead bodies occupying valuable land, then one day all remaining available land will be occupied by the dead and the living will have no place to live.

---

*Read ' Day-To-Day Buddhist Practice ' by the same author.*

There are still some people who object to the cremation of dead bodies. They say that cremation is against god's law, in the same way they have objected to many other things in the past. It will take some time for such people to understand that cremation is much more appropriate and effective than burial.

On the other hand Buddhists do not believe that one day someone will come and awaken the departed persons spirits from their graveyards or the ashes from their urns and decide who should go to heaven and who should go to hell.

The consciousness or mental energy of the departed person has no connection with the body left behind or his skeleton or his ashes. Many people believe that if the deceased is not given a proper burial or if a sanctified tombstone is not placed on the grave, then the soul of the deceased will wander to the four corners of the world and weep and wail and sometimes even return to disturb the relatives. Such a belief cannot be found anywhere in Buddhism.

Buddhists believe that when a person dies, rebirth will take place somewhere else according to his good or bad actions. As long as the person possesses the craving for existence, he must experience rebirth. Only the Arahants, who have gone beyond all passions will have no more rebirths and so after their death, they will attain their final goal *Nibbana*.

# 9

# DHAMMA AND OURSELVES
# AS REFUGE

## Why We Take Refuge
## in the Buddha

*Buddhists take refuge in the Buddha not out of fear of Him, but to gain inspiration and right understanding for their self-purification.*

BUDDHISTS do not take refuge in the Buddha with the belief that He is a god or son of god. The Buddha never claimed any divinity. He was the Enlightened One, the most Compassionate, Wise, and Holy One who ever lived in this world. Therefore, people take refuge in the Buddha as a Teacher or Master who has shown the real path of emancipation. They pay homage to Him to show their gratitude and respect, but they do not ask for material favours. Buddhists do not pray to the Buddha thinking that He is a god who will reward them or punish or curse them. They recite verses or some sutras not in the sense of supplication but as a means of recalling His great virtues and good qualities to get more inspiration and guidance for themselves and to develop the confidence to follow His Teachings. There are critics who condemn this attitude of taking refuge in the Buddha. They do not know the true meaning of the concept of taking refuge in and paying homage to a great religious Teacher. They have learned only about praying which is the only thing that some people do in the name of religion. When Buddhists seek refuge it means they accept the Buddha, Dhamma and the Sangha as the means by which they can eradicate all the causes of their fear and other mental disturbances. Many people, especially those with animistic beliefs, seek protection in certain objects around them which they believe are inhabited by spirits.

The Buddha advised against the futility of taking refuge in hills, woods, groves, trees and shrines when people are fear-stricken. No such refuge is safe, no such refuge is Supreme. Not by resorting to such a refuge is one freed from all ill. He who has gone for refuge to the Buddha, the Dhamma and the Sangha sees with right knowledge the Four Noble Truths — Sorrow, the cause of Sorrow, the transcending of Sorrow, and the Noble Eightfold Path which leads to the cessation of Sorrow. This indeed is secure refuge. By seeking such refuge one is released from all Sorrow.

*(Dhammapada 188-192)*

In the *Dhajagga Sutta,* it is mentioned that by taking refuge in *Sakra,* the king of gods or any god, the followers would not be free from all their worldly problems and fears. The reason is, such gods are themselves not free from lust, hatred, illusion and fear, but the Buddha, Dhamma and the Sangha (i.e. the community who has attained perfection) are free from them. Only those who are free from unsatisfactoriness can show the way to lasting happiness.

Francis Story, a well known Buddhist scholar, gives his views on seeking refuge in the Buddha.

' I go for refuge to the Buddha. I seek the presence of the Exalted Teacher by whose compassion I may be guided through the torrents of Samsara, by whose serene countenance I may be uplifted from the mire of worldly thoughts and cravings, seeing there in the very assurance of Nibbanic Peace, which He himself attained. In sorrow and pain I turn to Him and in my happiness I seek His tranquil gaze. I lay before His Image not only flowers and incense, but also the burning fires of my restless heart, that they may be quenched and stilled. I lay down the burden of my pride and my selfhood, the heavy burden of my cares and aspirations, the weary load of this incessant birth and death. '

Sri Rama Chandra Bharati, an Indian poet, gives another meaningful explanation for taking refuge in the Buddha.

' I seek not thy refuge for the sake of gain,
Not fear of thee, nor for the love of fame,
Not as thou hailest from the solar race,
Not for the sake of gaining knowledge vast,
But drawn by the power of the boundless love,
And thy all-embracing peerless ken,
The vast Samsara's sea safe to cross,
I bend low, O lord, and become thy devotee. '

Some people say that since the Buddha was only a man, there is no meaning in taking refuge in Him. But they do not know that although the Buddha very clearly said that He was a man, He was no ordinary man like any of us. He was an *extraordinary* and *incomparably* holy person who possessed Supreme Enlightenment and great compassion toward every living being. He was a man freed from all human weaknesses, defilements and even from ordinary human emotions. Of Him it has been said, ' There is none so godless as the Buddha, and yet none so godlike. ' In the Buddha is embodied all the great virtues, sacredness, wisdom and enlightenment.

Another question that people very often raise is this: ' If the Buddha is not a god, if He is not living in this world today, how can He bless people? ' According to the Buddha, if people follow His advice by leading a religious life, they would certainly receive blessings. Blessing in a Buddhist sense means the joy we experience when we develop confidence and satisfaction. The Buddha once said, ' If anyone wishes to see me, he should look at my Teachings and practise them. ' *(Samyutta Nikaya)* Those who understand His Teachings easily see the real nature of the Buddha reflected in themselves. The image of the Buddha they maintain in their minds is more real than the image they see on the altar, which is merely a symbolic representation. ' Those who live in accordance with the Dhamma (righteous way of life) will be protected by that very Dhamma. ' *(Thera Gatha)* One who knows the real nature of existence and the fact of life through Dhamma will not have any fear and secure a harmonious way of life.

In other religions, the people worship their god by asking for favours to be granted to them. Buddhists do not worship the Buddha by asking for worldly favours, but they respect Him for His supreme achievement. When Buddhists respect the Buddha, they are indirectly elevating their own minds so that one day they also can get the same enlightenment to serve mankind if they aspire to become a Buddha.

Buddhists respect the Buddha as their Master. However, this respect does not imply an attachment to or a dependence on the Teacher. This kind of respect is in accordance with His Teaching which is as follows:

' Monks, even if a monk should take hold of the edge of my outer garment and should walk close behind me, step for step, yet if he should be covetous, strongly attracted by pleasures of the senses, malevolent in thought, of corrupt mind and purpose, of confused recollection, inattentive and not contemplative, scatter-brained, his sense-faculties uncontrolled, then he is far from me and I am far from him. '

' Monks, if the monk should be staying even a hundred miles away, yet he is not covetous, not strongly attracted by the pleasures of the senses, not malevolent in thought, not of corrupt mind and purpose, his collection firmly set, attentive, contemplative, his thoughts be one-pointed, restrained in his sense-faculties, then he is near me and I am near him. ' *(Samyutta Nikaya)*

# No Self Surrender

*Dependence on others means a surrender of one's effort and self-confidence.*

BUDDHISM is a gentle religion where equality, justice and peace reign supreme. To depend on others for salvation is negative, but to depend o. oneself is positive. Dependence on others means surrendering one's intelligence and efforts.

Everything which has improved and uplifted humanity has been done by man himself. Man's improvement must come from his own knowledge, understanding, effort and experience and not from heaven. Man should not be a slave even to the great forces of nature because even though he is crushed by them he remains superior by virtue of his understanding of them. Buddhism carries the Truth further: it shows that by means of understanding, man can also control his environment and circumstances. He can cease to be crushed by them and use their power to raise himself to great heights of spirituality and nobility.

Buddhism gives due credit to man's intelligence and effort for his achievements rather than to supernatural beings. True religion means faith in the good of man rather than faith in unknown forces. In that respect, Buddhism is not merely a religion, but a noble method to gain peace and eternal salvation through living a respectable way of life. From the very outset, Buddhism appeals to the cultured and the intellectual minds. Every cultured man in the world today respects the Buddha as a rational Teacher.

The Buddha taught that what man needs for his happiness is not a religion with a mass of dogmas and theories but knowledge — knowledge of the cosmic nature and its relationship to the law of cause and effect. Until this principle that life is merely an imperfect manifestation of nature is fully understood, no man can be fully emancipated.

The Buddha has given a new explanation of the universe. It is a new vision of eternal happiness, the achievement of perfection. The winning of the human goal in Buddhism is the permanent state beyond impermanency, the attainment of *Nibbana* beyond all the worlds of change, and the final deliverance from the miseries of existence.

# No Sinners

*In Buddhism, actions are merely termed as unskilful or unwholesome, not as sinful.*

Buddhists do not regard man as sinful by nature or ' in rebellion against god '. Every human being is a person of great worth who has within himself a vast store of good as well as evil habits. The good in a person is always waiting for a suitable opportunity to flower and to ripen. Remember the saying, ' There is so much that is good in the worst of us and so much that is bad in the best of us. '

Buddhism teaches that everyone is responsible for his own good and bad deeds, and that each individual can mould his own destiny. Says the Buddha, ' These evil deeds were only done by you, not by your parents, friends, or relatives; and you yourself will reap the painful results. ' *(Dhammapada 165)*

Man's sorrow is his own making and is not handed down by a family curse or an original sin of a mythical primeval ancestor.

Buddhists do not accept the belief that this world is merely a place of trial and testing. This world can be made a place where we can attain the highest perfection. And perfection is synonymous with happiness. To the Buddha, man is not an experiment in life created by somebody which can be done away with when unwanted. If a sin could be forgiven, people might take advantage and commit more and more sins. The Buddhist has no reason to believe that the sinner can escape the consequences by the grace of an external power. If a man thrusts his hand into a furnace, his hand will be burnt, and all the prayer in the world will not remove the scars. The same is with the man who walks into the fires of evil action. The Buddha's approach to the problems of suffering is not imaginary, speculative or metaphysical, but essentially empirical.

According to Buddhism, there is no such thing as sin as explained by other religions. To the Buddhists, sin is unskilful or unwholesome action — *Akusala Kamma* which creates *Papa* — the downfall of man. The wicked man is an ignorant man. He needs instruction more than he needs punishment and condemnation. He is not regarded as violating god's will or as a person who must beg for divine mercy and forgiveness. He needs only guidance for his enlightenment.

All that is necessary is for someone to help him use his reason to realise that he is responsible for his wrong action and that he must pay for the consequences. Therefore the belief in confession is foreign to Buddhism.

The purpose of the Buddha's appearance in this world is not to wash away the sins committed by human beings nor to punish or to destroy the wicked people, but to make the people understand how foolish it is to commit evil and to point out the reaction of such evil deeds. Consequently there are no commandments in Buddhism, since no one can command another for his spiritual upliftment. The Buddha has encouraged us to develop and use our understanding. He has shown us the path for our liberation from suffering. The precepts that we undertake to observe are not commandments: they are observed voluntarily. The Buddha's Teaching is thus: ' Please pay attention; take this advice and think it over. If you think it is suitable for you to practise my advice, then try to practise it. You can see the results through your own experience. ' There is no religious value in blindly observing any commandment without proper conviction and understanding. However, we should not take advantage of the liberty given by the Buddha to do anything we like. It is our duty to behave as cultured, civilised and understanding human beings to lead a religious life. If we can understand this, commandments are not important. As an enlightened teacher, the Buddha advised us on how to lead a pure life without imposing commandments and using the fear of punishment.

# Do It Yourself

*Self confidence plays an important part in every aspect of man's life.*

KNOWING that no external sources, no faith or rituals can save him, the Buddhist feels the need to rely on his own efforts. He gains confidence through self-reliance. He realises that the whole responsibility of his present life as well as his future life depends completely on himself alone. Each must seek salvation for himself. Achieving salvation can be compared to curing a disease: if one is ill, one must go to a doctor. The doctor diagnoses the ailment and prescribes medicine. The medicine must be taken by the person himself. He cannot depute someone else to take the medicine for him. No one can be cured by simply admiring the medicine or just praising the doctor for his good prescription.

In order to be cured, he himself must faithfully follow the instructions given by the doctor with regard to the manner and frequency in taking his medicine, his daily diet and other relevant medical restraints. Likewise, a person must follow the precepts, instructions or advice given by the Buddha (who gives prescriptions for liberation) by controlling or subduing one's greed, hatred and ignorance. No one can find salvation by simply singing praises of the Buddha or by making offerings to Him. Neither can one find salvation by celebrating certain important occasions in honour of the Buddha. Buddhism is not a religion where people can attain salvation by mere prayers or begging to be saved. They must strive hard by controlling their selfish desires and emotions in order to gain salvation.

# Man is Responsible for Everything

*When a man has learned how to live as a real human being without disturbing others, he can live peacefully without any fear in his heart.*

According to the Buddha, man himself is the maker of his own destiny. He has none to blame for his lot since he alone is responsible for his own life. He makes his own life for better or for worse.

The Buddha says: man creates everything. All our griefs, perils and misfortunes are of our own creation. We spring from no other source than our own imperfections of heart and mind. We are the results of our good and bad actions committed in the past under the influence of greed and delusion. And since we ourselves brought them into being, it is within our power to overcome bad effects and cultivate good natures.

The human mind, like that of an animal, is sometimes governed by animal instinct. But unlike the animal mind, the human mind can be trained for higher values. If man's mind is not properly

*Read the booklet ' You are Responsible ' by the same author.*

cultured, that uncultured mind creates a great deal of trouble in this world. Sometimes man's behaviour is more harmful and more dangerous than animal behaviour. Animals have no religious problems, no language problems, no political problems, no social and ethical problems, no colour-bar problems. They fight only for their food, shelter and sex. But, there are thousands of problems created by mankind. Their behaviour is such that they would not be able to solve any of these problems without creating further problems. Man is reluctant to admit his weaknesses. He is not willing to shoulder his responsibilities. His attitude is always to blame others for his failures. If we become more responsible in our actions, we can maintain peace and happiness.

# Man is His Own Jailor

*Is there any truth in man's claim that he should be given freedom to do things as he likes?*

When we consider human freedom, it is very difficult to find out whether man is really free to do anything according to his own wishes. Man is bound by many conditions both external and internal: he is asked to obey the laws that are imposed on him by the government; he is bound to follow certain religious principles; he is required to co-operate with the moral and social conditions of the society in which he lives; he is compelled to follow certain national and family customs and traditions. In modern society, he is inclined to disagree with life; he is expected to conform by adapting himself to the modern way of life. He is bound to co-operate with natural laws and cosmic energy, because he is also part of the same energy. He is subjected to the weather and climatic conditions of the region. Not only does he have to pay attention to his life or to physical elements, but he has also to make up his mind to control his own emotions. In other words, he has no freedom to think freely because he is overwhelmed by new thoughts which may contradict or do away with his previous thoughts and convictions. At the same time, he may believe that he has to obey and work according to the will of god, and not follow his own free-will.

Taking into consideration all the above changing conditions to which man is bound, we can ask ' Is there any truth in man's claim that he should be given freedom to do things as he likes? '

Why does man have his hands tied so firmly? The reason is that there are various bad elements within man. These elements are dangerous and harmful to all living creatures. For the past few thousand years, all religions have been trying to tame this unreliable attitude of man and to teach him how to live a noble life. But it is most unfortunate that man is still not ready to be trustworthy, however good he may appear to be. Man still continues to harbour all these evil elements within himself. These evil elements are not introduced or influenced by external sources but are created by man himself. If these evil forces are man-made, then man himself must work hard to get rid of them after realising their danger. Unfortunately the majority of men are cruel, cunning, wicked, ungrateful, unreliable, unscrupulous. If man is allowed to live according to his own free-will without moderation and restraint, he would most definitely violate the peace and happiness of innocent people. His behaviour would probably be much worse than that of dangerous living beings. Religion is required to train him to lead a respectable life and to gain peace and happiness here and hereafter.

Another obstacle confronting religious life and spiritual progress is racial arrogance. The Buddha advised His followers not to bring forward any racial issue when they come to practise religion. Buddhists are taught to sink their own racial origin and caste or class distinction. People of all religions should not discriminate against any groups of people by bringing forward their personal traditional way of life. They should treat everyone equally, especially in the religious field. Unfortunately, followers of different religions create more discriminations and hostility towards other religious groups when performing their religious activities.

While working with others, they should not disturb their feelings because of their so-called traditions and customs. They can follow traditions and customs that are in keeping with the religious principles and moral codes of their religions.

Racial arrogance is a great hindrance to religion and spiritual progress. The Buddha once used the simile of ocean water to illustrate the harmony which can be experienced by people who have learnt to cast aside their racial arrogance: Different rivers have different names. The water of the individual rivers all flow into the ocean and become ocean water. In a similar manner, all those who have come from different communities and different castes, must forget their differences and think of themselves only as human beings.

# You Protect Yourself

*' Protecting oneself one protects others '*
*' Protecting others one protects oneself. '*

ONCE the Blessed One told His monks the following story:

' There was once a pair of jugglers who did their acrobatic feats on a bamboo pole. One day the master said to his apprentice: 'Now get on my shoulders and climb up the bamboo pole.' When the apprentice had done so, the master said: 'Now protect me well and I shall protect you. By watching each other in that way, we shall be able to show our skill, we shall make a good profit and you can get down safely from the bamboo pole'. But the apprentice said: 'Not so, master. You! O Master, should protect yourself, and I too shall protect myself. Thus self-protected and self-guarded we shall safely do our feats.'

' This is the right way, ' said the Blessed One and spoke further as follows:

' It is just as the apprentice said: 'I shall protect myself,' in that way the Foundation of Mindfulness should be practised. 'I shall protect others,' in that way the Foundation of Mindfulness should be practised. Protecting oneself one protects others; protecting others one protects oneself.

' And how does one, in protecting oneself, protect others? By the repeated and frequent practice of meditation.

' And how does one, by protecting others, protect oneself? By patience and forbearance, by a non-violent and harmless life, by loving kindness and compassion. '*(Satipatthana, Samyutta, No:.19)*.

' Protecting oneself one protects others '
' Protecting others one protects oneself '

These two sentences supplement each other and should not be taken (or quoted) separately.

Nowadays, when social service is so greatly stressed, people may for instance, be tempted to quote, in support of their ideas, only the second sentence. But any such one-sided quotation would misrepresent the Buddha's statement. It has to be remembered that, in our story the Buddha expressly approved the words of the apprentice, which is that one has first to carefully watch one's own steps if one wishes to protect others from harm. He who is sunk in the mire himself cannot help others out of it. In that sense, self-protection is not selfish protection. It is the cultivation of self-control, and ethical and spiritual self-development.

Protecting oneself one protects others — the truth of this statement begins at a very simple and practical level. At the material level, this truth is so self-evident that we need not say more than a few words about it. It is obvious that the protection of our own health will go far in protecting the health of our closer or wider environment, especially where contagious diseases are concerned. Caution and circumspection in all our doings and movements will protect others from harm that may come to them through our carelessness and negligence. By careful driving, abstention from alcohol, by self-restraint in situations that might lead to violence — in all these and many other ways we shall protect others by protecting ourselves.

We come now to the ethical level of that truth. Moral self-protection will safeguard others, individual and society, against our own unrestrained passions and selfish impulses. If we permit the Three Roots of everything evil, Greed, Hate and Delusion, to take a firm hold in our hearts, then that which grows from those evil roots will spread around like the jungle creeper which suffocates and kills the healthy and noble growth. But if we protect ourselves against these Three Roots of Evil, fellow beings too will be safe from our reckless greed for possession and power, from our unrestrained lust and sensuality, from our envy and jealousy. They will be safe from the disruptive, or even destructive and murderous, consequences of our hate and enmity, from the outbursts of our anger, from our spreading an atmosphere of antagonism and quarrelsomeness which may make life unbearable for those around us. But the harmful effects of our greed and hate on others are not limited to cases when they become the passive objects or victims of our hate, or their possession the object of our greed. Greed and hate have an infectious power, which can multiply the evil effects. If we ourselves think of nothing else than to crave and grasp, to acquire and possess, to hold and cling, then we may rouse or strengthen these possessive instincts in others too. Our bad example may become the standard of behaviour of our environment for instance among our own children, our colleagues, and so on. Our own conduct may induce others to join us in the common satisfaction of rapacious desires; or we may arouse feelings of resentment and competitiveness in others who wish to beat us in the race. If we are full of sensuality we may kindle the fire of lust in others. Our own hate may cause the hate and vengeance of others. It may also happen that we ally ourselves with others or instigate them to common acts of hate and enmity.

# How to Save Yourself

*Oneself, indeed, is one's saviour, for what other saviour would there be?*
*With oneself well controlled the problem of looking for an external saviour is solved. (Dhammapada 166)*

As the Buddha was about to pass away, His disciples came from everywhere to be near Him. While the other disciples were constantly at His side and in deep sorrow over the expected loss of their Master, a monk named Attadatta went into his cell and practised meditation. The other monks, thinking that he was unconcerned about the welfare of the Buddha, were upset and reported the matter to Him. The monk, however, addressed the Buddha thus, ' Lord as the Blessed One would be passing away soon, I thought the best way to honour the Blessed One would be by attaining Arahantship during the lifetime of the Blessed One itself. ' The Buddha was pleased by his attitude and his conduct and said that one's spiritual welfare should not be abandoned for the sake of others.

In this story is illustrated one of the most important aspects of Buddhism. A person must constantly be on the alert to seek his own deliverance from *Samsara,* and his ' salvation ' must be brought about by the individual himself. He cannot look to any external force or agency to help him to attain *Nibbana.*

People who do not understand Buddhism criticize this concept and say that Buddhism is a selfish religion which only talks about the concern for one's own freedom from pain and sorrow. This is not true at all. The Buddha states clearly that one should work ceaselessly for the spiritual and material welfare of all beings,

For further clarification on devas, refer to sections entitled *Belief in Deities — Devas, Spirit World* and *The Significance of Transference of Merit to the Departed* in this book while at the same time diligently pursuing one's own goal of attaining *Nibbana*. Selfless service is highly commended by the Buddha.

Again, people who do not understand Buddhism may ask, ' It may be alright for the fortunate human beings, in full command of their mental powers, to seek *Nibbana* by their own efforts. But what about those who are mentally and physically or even materially handicapped? How can they be self-reliant? Do they not need the help of some external force, some god or deva to assist them? '

The answer to this is that Buddhists do not believe that the final release must necessarily take place in one life time. The process can take a long time, over the period of many births. One has to apply oneself, to the best of one's ability, and slowly develop the powers of self reliance. Therefore, even those who are handicapped mentally, spiritually and materially must make an effort, however small, to begin the process of deliverance.

Once the wheels are set in motion, the individual slowly trains himself to improve his powers of self-reliance. The tiny acorn will one day grow into a mighty oak, but not overnight. Patience is an essential ingredient in this difficult process.

For example, we know from experience how many parents do everything in their power to bring up their children according to the parents' hopes and aspirations. And yet when these children grow up, they develop in their own way, not necessarily the way the parents wanted them to be. In Buddhism, we believe that while others can exert an influence on someone's life, the individual will in the end create his own *kamma* and be responsible for his own actions. No human being or deva can, in the final analysis, direct or control an individual's attainment of 'the ultimate salvation. This is the meaning of self-reliance.

This does not mean that Buddhism teaches one to be selfish. In Buddhism, when someone seeks, by his own effort, to attain *Nibbana,* he is determined not to kill, steal, tell lies, lust after others, or lose the control of his senses through intoxication. When he controls himself thus he automatically contributes to the happiness of others. So is not this so-called ' selfishness ' a good thing for the general welfare of others?

On a more mundane level it has been asked how the lower forms of life can extricate themselves from a mere meaningless round of existence. Surely in that helpless state some benevolent external force is necessary to pull the unfortunate being from the quicksand. To answer this question we must refer to our knowledge of the evolution theory. It is clearly stated that life began in very primitive forms — no more than a single cell floating in the water. Over millions of years these basic life forms evolved and became more complex, more intelligent. It is at this more intelligent level that life forms are capable of organization, independent thought, conceptualization and so on.

When Buddhists talk about the ability to save oneself, they are referring to life forms at this higher level of mental development. In the earlier stages of evolution kammic and mental forces remain dormant, but over countless rebirths, a being raises itself to the level of independent thought and becomes capable of rational rather than instinctive behaviour. It is at this stage that the being becomes aware of the meaninglessness of undergoing endless rebirths with its natural concomitants of pain and sorrow. It is then that the being is capable of making its determination to end rebirth and seek happiness by gaining enlightenment and *Nibbana*. With this high level of intelligence, the individual is indeed capable of self-improvement and self-development.

We all know human beings are born with very varying levels of intelligence and powers of reasoning. Some are born as geniuses, while at the other end of the spectrum, others are born with very low intelligence. Yet every being has some ability to distinguish between choices or options, especially when they concern survival. If we extend this fact of survival even to the animal world we can distinguish between higher and lower animals, with this same ability (in varying degrees of course) to make choices for the sake of survival.

Hence, even a lower form of life has the potential to create a good *kamma,* however limited its scope. With the diligent application of this and the gradual increase of good *kamma* a being can raise itself to higher levels of existence and understanding.

To look at this problem from another angle, we can consider one of the earliest stories that have been told to show how the Buddha-to-be first made the initial decision to strive for Enlightenment. A great many rebirths before the Buddha was born as Siddharta, he was born as an ordinary man.

One day while travelling in a boat with his mother, a great storm arose and the boat capsized, throwing the occupants into the angry sea. With no thought for his personal safety, the future Buddha carried his mother on his back and struggled to swim to dry land. But so great was the expanse of water ahead of him that he did not know the best route to safety. When he was in this dilemma, not knowing which way to turn, his bravery was noticed by one of the devas. This deva could not physically come to his aid, but he was able to make the future Buddha know the best route to take. The young man listened to the deva and both he and his mother were saved. There and then he made a firm determination not to rest until he had finally gained Enlightenment.

This story illustrates the fact that Buddhists can and do seek the help of devas in their daily life. A deva is a being who by virtue of having acquired great merit (like the king of the devas) is born with the power to help other beings. But this power is limited to material and physical things. In our daily existence, we can seek help of the devas (when misfortune strikes, when we need to be comforted, when we are sick or afraid, and so on).

The fact that we seek the aid of these devas means that we are still tied to the material world. We must accept the fact that by being born we are subject to physical desires and needs. And it is not wrong to satisfy these needs on a limited scale. When the Buddha advocated the Middle Path, He said that we should neither indulge ourselves in luxury nor completely deny ourselves the basic necessities of life.

However, we should not stop at that. While we accept the conditions of our birth, we must also make every effort, by following the Noble Eightfold Path, to reach a level of development where we realize that attachment to the material world creates only pain and sorrow.

As we develop our understanding over countless births, we crave less and less for the pleasures of the senses. It is at this stage that we become truly self-reliant. At this stage, the devas cannot help us anymore, because we are not seeking to satisfy our material needs.

A Buddhist who really understands the fleeting nature of the world practises detachment from material goods. He is not unduly attached to worldly goods. Therefore, he shares these goods freely with those who are more unfortunate than he is — he practises generosity. In this way again a Buddhist contributes to the welfare of others.

When the Buddha gained Enlightenment as a result of His own efforts, He did not selfishly keep this knowledge to Himself. Rather, He spent no less than forty five years imparting His knowledge not only to men and women but even to the devas. This is Buddhism's supreme example of selflessness and concern for the well-being of all living things.

It is often said that the Buddha helped devotees who were in trouble not through the performance of miracles such as restoring the dead to life and so on, but through His acts of wisdom and compassion.

In one instance, a woman named Kisa Gotami went to seek the help of the Buddha in restoring her dead child to life. Knowing that He could not reason with her as she was so distressed and overwhelmed with grief, the Buddha told her that she should first obtain a handful of mustard seeds from a person who had never lost a dear one through death. The distracted woman ran from house to house and while everyone was only too willing to give her the mustard seeds, no one could honestly say that he or she had not lost a dear one through death. Slowly, Kisa Gotami came to the realization that death is a natural occurrence to be experienced by any being that is born. Filled with this realisation she returned to the Buddha and thanked Him for showing her the truth about death.

Now, the point here is that the Buddha was more concerned with the woman's understanding about the nature of life than giving her temporary relief by restoring her child to life — the child would have grown old and still have died. With her greater realisation Kisa Gotami was able not only to come to terms with the phenomenon of death but also to learn about the cause of sorrow through attachment. She was able to realise that attachment causes sorrow, that when attachment is destroyed, then sorrow is also destroyed.

Therefore in Buddhism, a person can seek the help of external agencies (like devas) in the pursuit of temporal happiness, but in the later stages of development when attachment to the worldly conditions ceases, there begins the path towards renunciation and enlightenment for which one must stand alone. When a man seeks to gain liberation, to break away from the endless cycle of birth and death, to gain realisation and enlightenment, he can only do this by his own efforts, by his own concentrated will power.

Buddhism gives great dignity to man. It is the only religion which states that a human being has the power to help and free himself. In the later stages of his development, he is not at the mercy of any external force or agency which he must constantly please by worshipping or offering sacrifices.

# 10

# PRAYER, MEDITATION AND RELIGIOUS PRACTICES

## Faith, Confidence and Devotion

*Right understanding points the way to confidence; confidence paves the way to wisdom.*

FAITH in the theistic sense is not found in Buddhism because of its emphasis on understanding. Theistic faith is a drug for the emotional mind and demands belief in things which cannot be known. Knowledge destroys faith and faith destroys itself when a mysterious belief is examined under the daylight of reason. Confidence cannot be obtained by faith since it places less emphasis on reason, but only by understanding.

   Referring to the unintelligible and *'blind'* nature of faith, Voltaire said, ' Faith is to believe in something which your reason tells you cannot be true; for if your reason approved of it, there could be no question of blind faith. '

Confidence, however, is not the same as faith. For confidence is not a mental acceptance of that which cannot be known. Confidence is an assured expectation, not of an unknown beyond, but of what can be tested as experienced and understood personally. Confidence is like the understanding that a student has in his teacher who explains in the class-room the inverse square law of gravitation as stated by Newton. He should not adopt an unquestioning belief of his teacher and his text-book. He studies the fact, examines the scientific arguments, and makes an assessment of the realiability of the information. If he has doubts, he should reserve his judgement until such time as when he is able to investigate the accuracy of the information for himself. To a Buddhist, confidence is a product of reason, knowledge and experience. When it is developed, confidence can never be blind faith. Confidence becomes a power of the mind.

In his book, *What The Buddha Taught* Walpola Rahula says:

' The question of belief arises when there is no seeing — seeing in every sense of the word. The moment you see, the question of belief disappears. If I tell you that I have a gem hidden in the folded palm of my hand, the question of belief arises because you do not see it yourself. But if I unclench my fist and show you the gem, then you see it for yourself, and the question of belief does not arise. So the phrase in ancient Buddhist texts reads: 'Realizing, as one sees a gem (or a myrobalan fruit) in the palm '.'

## The Meaning of Prayer

*Nature is impartial; it cannot be flattered by prayers. It does not grant any special favours on request.*

MAN is not a fallen creature who begs for his needs as he awaits mercy. According to Buddhism, man is a potential master of himself. Only because of his deep ignorance does man fail to realise his full potential. Since the Buddha has shown this hidden power, man must cultivate his mind and try to develop it by realising his innate ability.

Buddhism gives full responsibility and dignity to man. It makes man his own master. According to Buddhism, no higher being sits in judgement over his affairs and destiny. That is to say, our life, our society, our world, is what you and I want to make out of it, and not what some other unknown being wants it to be.

Remember that nature is impartial; it cannot be flattered by prayers. Nature does not grant any special favours on request. Thus in Buddhism, prayer is meditation which has self-change as its object. Prayer in meditation is the reconditioning of one's nature. It is the transforming of one's inner nature accomplished by the purification of the three faculties — thought, word and deed. Through meditation, we can understand that 'we become what we think', in accordance with the discoveries of psychology. When we pray, we experience some relief in our minds; that is, the psychological effect that we have created through our faith and devotion. After reciting certain verses we also experience the same result. Religious names or symbols are important to the extent that they help to develop devotion and confidence.

The Buddha Himself has clearly expressed that neither the recital of holy scriptures, nor self-torture, nor sleeping on the ground, nor the repetition of prayers, penances, hymns, charms, mantras, incantations and invocations can bring the real happiness of *Nibbana*.

Regarding the use of prayers for attaining the final goal, the Buddha once made an analogy of a man who wants to cross a river. If he sits down and prays imploring that the far bank of the river will come to him and carry him across, then his prayer will not be answered. If he really wants to cross the river, he must make some effort; he must find some logs and build a raft, or look for a bridge or construct a boat or perhaps swim. Somehow he must work to get across the river. Likewise, if he wants to cross the river of Samsara, prayers alone are not enough. He must work hard by living a religious life, by controlling his passions, calming his mind, and by getting rid of all the impurities and defilements in his mind. Only then can he reach the final goal. Prayer alone will never take him to the final goal.

If prayer is necessary, it should be to strengthen the mind and not to beg for gains. The following prayer of a well-known poet, teaches us how to pray. Buddhists will regard this as meditation to cultivate the mind:

> ' *Let me not pray to be sheltered from dangers,*
> *but to be fearless in facing them.*
> *Let me not beg for the stilling of my pain,*
> *but for the heart to conquer it.*
> *Let me not crave in anxious fear to be saved,*
> *but for the patience to win my freedom.* '

# Meditation

*Meditation is the psychological approach to mental culture, training and purification.*

IN place of prayer, Buddhists practise meditation for mental culture and for spiritual development. No one can attain *Nibbana* or salvation without developing the mind through meditation. Any amount of meritorious deeds alone will not lead a person to attain the final goal without the corresponding mental purification. Naturally, the untrained mind is very elusive and persuades people to commit evil and become slaves of the senses. Imagination and emotions always mislead man if his mind is not properly trained. One who knows how to practise meditation will be able to control one's mind when it is misled by the senses.

Most of the troubles which we are confronting today are due to the untrained and uncultured mind. It is already established that meditation is the remedy for many physical and mental sicknesses. Medical authorities and great psychologists the world over say that mental frustration, worries, miseries, anxieties, tension and fear are the causes of many diseases, stomach ulcers, gastritis, nervous complaints and mental sickness. And even latent sickness will be aggravated through such mental conditions.

When the conscious '*I*' frets too much, worries too much, or grieves too long and too intensely, then troubles develop in the body. Gastric ulcers, tuberculosis, coronary diseases and a host of functional disorders are the products of mental and emotional imbalance. In the case of children, the decay of the teeth and defective eye-sight are frequently related to emotional disorders.

Many of these sicknesses and disorders can be avoided if people could spend a few minutes a day to calm their senses through the practice of meditation. Many people do not believe this or are too lazy to practise meditation owing to lack of understanding. Some people say that meditation is only a waste of time. We must remember that every spiritual master in this world attained the highest point of his life through the practice of meditation. They are honoured today by millions of people because they have done tremendous service to mankind with their supreme knowledge and patience which they obtained through the practice of meditation.

Meditation should not be a task to which we force ourselves ' with gritted teeth and clenched fists '; it should rather be something that draws us, because it fills us with joy and inspiration. So long as we have to force ourselves, we are not yet ready for meditation. Instead of meditating we are violating our true nature. Instead of relaxing and letting go, we are holding on to our ego, to our will power. In this way meditation becomes a game of ambition, of personal achievement and aggrandizement. Meditation is like love: a spontaneous experience — not something that can be forced or acquired by strenuous effort.

Therefore Buddhist meditation has no other purpose than to bring the mind back into the present, into the state of fully awakened consciousness, by clearing it from all obstacles that have been created by habit or tradition.

The Buddha obtained His Enlightenment through the development of His mind. He did not seek divine power to help Him. He gained His wisdom through self-effort by practising meditation. To have a healthy body and mind and to have peace in life, one must learn how to practise meditation.

## Nature of Modern Life

Today we are living in a world where people have to work very hard physically and mentally. Without hard work, there is no place for people in the modern society. Very often keen competition is going on everywhere. One is trying to beat the other in every sphere of life and man has no rest at all. Mind is the nucleus of life. When there is no real peace and rest in the mind, the whole life will collapse. People naturally try to overcome their miseries through pleasing the senses: they drink, gamble, sing and dance — all the time having the illusion that they are enjoying the real happiness of life. Sense stimulation is not the real way to have relaxation. The more we try to please the senses through sensual pleasures, the more will we become slaves to the senses. There will be no end to our craving for satisfaction. The real way to relax is to calm the senses by the control of mind. If we can control the mind, then we will be able to control everything. When the mind is fully controlled and purified, it will be free from mental disturbances. When the mind is free from mental disturbances it can see many things which others cannot see with their naked eyes. Ultimately, we will be able to attain our salvation and find peace and happiness.

To practise meditation, one must have strong determination, effort and patience. Immediate results cannot be expected. We must remember that it takes many years for a person to be qualified as a doctor, lawyer, mathematician, philosopher, historian or a scientist. Similarly to be a good meditator, it will •

take sometime for the person to control the elusive mind and to calm the senses. Practising meditation is like swimming in a river against the current. Therefore one must not lose patience for not being able to obtain rapid results. At the same time the meditator must also cultivate his morality. A congenial place for meditation is another important aspect. The meditator must have an object for his meditation, for without an object the jumping mind is not easy to trap. The object must not create lust, anger, delusion, and emotion in the meditator's mind.

When we start to meditate, we switch the mind from the old imaginative way of thinking, or habitual thought into a new unimpeded or unusual way of thinking. While meditating when we breathe in mindfully, we absorb cosmic energy. When we breathe out mindfully with *Metta* — loving kindness, we purify the atmosphere. Intellect is necessary for the overcoming of emotionality and spiritual confusion as intuition is necessary for overcoming intellectual limitation and conceptual abstraction.

We spend most of our time on our body: to feed it, to clothe it, to cleanse it, to wash it, to beautify it, to relax it, but how much time do we spend on our mind for the same purposes?

Some people take the Buddha Image as an object and concentrate on it. Some concentrate on inhaling and exhaling. Whatever may be the method, if anyone tries to practise meditation, he is sure to find relaxation. Meditation will help him a great deal to have physical and mental health and to control the mind when it is necessary.

Man can do the highest service to society by simply abstaining from evils. The cultured mind that is developed through meditation performs a most useful service to others. Meditation is not simply a waste of man's valuable time. The advanced mind of a meditator can solve so many human problems and is very useful to enlighten others. Meditation is very useful to help a person live peacefully despite various disturbances that are so prevalent in this modern world. We cannot be expected to retire to a jungle or forest to live in ivory towers — 'far from the madding crowd'.

By practising right meditation we can have an abode for temporary oblivion. Meditation has the purpose of training a person to face, understand and conquer this very world in which we live. Meditation teaches us to adjust ourselves to bear with the numerous obstacles to life in the modern world.

Some people practise meditation in order to satisfy their material desires; they want to further their material gains. They want to use meditation to get better jobs. They want to earn more money or to operate their business more efficiently. Perhaps they fail to understand that the aim of meditation is not to increase but to decrease desires. Materialistic motives are hardly suitable for proper meditation, the goal of which lies beyond worldly affairs. One should meditate to try to attain something that even money cannot buy or bring.

If you practice meditation, you can learn to behave like a gentleman even though you are disturbed by others. Through meditation you can learn how to relax the body and to calm the mind; you can learn to be tranquil and happy within.

Just as an engine gets overheated and damaged when it is run for a prolonged period and requires cooling down to overcome this, so also the mind gets overtaxed when we subject it to a sustained degree of mental effort and it is only through meditation that relaxation or cooling can be achieved. Meditation strengthens the mind to control human emotion when it is disturbed by negative thoughts and feelings such as jealousy, anger, pride and envy.

If you practise meditation, you can learn to make the proper decision when you are at a cross-roads in life and are at a loss as to which way to turn. These qualities cannot be purchased from anywhere. No amount of money or property can buy these qualities, yet you can attain them through meditation. And finally the ultimate object of Buddhist meditation is to eradicate all defilements from the mind and to attain the final goal — *Nibbana*.

Nowadays, however, the practice of meditation has been abused by people. They want immediate and quick results, just as they expect quick returns for everything they do in daily life. In Buddhism, as is the case with other eastern cultures, patience is a most important quality. The mind must be brought under control in slow degrees and one should not try to reach for the higher states without proper training. We have heard of over-enthusiastic young men and women literally going out of their minds because they adopted the wrong attitudes towards meditation. Meditation is a gentle way of conquering the defilements which pollute the mind. If people want ' success ' or ' achievement ' to boast to others that they have attained this or that level of meditation, they are abusing the method of mental culture. One must be trained in morality and one must clearly understand that to be successful in the discipline of meditation worldly achievements must not be equated with spiritual development. Ideally, it is good to work under an experienced teacher who will help his student to develop along the right path. But above all one must never be in a hurry to achieve too much too quickly.

# The Significance of Paritta Chanting

*Paritta chanting is the recital of some of the Sutras uttered by the Buddha in the Pali language for the blessing and protection of the devotees.*

PARITTA Chanting or Sutra Chanting is a well-known Buddhist practice conducted all over the world, especially in Theravada Buddhist countries where the Pali language is used for recitals. Many of these are important sutras from the basic teachings of the Buddha which were selected by His disciples. Originally, these sutras were recorded on *ola* leaves about two thousand years ago. Later, they were compiled into a book known as the ' Paritta Chanting Book '. The names of the original books from which these sutras were selected are the *Anguttara Nikaya, Majjhima Nikaya, Digha Nikaya, Samyutta Nikaya* and *Kuddaka Nikaya* in the *Sutra Pitaka.*

The sutras that Buddhists recite for protection are known as *Paritta Chanting.* Here ' *protection* ' means shielding ourselves from various forms of evil spirits, misfortune, sickness and influence of the planetary systems as well as instilling confidence in the mind. The vibrant sound of the chanting creates a very pleasing atmosphere in the vicinity. The rhythm of the chanting is also important. One might have noticed that when monks recite these sutras, different intonations are adopted to harmonise with different sutras intended for different quarters. It was found very early during man's spiritual development that certain rhythms of the human voice could produce significant psychological states of peacefulness and serenity in the minds of ardent listeners. Furthermore, intonation at certain levels would appeal to devas, whilst certain rhythms would create a good influence over lower beings like animals, snakes, or even spirits or ghosts. Therefore, a soothing and correct rhythm is an important aspect of Paritta Chanting.

The use of these rhythms is not confined to Buddhism alone. In every religion, when the followers recite their prayers by using the holy books, they follow certain rhythms. We can observe this when we listen to Quran reading by Muslims and the Veda Mantra Chanting by Hindu priests in the Sanskrit language. Some lovely chanting is also carried out by certain Christian groups, especially the Roman Catholic and Greek Orthodox sects.

When the sutras are chanted, three great and powerful forces are activated. These are the forces of the Buddha, Dhamma and the Sangha. Buddhism is the combination of these ' Three Jewels ' and when invoked together they can bring great blessings to mankind.

(1) *The Buddha.* He had cultivated all the great virtues, wisdom and enlightenment, developed His spiritual power and

gave us His noble Teachings. Even though the physical presence of the Teacher is no more with us, His Teachings have remained for the benefit of mankind. Similarly, the man who discovered electricity is no more with us, yet by using his knowledge, the effect of his wisdom still remains. The illumination that we enjoy today is the result of his wisdom. The scientists who discovered atomic energy are no longer living, but the knowledge to use it remains with us. Likewise the Noble Teachings given us through the Buddha's wisdom and enlightenment, are a most effective power for people to draw inspiration from. When you remember Him and respect Him, you develop confidence in Him. When you recite or listen to the words uttered by Him, you invoke the power of His blessings.

(2) *Dhamma.* It is the power of truth, justice and peace discovered by the Buddha which provides spiritual solace for devotees to maintain peace and happiness. When you develop your compassion, devotion and understanding, this power of the Dhamma protects you and helps you to develop more confidence and strength in your mind. Then your mind itself becomes a very powerful force for your own protection. When it is known that you uphold the Dhamma, people and other beings will respect you. The power of the Dhamma protects you from various kinds of bad influence and evil forces. Those who cannot understand the power of the Dhamma and how to live in accordance with the Dhamma, invariably surrender themselves to all forms of superstitious beliefs and subject themselves to the influence of many kinds of gods, spirits and mystical powers which require them to perform odd rites and rituals. By so doing, they only develop more fear and suspicion born out of ignorance. Large sums of money are spent on such practices and this could be easily avoided if people were to develop their confidence in the Dhamma. Dhamma is also described as ' nature ' or ' natural phenomena ' and ' cosmic law '. Those who have learnt the nature of these forces can protect themselves through the

Dhamma. When the mind is calmed through perfect knowledge disturbances cannot create fear in the mind.

(3)    *The Sangha.* It refers to the holy order of monks who have renounced their worldly life for their spiritual development. They are considered as disciples of the Buddha, who have cultivated great virtues to attain sainthood or Arahantahood. We pay respect to the Sangha community as the custodians of the Buddha Sasana or those who had protected and introduced the Dhamma to the world over the last 2,500 years. The services rendered by the Sangha community has guided mankind to lead a righteous and noble life. They are the living link with the Enlightened One who bring His message to us through the recital of the words uttered by Him.

The chanting of sutras for blessing was started during the Buddha's time. Later, in certain Buddhist countries such as Sri Lanka, Thailand and Burma, this practice was developed further by organising prolonged chanting for one whole night or for several days. With great devotion, devotees participated in the chanting sessions by listening attentively and intelligently. There were some occasions when the Buddha and His disciples chanted sutras to bring spiritual solace to people suffering from epidemics, famines, sickness and other natural disasters. On one occasion, when a child was reported to be affected by some evil influence, the Buddha instructed His monks to recite sutras to give protection to the child from the evil forces.

The blessing service, by way of chanting, was effective. Of course, there were instances when the sutra chanting could not be effective if the victims had committed some strong bad *kamma*. Nevertheless, certain minor bad kammic effects can be overcome by the vibrant power combined with the great virtues and compassion of those holy people who chant these sutras. Here, the overcoming of a bad kammic effect does not mean the complete eradication of the effect, but only a temporary suspension of such an effect.

Devotees who were tired or fatigued have experienced relief and calmness after listening to the chanting of sutras. Such an experience is different from that provided by music because music can create excitement in our mind and pander to our emotions but does not create spiritual devotion and confidence.

For the last 2,500 years, Buddhist devotees have experienced the good effects of sutra chanting. We should try to understand how and why the words uttered by the Buddha for blessing purposes could be so effective even after His passing away. It is mentioned in the Buddha's teaching that ever since He had the aspiration to become a Buddha during His previous births, He had strongly upheld one particular principle, namely, to abstain from ' telling lies '. Without abusing or misusing His words, He spoke gently without hurting the feelings of others. The power of Truth has become a source of strength in the words uttered by the Buddha with great compassion. However, the power of the Buddha's word alone is not enough to secure blessing without the devotion and understanding of the devotees.

The miraculous effect experienced by many people in ridding themselves of their sickness and many other mental disturbances through the medium of the Buddhist sutras, enabled them to develop their faith and confidence in this form of religious service.

# Are Buddhists Idol Worshippers?

*Buddhists are not idol worshippers but ideal worshippers.*

ALTHOUGH it is customary amongst Buddhists to keep Buddha images and to pay their respects to the Buddha, Buddhist are not idol worshippers. Idolatry generally means erecting images of unknown gods and goddesses in various shapes and sizes and to

For a more detailed treatment of the subject, read the booklet ' Are Buddhists Idol-worshippers? ' by the same author.

pray directly to these images. The prayers are a request to the gods for guidance and protection. The gods and goddesses are asked to bestow health, wealth, property and to provide for various needs; they are asked to forgive transgressions.

The ' worshipping ' at the Buddha image is quite a different matter. Buddhists revere the image of the Buddha as a gesture to the greatest, wisest, most benevolent, compassionate and holy man who has ever lived in this world. It is a historical fact that this great man actually lived in this world and has done a great service to mankind. The worship of the Buddha really means paying homage, veneration and devotion to Him and what He represents, and not to the stone or metal figure.

The image is a visual aid that helps one to recall the Buddha in the mind and to remember His great qualities which inspired millions of people from generation to generation throughout the civilized world. Buddhists use the statue as a symbol and as an object of concentration to gain a peace of mind. When Buddhists look upon the image of the Buddha, they put aside thoughts of strife and think only of peace, serenity, calmness and tranquility. The statue enables the mind to recall this great man and inspires devotees to follow His example and instructions. In their mind, the devout Buddhists feel the living presence of the Master. This feeling makes their act of worship become vivid and significant. The serenity of the Buddha image influences and inspires them to observe the right path of conduct and thought.

An understanding Buddhist never asks favours from the image nor does he request forgiveness for evil deeds committed. An understanding Buddhist tries to control his mind, to follow the Buddha's advice, to get rid of worldly miseries and to find his salvation.

Those who criticize Buddhists for practising idol worship are really misinterpreting what Buddhists do. If people can keep the photographs of their parents and grandparents to cherish in their memory, if people can keep the photographs of kings, queens, prime ministers, great heroes, philosophers, and poets, there is certainly no reason why Buddhists cannot keep their beloved Master's picture or image to remember and respect Him.

What harm is there if people recite some verses praising the great qualities of their Master? If people can lay wreaths on the graves of beloved ones to express their gratitude, what harm is there if Buddhists too offer some flowers, joss-sticks, incense, etc., to their beloved Teacher who devoted His life to help suffering humanity? People make statues of certain conquering heroes who were in fact murderers and who were responsible for the death of millions of innocent people. For the sake of power, these conquerors committed murder with hatred, cruelty and greed. They invaded poor countries and created untold suffering by taking away lands and properties of others, and causing much destruction. Many of these conquerors are regarded as national heroes; memorial services are conducted for them and flowers are offered on their graves and tombs. What is wrong then, if Buddhists pay their respects to their world honoured Teacher who sacrificed His worldly pleasures for the sake of Enlightenment to show others the Path of Salvation?

Images are the language of the subconscious. Therefore, the image of the Enlightened One is often created within one's mind as the embodiment of perfection, the image will deeply penetrate into the subconscious mind and (if it is sufficiently strong enough) can act as an automatic brake against impulses. The recollection of the Buddha produces joy, invigorates the mind and elevates man from states of restlessness, tension and frustration. Thus the worship of the Buddha is not a prayer in its usual sense but a meditation. Therefore, it is not idol worship, but 'ideal' worship. Thus Buddhists can find fresh strength to build a shrine of their lives. They cleanse their hearts until they feel worthy to bear the image in their innermost shrine. Buddhists pay respects to the great person who is represented by the image. They try to gain inspiration from His Noble personality and emulate Him. Buddhists do not see the Buddha image as a dead idol of wood or metal or clay. The image represents something vibrant to those who understand and are purified in thought, word and deed.

The Buddha images are nothing more than symbolic representations of His great qualities. It is not unnatural that the deep respect for the Buddha should be expressed in some of the finest and most beautiful forms of art and sculpture the world has ever known. It is difficult to understand why some people look down on those who pay respect to images which represent holy religious teachers.

The calm and serene image of the Buddha has been a common concept of ideal beauty. The Buddha's image is the most precious, common asset of Asian cultures. Without the image of the Buddha, where can we find a serene, radiant and spiritually emancipated personality?

But the image of the Buddha is appreciated not only by Asians or Buddhists. Anatole France in his autobiography writes, ' On the first of May, 1890, chance led me to visit the Museum in Paris. There standing in the silence and simplicity of the gods of Asia, my eyes fell on the statue of the Buddha who beckoned to suffering humanity to develop understanding and compassion. If ever a god walked on this earth, I felt here was He. I felt like kneeling down to Him and praying to Him as to a God. '

Once a general left an image of the Buddha as a legacy to Winston Churchill. The general said, ' If ever your mind gets perturbed and perplexed, I want you to see this image and be comforted. ' What is it that makes the message of the Buddha so attractive to people who have cultivated their intellect? Perhaps the answer can be seen in the serenity of the image of the Buddha.

Not only in colour and line did men express their faith in the Buddha and the graciousness of His Teaching. Human hands wrought in metal and stone to produce the Buddha image that is one of the greatest creations of the human genius. Witness the famous image in the *Abhayagiri Vihara* in Sri Lanka, or the Buddha image of *Sarnath* or the celebrated images of *Borobudur*. The eyes are full of compassion and the hands express fearlessness, or goodwill and blessings, or they unravel some thread of thought or call the earth to witness His great search for Truth. Wherever the Dhamma went, the image of the great Teacher went with it, not only as an object of worship but also as an object of meditation and reverence. ' I know nothing, ' says Keyserling, ' more grand in this world than the figure of the Buddha. It is an absolutely perfect embodiment of spirituality in the visible domain. '

A life so beautiful, a heart so pure and kind, a mind so deep and enlightened, a personality so inspiring and selfless — such a perfect life, such a compassionate heart, such a calm mind, such a serene personality is really worthy of respect, worthy of honour and worthy of offering. The Buddha is the highest perfection of mankind.

The Buddha image is the symbol, not of a person, but of Buddhahood — that to which all men can attain though few do. For Buddhahood is not for one but for many: ' The Buddhas of the past ages, the Buddhas that are yet to come, the Buddha of the present age; humbly I each day adore. '

However, it is not compulsory for every Buddhist to have a Buddha image to practise Buddhism. Those who can control their mind and the senses, can certainly do so without an image as an object. If Buddhists truly wish to behold the Buddha in all the majestic splendour and beauty of His ideal presence, they must translate His Teachings into practice in their daily lives. It is in the practice of His Teachings that they can come closer to Him and feel the wonderful radiance of His undying wisdom and compassion. Simply respecting the images without following His Sublime Teachings is not the way to find salvation.

We must also endeavour to understand the spirit of the Buddha. His Teaching is the only way to save this troubled world. In spite of the tremendous advantages of science and technology, people in the world today are filled with fear, anxiety and despair. The answer to our troubled world is found in the Teachings of the Buddha.

# Religious Significance of Fasting

*Many people in the world face untimely death owing to over-eating.*

IN Buddhism, fasting is recognised as one of the methods for practising self-control. The Buddha advised monks not to take solid food after noon. Lay people who observe the Eight Precepts on full moon days also abstain from taking any solid food after noon.

Critics sometimes regard these practices as religious fads. They are not religious fads but practices based on a moral and psychological insight.

In Buddhism, fasting is an initial stage of self-discipline to acquire self-control. In every religion, there is a system of fasting. By fasting and sacrificing a meal once a day or for any period, we can contribute our food to those who are starving or who do not have even a proper meal each day.

' A man who eats too much ', writes Leo Tolstoy, ' cannot strive against laziness, while a gluttonous and idle man will never be able to contend with sexual lust. Therefore, according to all moral teachings, the effort towards self-control commences with a struggle against the lust of gluttony — commences with fasting just as the first condition of a good life is self-control, so the first condition of a life of self-control is fasting. '

Sages in various countries who practised self-control began with a system of regulated fasting and succeeded in attaining unbelievable heights of spirituality. An ascetic was kicked and tortured, and then his hands and feet were severed on the orders of a rakish king. But the ascetic, according to the Buddhist story, endured the torture with equanimity and without the slightest anger or hatred. Such religious people have developed their mental power through restraining from sensual indulgence.

# Vegetarianism

*One should not judge the purity or impurity of man simply by observing what he eats.*

IN the *Amagandha Sutta,* the Buddha said:

> ' *Neither meat, nor fasting, nor nakedness,*
> *Nor shaven heads, nor matted hair, nor dirt,*
> *Nor rough skins, nor fire-worshipping,*
> *Nor all the penances here in this world,*
> *Nor hymns, nor oblation, nor sacrifice,*
> *Nor feasts of the season,*
> *Will purify a man overcome with doubt. '*

Taking fish and meat by itself does not make a man become impure. A man makes himself impure by bigotry, deceit, envy, self-exaltation, disparagement and other evil intentions. Through his own evil thoughts and actions, man makes himself impure. There is no strict rule in Buddhism that the followers of the Buddha should not take fish and meat. The only advice given by the Buddha is that they should not be involved in killing intentionally or they should not ask others to kill any living being for them. However, those who take vegetable food and abstain from animal flesh are praiseworthy.

Though the Buddha did not advocate vegetarianism for the monks, He did advise the monks to avoid taking ten kinds of meat for their self respect and protection. They are: humans, elephants, horses, dogs, snakes, lions, tigers, leopards, bears hyenas. Some animals attack people when they smell the flesh of their own kind. *(Vinaya Pitaka)*

When the Buddha was asked to introduce vegetarianism amongst His disciples (monks) by Devadatta, one of His disciples, the Buddha refused to do so. As Buddhism is a free religion, His advice was to leave the decision regarding vegetarianism to the individual disciple. It clearly shows that the Buddha had not considered this as a very important religious observance. The Buddha did not mention anything about vegetarianism for the lay Buddhists in His Teaching.

Jivaka Komarabhacca, the doctor, discussed this controversial issue with the Buddha: ' Lord, I have heard that animals are slaughtered on purpose for the recluse Gotama, and that the recluse Gotama knowingly eats the meat killed on purpose for him. Lord, do those who say animals are slaughtered on purpose for the recluse Gotama, and the recluse Gotama knowingly eats the meat killed on purpose for him. Do they falsely accuse the Buddha? Or do they speak the truth? Are your declarations and supplementary declarations not thus subject to be ridiculed by others in any manner? '

' Jivaka, those who say: 'Animals are slaughtered on purpose for the recluse Gotama, and the recluse Gotama knowingly eats the meat killed on purpose for him', do not say according to what I have declared, and they falsely accuse me. Jivaka, I have declared that one should not make use of meat if it is seen, heard or suspected to have been killed on purpose for a monk. I allow the monks meat that is quite pure in three respects: if it is not seen, heard or suspected to have been killed on purpose for a monk. ' (Jivaka Sutta)

In certain countries, the followers of the Mahayana school of Buddhism are strict vegetarians. While appreciating their observance in the name of religion, we should like to point out that they should not condemn those who are not vegetarians. They must remember that there is no precept in the original Teachings of the Buddha that requires all Buddhists to be vegetarians. We must realise that Buddhism is known as the Middle Path. It is a liberal religion and the Buddha's advice was that it is not necessary to go to extremes to practise His Teachings.

Vegetarianism alone does not help a man to cultivate his humane qualities. There are kind, humble, polite and religious people amongst non-vegetarians. Therefore, one should not condone the statement that a pure, religious man *must* practise vegetarianism.

On the other hand, if anybody thinks that people cannot have a healthy life without taking fish and meat, it does not necessarily follow that they are correct since there are millions of pure vegetarians all over the world who are stronger and healthier than the meat-eaters.

People who criticize Buddhists who eat meat do not understand the Buddhist attitude towards food. A living being needs nourishment. We eat to live. As such a human being should supply his body with the food it needs to keep him healthy and to give him energy to work. However, as a result of increasing wealth, more and more people, especially in developed countries, eat simply to satisfy their palates. If one craves after any kind of food, or kills to satisfy his greed for meat, this is wrong. But if one eats without greed and without directly being involved in the act of killing but merely to sustain the physical body, he is practising self restraint.

# The Moon and Religious Observances

*The outstanding events in the life of the Buddha took place on full moon days.*

MANY people would like to know the religious significance of the full moon and new moon days. To Buddhists, there is a special religious significance especially on full moon day because certain important and outstanding events connected with the life of Lord Buddha took place on full moon days. The Buddha was born on a full moon day. His renunciation took place on a full moon day. His Enlightenment, the delivery of His first sermon, His passing away into Nibbana and many other important events associated with His life-span of eighty years, occurred on full moon days.

Buddhists all over the world have a high regard for full moon days. They celebrate this day with religious fervour by observing precepts, practising meditation and by keeping away from the sensual worldly life. On this day they direct their attention to spiritual development. Apart from Buddhists, it is understood that other co-religionists also believe that there is some religious significance related to the various phases of the moon. They also observe certain religious disciplines such as fasting and praying on full moons days.

Ancient belief in India says that the moon is the controller of the waters, and circulating through the universe, sustaining all living creatures, is the counterpart on earth of the liquor heaven, ' *amrta* ' the drink of the gods. Dew and rain become vegetable sap, sap becomes the milk of the cow, and the milk is then converted into blood — Amrta water, sap, milk and blood, represent but different states of the one elixir. The vessel or cup of this immortal fluid is the moon.

It is believed that the moon, like the other planets, exerts a considerable degree of influence on human beings. It has been observed that people suffering from mental ailments invariably have their passions and emotional feelings affected during full moon days. The word 'lunatic' derived from the word 'lunar' (or moon) is most significant and indicates very clearly the influence of the moon on human life. Some people, suffering from various forms of illness invariably find their sickness aggravated during such periods. Researchers have found that certain phases of the moon not only affect humans and animals, but also influence plant life and other elements. Low-tides and high-tides are a direct result of the overpowering influence of the moon.

Our human body consists of about seventy percent liquid. It is accepted by physicians that our bodily fluids flow more freely at the time of full moon. People suffering from asthma, bronchitis and even certain skin diseases, find their ailments aggravated under the influence of the moon. More than five thousand years ago, people had recognised the influence of the moon on cultivation. Farmers were very particular about the effect of the moon on their crops. They knew that certain grains and paddy would be affected if blooming took place during a full moon period. Medical science had also ascertained the different reactions of certain medicines under different facets of the moon, because of the influence of the moon on human beings.

In view of the possible influence of the moon, the ancient sages advised the people to refrain from various commitments on this particular day and take it easy for the day. They are advised to relax their minds on this particular day and to devote their time to spiritual pursuits. All those who have developed their minds to a certain extent can achieve enlightenment since the brain is in an awakened state. Those who have not trained their minds through religious discipline are liable to be subjected to the strong influence of the moon. The Buddha attained His Enlightenment on a full moon day for He had been developing and attuning it correctly for a long period.

In days gone by, full moon and new moon days were declared public holidays in many Buddhist countries and people were encouraged to devote their time to spiritual development. It was only during the colonial period that holidays were switched over to Sundays. In view of this, some Buddhist countries are now trying to re-introduce the former lunar system of holidays. It is advisable to observe full moon day as a religious day to concentrate on peace and happiness by calming down the senses. Many Buddhists observe the eight precepts on full moon days, to be free from family commitments and to keep away from worldly pleasures in order to have peace of mind for their spiritual development. The effect of the moon on life and earth has been analysed scientifically.

One writer says:

' I have been reading an article in an American science magazine recently where the writer brings together the present research on the subject of the moon to prove how decisively this age old object of the skies influences our lives, particularly at each of the four phases it passes through in its 28-day cycle. '

This research, by the way, was done at the American Universities of Yale, Duke and Northwestern and they have ' independently ' come up with the astonishing evidence that the moon plays a big part in our daily life and indeed, in the lives of all living things.

We are assured that there is nothing very occult in this phenomenon put that the phases of the moon do in fact stimulate various bodily actions like modifying metabolism, electrical charges and blood acidity.

One of the key experiments performed to establish this fact was on fiddler crabs, mice and some plants. They were all placed in chambers where weather conditions could not affect them, but were subjected to air pressure, humidity, light and temperature under controlled conditions.

The hundreds of observations made showed a remarkable fact, namely that all the animals and plants operated on a 28-day cycle. Metabolism which was found to have dropped at the time of the new moon was twenty percent higher at the time of the phase of the full moon. This difference is described as a striking variation.

Once a nurse in Florida told a doctor that she noticed a lot more bleeding occured when the moon is full. Like all doctors who are sceptical about such beliefs, he laughed at this statement.

But the nurse, undeterred, produced records of surgical operations which clearly showed that during full moon, more patients had to be returned to the operating theatre than at any other time for treatment for excessive bleeding after operations. To satisfy himself, this doctor started keeping records on his own and he came to a similar conclusion. When we consider all those occurences, we can understand why our ancestors and religious teachers had advised us to change our daily routine and to relax physically and mentally on full moon and new moon days. The practise of religion is the most appropriate method for people to experience mental peace and physical relaxation. The Buddhists are merely observing the wisdom of the past when they devote more time to activities of a spiritual nature on New Moon and Full Moon days.

PART FOUR

# HUMAN LIFE IN SOCIETY

# 11

# LIFE AND CULTURE

## Traditions, Customs and Festivals

*Buddhism is open to traditions and customs provided they are not harmful to the welfare of others.*

THE Buddha advised us not to believe in anything simply because it is the traditional custom. However, we are not advised to suddenly do away with all traditions. ' You must try to experiment with them and put them thoroughly to test. If they are reasonable and conducive both to your happiness and to the welfare of others, only then should you accept and practise these traditions and customs. ' *(Kalama Sutta)* This is certainly one of the most liberal declarations ever made by any religious teacher. This tolerance of other's traditions and customs is not known to some other religionists. These religionists usually advise their new converts to give up all their traditions, customs and culture without observing whether they are good or bad. While preaching the Dhamma, Buddhist missionaries have never advised the people to give up their traditions as long as they are reasonable. But the customs and traditions must be within the framework of religious principles. In other words, one should not violate the religious precepts in order to follow one's traditions. If people are very keen to follow their own traditions which have no religious value at all, they can do so provided that they do not practise these traditions in the name of religion. Even then, such practices must be harmless to oneself and to all other living creatures.

## Rites and Rituals

These are included within customs and traditions. The rites and rituals are an ornamentation or a decoration to beautify a religion in order to attract the public. They provide a psychological help to some people. But one can practise religion without any rites and rituals. Certain rites and rituals that people consider as the most important aspect of their religion for their salvation are not considered as such in Buddhism. According to the Buddha, one should not cling to such practices for his spiritual development or mental purity.

## Festivals

Genuine and sincere Buddhists do not observe Buddhist festivals by enjoying themselves under the influence of liquor and merry-making or holding feasts by the slaughtering of animals. The true Buddhists observe festival days in an entirely different manner. On the particular festival day, they would devote their time to abstaining from all evil. They would practise charity and help others to relieve themselves from their suffering. They may entertain friends and relatives in a respectable way.

The festivals that have been incorporated with religion sometimes could pollute the purity of a religion. On the other hand a religion without festivals can become very dull and lifeless to many people. Usually children and youths come to religion through religious festivals. To them the attraction of a religion is based on its festivals. However, to a meditator, festivals can become a nuisance.

Of course, some people will not be satisfied with religious observances only during a festival. They naturally like to have some sort of merry-making and outward show. Rites, rituals, ceremonies, processions and festivals are organised to quench that thirst for emotional satisfaction through religion. No one can say that such practices are wrong, but devotees have to organise those ceremonies in a cultured manner, without causing a nuisance to others.

# Buddhism and Women

*A female child may prove even to be a better offspring than a male.*

WOMEN'S position in Buddhism is unique. The Buddha gave women full freedom to participate in a religious life. The Buddha was the first religious Teacher who gave this religious freedom to women. Before the Buddha, women's duties had been restricted to the kitchen; women were not even allowed to enter any temple or to recite any religious scripture. During the Buddha's time, women's position in society was very low. The Buddha was criticized by the prevailing establishment when He gave this freedom to women. His move to allow women to enter the Holy Order was extremely radical for the times. Yet the Buddha allowed

---

*For a deeper discussion on this subject, read the booklet 'Status of Women in Buddhism' by the same author.*

women to prove themselves and to show that they too had the capacity like men to attain the highest position in the religious way of life by attaining Arahantahood. Every woman in the world must be grateful to the Buddha for showing them the real religious way of living and for giving such freedom to them for the first time in world history.

A good illustration of the prevailing attitude towards women during the Buddha's time is found in these words of Mara:

' No woman, with the two-finger wisdom *(narrow)* which is hers, could ever hope to reach thóse heights which are attained only by the sages. '

Undoubtedly, the Buddha was vehement in contradicting such attitudes. The nun *(bhikkhuni)* to whom Mara addressed these words, gave the following reply:

' When one's mind is well concentrated and wisdom never fails, does the fact of being a woman make any difference? '

King Kosala was very disappointed when he heard that his Queen had given birth to a baby girl. He had expected a boy. To console the sad King, the Buddha said:

' A female child, O Lord of men, may prove
Even a better offspring than a male.
For she may grow up wise and virtuous,
Her husband's mother reverencing, true wife,
The boy that she may bear may do great deeds,
And rule great realms, yes, such a son
Of noble wife becomes his country's guide, '

*(Samyutta Nikaya)*

The Buddha has confirmed that man is not always the only wise one; woman is also wise.

Nowadays many religionists like to claim that their religions give women equal rights. We only have to look at the world around us today to see the position of women in many societies. It seems that they have no property rights, are discriminated in various fields and generally suffer abuse in many subtle forms.

Even in western countries, women like the Suffragettes had to fight very hard for their rights. According to Buddhism, it is not justifiable to regard women as inferior. The Buddha Himself was born as a woman on several occasions during His previous births in Samsara and even as a woman He developed the noble qualities and wisdom until He gained Enlightenment or Buddhahood.

# Buddhism and Politics

*The Buddha had gone beyond all worldly affairs, but still gave advice on good government.*

THE Buddha came from a warrior caste and was naturally brought into association with kings, princes and ministers. Despite His origin and association, He never resorted to the influence of political power to introduce His teaching, nor allowed His Teaching to be misused for gaining political power. But today, many politicians try to drag the Buddha's name into politics by introducing Him as a communist, capitalist, or even an imperialist. They have forgotten that the new political philosophy as we know it really developed in the West long after the Buddha's time. Those who try to make use of the good name of the Buddha for their own personal advantage must remember that the Buddha was the Supremely Enlightened One who had gone beyond all worldly concerns.

There is an inherent problem of trying to intermingle religion with politics. The basis of religion is morality, purity and faith, while that for politics is power. In the course of history, religion has often been used to give legitimacy to those in power and their exercise of that power. Religion was used to justify wars and conquests, persecutions, atrocities, rebellions, destruction of works of art and culture.

When religion is used to pander to political whims, it has to forego its high moral ideals and become debased by worldly political demands.

The thrust of the Buddha Dhamma is not directed to the creation of new political institutions and establishing political arrangements. Basically, it seeks to approach the problems of society by reforming the individuals constituting that society and by suggesting some general principles through which the society can be guided towards greater humanism, improved welfare of its members, and more equitable sharing of resources.

There is a limit to the extent to which a political system can safeguard the happiness and prosperity of its people. No political system, no matter how ideal it may appear to be, can bring about peace and happiness as long as the people in the system are dominated by greed, hatred and delusion. In addition, no matter what political system is adopted, there are certain universal factors which the members of that society will have to experience: the effects of good and bad *kamma,* the lack of real satisfaction or everlasting happiness in the world characterised by *dukkha* (unsatisfactoriness), *anicca* (impermanence), and *anatta* (egolessness). To the Buddhist, nowhere in Samsara is there *real freedom,* not even in the heavens or the world of *Brahmas.*

Although a good and just political system which guarantees basic human rights and contains checks and balances to the use of power is an important condition for a happy life in society, people should not fritter away their time by endlessly searching for the ultimate political system where men can be completely free, because complete freedom cannot be found in any system but only in minds which are free. To be free, people will have to look within their own minds and work towards freeing themselves from the chains of ignorance and craving. Freedom in the truest sense is only possible when a person uses Dhamma to develop his character through good speech and action and to train his mind so as to expand his mental potential and achieve his ultimate aim of enlightenment.

While recognising the usefulness of separating religion from politics and the limitations of political systems in bringing about peace and happiness, there are several aspects of the Buddha's teaching which have close correspondence to the political arrangements of the present day. Firstly, the Buddha spoke about the equality of all human beings long before Abraham Lincoln, and that classes and castes are artificial barriers erected by society. The only classification of human beings, according to the Buddha, is based on the quality of their moral conduct. Secondly, the Buddha encouraged the spirit of social co-operation and active participation in society. This spirit is actively promoted in the political process of modern societies. Thirdly, since no one was appointed as the Buddha's successor, the members of the Order were to be guided by the Dhamma and Vinaya, or in short, the Rule of Law. Until today every member of the Sangha is to abide by the Rule of Law which governs and guides their conduct.

Fourthly, the Buddha encouraged the spirit of consultation and the democratic process. This is shown within the community of the Order in which all members have the right to decide on matters of general concern. When a serious question arose demanding attention, the issues were put before the monks and discussed in a manner similar to the democratic parliamentary system used today. This self-governing procedure may come as a surprise to many to learn that in the assemblies of Buddhists in India 2,500 years and more ago are to be found the rudiments of the parliamentary practice of the present day. A special officer similar to ' Mr. Speaker ' was appointed to preserve the dignity of the assembly. A second officer, who played a role similar to the Parliamentary Chief Whip, was also appointed to see if the quorum was secured. Matters were put forward in the form of a motion which was open to discussion. In some cases it was done once, in others three times, thus anticipating the practice of Parliament in requiring that a bill be read a third time before it becomes law. If the discussion showed a difference of opinion, it was to be settled by the vote of the majority through balloting.

The Buddhist approach to political power is the moralization and the responsible use of public power. The Buddha preached non-violence and peace as a universal message. He did not approve of violence or the destruction of life, and declared that there is no such thing as a ' just ' war. He taught: ' The victor breeds hatred, the defeated lives'in misery. He who renounces both victory and defeat is happy and peaceful. ' Not only did the Buddha teach non-violence and peace, He was perhaps the first and only religious teacher who went to the battlefield personally to prevent the outbreak of a war. He diffused tension between the Sakyas and the Koliyas who were about to wage war over the waters of Rohini. He also dissuaded King Ajatasattu from attacking the Kingdom of the *Vajjis.*

The Buddha discussed the importance and the prerequisites of a good government. He showed how the country could become corrupt, degenerate and unhappy when the head of the government becomes corrupt and unjust. He spoke against corruption and how a government should act based on humanitarian principles.

The Buddha once said, ' When the ruler of a country is just and good, the ministers become just and good; when the ministers are just and good, the higher officials become just and good; when the higher officials are just and good, the rank and file become just and good; when the rank and file become just and good, the people become just and good. ' *(Anguttara Nikaya)*

In the *Cakkavatti Sihananda Sutta,* the Buddha said that immorality and crime, such as theft, falsehood, violence, hatred, cruelty, could arise from poverty. Kings and governments may try to suppress crime through punishment, but it is futile to eradicate crimes through force.

In the *Kutadanta Sutta,* the Buddha suggested economic development instead of force to reduce crime. The government should use the country's resources to improve the economic conditions of the country. It could embark on agricultural and rural development, provide financial support to entrepreneurs and business, provide adequate wages for workers to maintain a decent life with human dignity.

In the *Jataka,* the Buddha had given 10 rules for Good Government, known as ' *Dasa Raja Dharma* '. These ten rules can be applied even today by any government which wishes to rule the country peacefully. The rules are as follows:
1. be liberal and avoid selfishness,
2. maintain a high moral character,
3. be prepared to sacrifice one's own pleasure for the well-being of the subjects,
4. be honest and maintain absolute integrity,
5. be kind and gentle,
6. lead a simple life for the subjects to emulate,
7. be free from hatred of any kind,
8. exercise non violence,
9. practise patience, and
10. respect public opinion to promote peace and harmony.

Regarding the behaviour of rulers, He further advised:
(a) A good ruler should act impartially and should not be biased and discriminate between one particular group of subjects against another.
(b) A good ruler should not harbour any form of hatred against any of his subjects.
(c) A good ruler should show no fear whatsoever in the enforcement of the law, if it is justifiable.
(d) A good ruler must possess a clear understanding of the law to be enforced. It should not be enforced just because the ruler has the authority to enforce the law. It must be done in a reasonable manner and with common sense.

*(Cakkavatti Sihananda Sutta)*

In the *Milinda Panha,* it is stated: ' If a man, who is unfit, incompetent, immoral, improper, unable and unworthy of kingship, has enthroned himself a king or a ruler with great authority, he is subject to be tortured... to be subject to a variety of punishment by the people, because, being unfit and unworthy, he has placed himself unrighteously in the seat of sovereignty. The ruler, like others who violate and trangress moral codes and basic rules of all social laws of mankind, is equally subject to punishment; and moreover, to be censured is the ruler who conducts himself as a robber of the public. ' In a Jataka story, it is mentioned that a ruler who punishes innocent people and does not punish the culprit is not suitable to rule a country.

The king always improves himself and carefully examines his own conduct in deeds, words and thoughts, trying to discover and listen to public opinion as to whether or not he had been guilty of any faults and mistakes in ruling the kingdom. If it is found that he rules unrighteously, the public will complain that they are ruined by the wicked ruler with unjust treatment, punishment, taxation, or other oppressions including corruption of any kind, and they will react against him in one way or another. On the contrary, if he rules righteously they will bless him: ' Long live His Majesty. ' *(Majjhima Nikaya)*

The Buddha's emphasis on the moral duty of a ruler to use public power to improve the welfare of the people had inspired Emperor Asoka in the Third Century B.C. to do likewise. Emperor Asoka, a sparkling example of this principle, resolved to live according to and preach the Dhamma and to serve his subjects and all humanity. He declared his non-aggressive intentions to his neighbours, assuring them of his goodwill and sending envoys to distant kings bearing his message of peace and non-aggression. He promoted the energetic practice of the socio-moral virtues of honesty, truthfulness, compassion, benevolence, non-violence, considerate behaviour towards all, non-extravagance, non-acquisitiveness, and non-injury to animals. He encouraged religious freedom and mutual respect for each other's creed. He went on periodic tours preaching the Dhamma to the rural people. He undertook works of public utility, such as founding of hospitals for men and animals, supplying of medicine, planting of roadside trees and groves, digging of wells, and construction of watering sheds and rest houses. He expressly forbade cruelty to animals.

Sometimes the Buddha is said to be a social reformer. Among other things, He condemned the caste system, recognised the equality of people, spoke on the need to improve socio-economic conditions, recognised the importance of a more equitable distribution of wealth among the rich and the poor, raised the status of women, recommended the incorporation of humanism in government and administration, and taught that a society should not be run by greed but with consideration and compassion for the people. Despite all these, His contribution to mankind is much greater because He took off at a point which no other social reformer before or ever since had done, that is, by going to the deepest roots of human ill which are found in the human mind. It is only in the human mind that true reform can be effected. Reforms imposed by force upon the external world have a very short life because they have no roots. But those reforms which spring as a result of the transformation of man's inner consciousness remain rooted. While their branches spread outwards, they draw their nourishment from an unfailing source — the subconscious imperatives of the life-stream itself. So reforms come about when men's minds have prepared the way for them, and they live as long as men revitalise them out of their own love of truth, justice and their fellow men.

The doctrine preached by the Buddha is not one based on ' Political Philosophy '. Nor is it a doctrine that encourages men to worldly pleasures. It sets out a way to attain Nibbana. In other words, its ultimate aim is to put an end to craving *(Tanha)* that keeps men in bondage to this world. A stanza from the *Dhammapada* best summarises this statement: ' The path that leads to worldly gain is one, and the path that leads to Nibbana (by leading a religious life) is another '. However, this does not mean that Buddhists cannot or should not get involved in the political process, which is a social reality. The lives of the members of a society are shaped by laws and regulations, economic arrangements allowed within a country, institutional arrangements, which are influenced by the political arrangements of that society. Nevertheless, if a Buddhist wishes to be involved in politics, he should not misuse religion to gain political powers, nor is it advisable for those who have renounced the worldly life to lead a pure, religious life to be actively involved in politics.

# 12

# MARRIAGE, BIRTH CONTROL AND DEATH

## Buddhist Views on Marriage

*In Buddhism, marriage is regarded as entirely a personal, individual concern and not as a religious duty.*

MARRIAGE is a social convention, an institution created by man for the well-being and happiness of man, to differentiate human society from animal life and to maintain order and harmony in the process of procreation. Even though the Buddhist texts are silent on the subject of monogamy or polygamy, the Buddhist laity is advised to limit themselves to one wife. The Buddha did not lay rules on married life but gave necessary advice on how to live a happy married life. There are ample inferences in His sermons that it is wise and advisable to be faithful to one wife

---

*Read the book "Happy Married Life" by the same author for more details.*

and not to be sensual and to run after other women. The Buddha realised that one of the main causes of man's downfall is his involvement with other women *(Parabhava Sutta)*. Man must realise the difficulties, the trials and tribulations that he has to undergo just to maintain a wife and a family. These would be magnified many times when faced with calamities. Knowing the frailties of human nature, the Buddha did, in one of His precepts, advise His followers to refrain from committing adultery or sexual misconduct.

The Buddhist views on marriage are very liberal: in Buddhism, marriage is regarded entirely as a personal and individual concern, and not as a religious duty. There are no religious laws in Buddhism compelling a person to be married, to remain as a bachelor or to lead a life of total chastity. It is not laid down anywhere that Buddhists must produce children or regulate the number of children that they produce. Buddhism allows each individual the freedom to decide for himself all the issues pertaining to marriage. It might be asked why Buddhist monks do not marry, since there are no laws for or against marriage. The reason is obviously that to be of service to mankind, the monks have chosen a way of life which includes celibacy. Those who renounce the worldly life keep away from married life voluntarily to avoid various worldly commitments in order to maintain peace of mind and to dedicate their lives solely to serve others in the attainment of spiritual emancipation. Although Buddhist monks do not solemnize a marriage ceremony, they do perform religious services in order to bless the couples.

### Divorce

SEPARATION or divorce is not prohibited in Buddhism though the necessity would scarcely arise if the Buddha's injunctions were strictly followed. Men and women must have the liberty to separate if they really cannot agree with each other. Separation is preferable to avoid miserable family life for a long period of time. The Buddha further advises old men not to have young wives as the old and young are unlikely to be compatible, which can create undue problems, disharmony and downfall *(Parabhava Sutta)*.

A society grows through a network of relationships which are mutually inter-twined and inter-dependent. Every relationship is a whole hearted commitment to support and to protect others in a group or community. Marriage plays a very important part in this strong web of relationships of giving support and protection. A good marriage should grow and develop gradually from understanding and not impulse, from true loyalty and not just sheer indulgence. The institution of marriage provides a fine basis for the development of culture, a delightful association of two individuals to be nurtured, and to be free from loneliness, deprivation and fear. In marriage, each partner develops a complementary role, giving strength and moral courage to one another, each manifesting a supportive and appreciative recognition of the other's skills. There must be no thought of either man or woman being superior — each is complementary to the other, a partnership of equality, exuding gentleness, generosity, calm and dedication.

# Birth Control, Abortion and Suicide

*Although man has freedom to plan his family according to his own convenience, abortion is not justifiable.*

THERE is no reason for Buddhists to oppose birth control. They are at liberty to use any of the old or modern measures to prevent conception. Those who object to birth control by saying that it is against God's law to practise it, must realise that their concept regarding this issue is not reasonable. In birth control what is done is to *prevent* the coming into being of an existence. There is no killing involved and there is no *akusala kamma*. But if they take any action to have an abortion, this action is wrong because it involves taking away or destroying a visible or invisible life. Therefore, abortion is not justifiable.

According to the Teachings of the Buddha, five conditions must be present to constitute the evil act of killing. They are:

1. a living being
2. knowledge or awareness it is a living being
3. intention of killing
4. effort to kill, and
5. consequent death

When a female conceives, there is a being in her womb and this fulfils the first condition. After a couple of months, she knows that there is a new life within her and this satisfies the second condition. Then for some reason or other, she wants to do away with this being in her. So she begins to search for an abortionist to do the job and in this way, the third condition is fulfilled. When the abortionist does his job, the fourth condition is provided for and finally, the being is killed because of that action. So all the conditions are present. In this way, there is a violation of the First Precept ' not to kill ', and this is tantamount to killing a human being. According to Buddhism, there is no ground to say that we have the right to take away the life of another.

Under certain circumstances, people feel compelled to do that for their own convenience. But they should not justify this act of abortion as somehow or other they will have to face some sort of bad karmic results. In certain countries abortion is legalised, but this is to overcome some problems. Religious principles should never be surrendered for the pleasure of man. They stand for the welfare of the whole of mankind.

## Committing Suicide

Taking one's own life under any circumstances is morally and spiritually wrong. Taking one's own life owing to frustration or disappointment only causes greater suffering. Suicide is a cowardly way to end one's problems of life. A person cannot commit suicide if his mind is pure and tranquil. If one leaves this world with a confused and frustrated mind, it is most unlikely that he would be born again in a better condition. Suicide is an unwholesome or unskilful act since it is encouraged by a mind filled with greed, hatred and delusion. Those who commit suicide have not learnt how to face their problems, how to face the facts of life, and how to use their mind in a proper manner. Such people have not been able to understand the nature of life and worldly conditions.

Some people sacrifice their own lives for what they deem as a good and noble cause. They take their own life by such methods as self-immolation, bullet-fire, or starvation. Such actions may be classified as brave and courageous. However, from the Buddhist point of view, such acts are not to be condoned. The Buddha has clearly pointed out that the suicidal states of mind lead to further suffering.

# Why Does the World Population Increase?

*There is really no ground to think that this is the only period in which the population of the world has increased.*

IF Buddhists do not believe in the soul created by god, how are they going to account for the increase of population in the world today? This is a very common question that is asked by many people today. People who ask this question usually assume that there is only one world where living beings exist. One must consider that it is quite natural for the population to increase in such places where good climatic conditions, medical facilities, food and precautions are available to produce and to protect living beings.

One must also consider that there is really no ground to think that this is the only period in which the population in the world has increased. There are no means of comparison with any period of ancient history. Vast civilisations existed and have disappeared in Central Asia, the Middle East, Africa and Ancient America. No census figures on these civilisations are even remotely available. Population, as everything else in the universe, is subject to cycles of rise and fall. In cycles of alarming increases of birth rate, one might be consequently tempted to argue against rebirth in this or other worlds. For the last few thousand years, there has been no evidence to prove that there were more people in some parts of the world than there are today. The number of beings existing in the various world systems is truly infinite. If human lives can be compared to only one grain of sand, the number of beings in the universe is like the grains of sand on all the beaches in the world. When conditions are right and when supported by their good *kamma,* a few of these infinite number of beings are reborn as human beings. The advancement of medicine especially in the 19th and 20th centuries has enabled human beings to live longer and healthier lives.

This is a factor that contributes to population increase. Population can further increase unless sensible people take measures to control it. Hence, the credit or responsibility of increasing the population must be given to medical facilities and other circumstances available today. This credit or responsibility cannot be allotted to any particular religion or any external sources.

There is a belief among certain people that all unfortunate occurrences that destroy human lives are created by god in order to reduce the population of the world. Instead of giving so much suffering to his own creatures, why cannot he control the population? Why does he create more and more people in thickly populated countries where there is no proper food, clothing and other basic and necessary requirements? Those who believe that god created everything cannot give a satisfactory answer to this question. Poverty, unhappiness, war, hunger, disease, famine are not due to the will of god or to the whim of some devil, but to causes which are not so difficult to discover.

# Sex and Religion

*' The lower part of us is still animal. '*
*(Gandhi)*

THE sex impulse is the most dynamic force in human nature. So far-reaching is the sexual force that some measure of self-control is necessary even in ordinary existence. In the case of the spiritual aspirant, for whoever wants to bring his mind under complete control, a still greater measure of self-discipline is necessary. Such a powerful force in human character can be subdued only if the aspirant controls his thoughts and practises concentration. The conservation of the sexual force helps to develop this strength. For if he controls the sexual force, he will have more control over his whole make-up, over his lesser emotions.

Celibacy is one of the requirements for those who like to develop their spiritual development to perfection. However, it is not compulsory for each and every person to observe complete celibacy in order to practise Buddhism. The Buddha's advice is that observing celibacy is more congenial for a person who wants to cultivate his spiritual achievements. For ordinary Buddhist laymen, the precept is to abstain from sexual misconduct. Although perversion of the sexual force is not under this same category, the perverted person invariably suffers bad reactions either physically, or mentally or both.

There is a need for Buddhist laymen to exercise some degree of control over their sexual force. Man's sexual urge must be controlled properly otherwise man will behave worse than an animal when he is intoxicated with lust. Consider the sexual behaviour of what we call the 'lower animal'. Which really is often 'lower' — the animal or the man? Which acts in a normal, regular manner as regards sexual behaviour? And which runs off into all manner of irregularities and perversities? Often it is the animal that is the higher creature and man that is the lower. And why is this? It is simply because man who possesses the mental capacity which if rightly used, could make him master over his sex impulses, has actually used his mental powers in such deplorable fashion as to make himself more a slave to those impulses. Thus man can, at times, be considered lower than the animal.

Our ancestors played down this sexual impulse; they knew that it was strong enough without giving it any extra encouragement. But today we have blown it up with a thousand forms of incitation, suggestive advertisements, emphasis and display; and we have armed the sexual force with the doctrine that inhibition is dangerous and can even cause mental disorders.

Yet inhibition — the control of impulse is the first principle of any civilisation. In our modern civilisation, we have polluted the sexual atmosphere that surrounds us — so great is the mind-body urge for sexual gratification.

As a result of this sex exploitation by the hidden persuaders of modern society, the youth of today have developed an attitude toward sex that is becoming a public nuisance. An innocent girl has no freedom to move anywhere without being disturbed. On the other hand, females should be dressed in such a manner as not to arouse the hidden animal nature of youths.

Man is the only animal that does not have periods of natural sexual inactivity during which the body can recover its vitality. Unfortunately, commercial exploitation of the erotic nature in man has caused modern man to be exposed to a ceaseless barrage of sexual stimulation from every side. Much of the neuroses of present-day life is traceable to this unbalanced state of affairs. Men are expected to be monogamous, yet women are encouraged in every possible way to 'glamourise' themselves, not for the husband alone, but to excite in every man passions that society forbids him to indulge in.

Many societies try to enforce monogamous relationships. Thus a man with many failings can still be a moral man, meaning that he is faithful to the one wife that the law allows him to have. The danger here lies in the fact that thoughtful people who are intelligent enough to realise that these rules are artificial and not based on any transcendental, universally valid principles, are liable to fall into the error of thinking the same about all the other ethical laws.

Sex should be given its due place in normal human life; it should be neither unhealthily repressed nor morbidly exaggerated. And it should always be under the control of the will, as it can be if it is regarded sanely and placed in its proper perspective.

Sex should not be considered as the most important ingredient for one's happiness in a married life. Those who over-indulge can become slaves to sex which would ultimately ruin love and humane consideration in marriage. As in everything, one must be temperate and rational in one's sexual demands taking into consideration one another's intimate feelings and temperament.

Marriage is a bond of partnership for life entered into by a man and a woman. Patience, tolerance and understanding are the three principal qualities that should be developed and nurtured by the couple. Whilst love should be the knot tying the couple together, material necessities for sustaining a happy home should be made available by the male partner for the couple to share. The qualification for a good partnership in marriage should be ' ours ' and not ' yours ' or ' mine '. A good couple should 'open' their hearts to one another and to refrain from entertaining 'secrets'. Keeping secrets to oneself could lead to suspicion and suspicion is the element that could destroy love in a partnership. Suspicion breeds jealousy, jealousy creates anger, anger develops hatred, hatred turns into enmity and enmity could cause untold sufferings including bloodshed, suicide and even murder.

PART FIVE

A RELIGION FOR REAL
HUMAN PROGRESS

# 13

# NATURE, VALUE AND CHOICE OF RELIGIOUS BELIEFS

## Man and Religion

*Man is the only living being in this world who has discovered religion and performs worship and prayer.*

MAN developed religion in order to satisfy his desire to understand the life within him and the world outside him. The earliest religions had animistic origins, and they arose out of man's fear of the unknown and his desire to placate the forces which he thought inhabited inanimate objects. Over time these religions underwent changes, being shaped by the geographical, historical, socio-economic, political, and intellectual environment existing at that time.

Many of these religions have become organised and are flourishing to this day, backed by a strong following of devotees.

Many people are drawn to organised religions because of the pomp and ceremony, while there are some who prefer to practice their own personal religion, inwardly venerating their religious teachers and applying moral principles in their daily life. Because of the importance of practice, every religion claims to be a way of life, not merely a faith. In view of their various origins and paths of development which religions undergo, it is hardly surprising that the religions of man should differ in their approach, the understanding and interpretation of their followers, their goal and how it can be achieved, and their concept of reward and punishment for deeds performed.

In terms of approach, religious practices may be based on faith, fear, rationality or harmlessness: Faith forms the basis of many religious practices which were developed to overcome man's fear and to meet his needs. A religion of miraculous or mystical powers exploits that fear which arises from ignorance and makes promises of material gain based on greed. A religion of devotion is based on emotion and the fear of the supernatural which, it is so believed, can be appeased through rites and rituals. A religion of faith is based on the desire for gaining confidence in the face of the uncertainty of human life and destiny.

Some religious practices grew as a result of the development of man's knowledge, experience and wisdom. The rational approach to religion had been adopted in this case, incorporating the principles of human value and natural or universal laws. It is based on humanism and concentrates on the cultivation of humane qualities. A religion of cause and effect or *kamma* is based on the principle of self-help and assumes that the individual alone is responsible for his own happiness and suffering as well as salvation. A religion of wisdom is based on the application of reason and seeks to understand life and the reality of worldly conditions through analytical knowledge.

Harmlessness and goodwill are common elements found in religion. A religion of peace is based on the principle of causing no harm to oneself as well as others, and its followers are to cultivate a harmonious, liberal and peaceful life. A religion of goodwill or loving-kindness is based on the sacrifice and service for the welfare and happiness of others.

Religions differ according to the understanding capacity of their followers and the interpretations which religious authorities give to the religious doctrines and practices. In some religions, authorities have a strong say in enforcing religious laws and moral codes, while in others they only provide advice on the need and the way to follow these codes. Every religion will offer reasons to explain the existing human problems and inequalities and the way to remedy the situation. By way of explanation, some religions claim that man has to face these problems because he is on trial in this world. When such an explanation is given, another may ask, ' For what purpose? How can a man be judged on the basis of just one life when human beings generally differ in their experiences of physical, intellectual, social, economic and environmental factors and conditions? '

Every religion has its own concept of what is regarded to be the goal of spiritual life. For some religions, eternal life in heaven or paradise with the Lord is the final goal. For some the ultimate aim in life is the union of universal consciousness, because it is believed that life is a unit of consciousness and it must return to the same original consciousness. Some religions believe that the ending of suffering or repeated birth and death is the final goal. For others, even heavenly bliss or union with Brahma (creator) is secondary to the uncertainty of existence, no matter, whatever form it takes. And there are even some who believe that the present life itself is more than enough to experience the aim of life.

To attain the desired goal, every religion offers a method. Some religions ask their followers to surrender to God or depend on God for everything. Others call for stringent asceticism as the means of purging oneself of all evil through self mortification. Some others recommend the performance of animal sacrifices and many kinds of rites and rituals as well as the recital of mantras for their purification to gain the final goal. There is yet another which upholds diverse methods and devotions, intellectual realisation of truth, and concentration of the mind through meditation.

Each religion has a different concept of punishment for evil deeds. According to some religions, man is doomed forever by God for his transgressions in this one life. Some others say that action and reaction (cause and effect) operate due to natural laws and the effect of a deed will only be experienced for a certain period. Some religions maintain that this life is only one of so many, and a person will always have a chance to reform himself in stages until he finally evolves to attain the goal of Supreme Bliss.

Given such a wide variety of approaches, interpretations and goals of different religions adopted by mankind, it is useful for people not to hold dogmatic views about their religion but to be open to and tolerant of other religious views.

The Buddha said: ' One must not accept my teachings from reverence, but first try them as gold is tried by fire. '

After emphasising the importance of maintaining an open mind towards religious doctrines, it is useful to remember that a religion should be practised for the welfare, freedom and happiness of all living beings. That is, religious principles should be used positively to improve the quality of life of all beings. Yet today, humankind is corrupted and has gone astray from basic religious principles. Immoral and evil practices have become common among many people, and religious-minded people experience difficulties trying to maintain certain religious principles in modern life. At the same time, the standard of basic religious principles is also lowered to pander to the demands of polluted and selfish minds. Man should not violate universal moral codes to suit his own greed or indulgence; rather man should try to adjust himself according to these codes taught by religion.

Religious precepts have been introduced by enlightened religious teachers who have realised the noble way of life which leads to peace and happiness. Those who violate these precepts transgress the universal laws, which, according to Buddhism will bring bad effects through the working of moral causation.

This does not mean, on the other hand, that a person should slavishly follow what is found in his religion, regardless of its applicability to modern times. Religious laws and precepts should enable people to lead a meaningful life, and are not to be used to bind them to archaic practices and superstitious rituals and beliefs. A person who upholds the basic religious principles should give credit to human intelligence and live respectably with human dignity. There must be some changes in our religious activities to correspond to our education and the nature of our changing society, without at the same time sacrificing the noble universal principles. But it is recognised that making changes to any religious practices is always difficult because many conservative people are opposed to changes, even if they are for the better. Such conservative views are like a stagnant pool of water, while fresh ideas are like the waterfall where the water is constantly being renewed and is, therefore, usable.

**Distortion of Religion**

Despite the value of religion in moral upliftment, it is also true to say that religion is a fertile soil for the development of superstitions and devotional hypocrisy, wrapped under the cloak of religiosity. Many people use religion to escape from the realities of life and put on the garb of religion and religious symbols. They may even pray very often in places of worship, yet they are not sincerely religious minded and have not understood what religion stands for. When a religion has been debased by ignorance, greed for power and selfishness, people quickly point an accusing finger and say that religion is irrational. But ' Religion ' (the ritualistic external practice of any teaching) must be distinguished from the teaching itself. Before one criticizes, one must study the original teachings of the founder and see it there is anything intrinsically wrong with it.

Religion advises people to do good and be good, but they are not interested in acting thus. Instead they prefer to cling to the other practices which have no real religious values. Had they tried to culture their minds by eradicating jealousy, pride, cruelty and selfishness, at least they would have found the correct way to practise a religion. Unfortunately, they develop jealousy, pride, cruelty and selfishness instead of eradicating them. Many people pretend to be religious, but commit the greatest atrocities in the name of religion. They fight, discriminate and create unrest for the sake of religion, losing sight of its lofty purpose. From the increase in the performance of various so-called religious activities, we may get the impression that religion is progressing, but the opposite is really the case since very little mental purity and understanding are actually being practised.

Practising a religion is nothing more than the development of one's inner awareness, goodwill and understanding. Problems would have to be faced squarely by relying on one's spiritual strength. Running away from one's problems in the name of spiritualism is not courageous, much less to be regarded as spiritual. Under today's chaotic conditions, men and women are rapidly sliding downhill to their own destruction. The irony is that they imagine they are progressing towards a glorious civilisation that is yet to be realised.

In the midst of this confusion, imaginary and plastic religious concepts are propagated to create more temptation and confusion in man's mind. Religion is being misused for personal gain and power. Certain immoral practices, such as free sex, have been encouraged by some irresponsible religious groups to introduce their religion among youths. By arousing lustful feelings, these groups hope to seduce boys and girls into following their religion. Today religion has degenerated into a cheap commodity in the religious market giving scant regard to moral values and what they stand for. Some missionaries claim that the practice of morals, ethics and precepts are not important as long as a person has faith and prays to God, which is believed to be sufficient to grant him salvation. Having witnessed how some religious authorities have misled and blindfolded their followers in Europe, Karl Marx made a caustic remark: ' Religion is the sigh of the oppressed creature, the feelings of a heartless world, just as it is the soul of souless conditions. It is the opium of the people. '

Man needs a religion not for the reason of giving him a dream for his next life or providing him with some dogmatic ideas to follow, in such a way that he surrenders his human intelligence and becomes a nuisance to his fellow beings. A religion should be a reliable and reasonable method for people to live ' here and now ' as cultured, understanding beings, while setting a good example for others to follow. Many religions turn man's thoughts away from himself towards a supreme being, but Buddhism directs man's search for peace inwards to the potentialities that lie hidden within himself. ' *Dhamma* ' (meaning, to hold on) is not something a person searches outside himself, because in the final analysis, man is *Dhamma* and *Dhamma* is man. Therefore, true religion, which is *Dhamma,* is not something outside us that we acquire, but the cultivation and realisation of wisdom, compassion and purity that we develop within ourselves.

# Which is the Proper Religion?

*If any religion has the Four Noble Truths and the Eightfold Path, then it can be regarded as a proper religion.*

IT is a very difficult for a man to find out why there are so many different religions, and which religion is the true one. Followers of every religion are trying to show the superiority of their religion. Diversity has created some uniformity, but in matters of religion, men look upon each other with jealousy, hatred and disdain. The most respected religious practices in one religion are deemed ridiculous to others. To introduce their divine and peaceful messages some people have resorted to weapons and wars. Have they not polluted the good name of religion? It seems that certain religions are responsible for dividing instead of uniting mankind.

To find a true and proper religion, we must weigh with an unbiased mind what exactly is a false religion. False religions or philosophies include: materialism which denies surval after death; amoralism which denies good and evil; any religion which asserts that man is miraculousy saved or doomed; theistic evolution which holds that everything is preordained and everyone is destined to attain eventual salvation through mere faith.

Buddhism is free from unsatisfactory and uncertain foundations. Buddhism is realistic and verifiable. Its Truths have been verified by the Buddha, verified by His disciples, and always remain open to be verified by anyone who wishes to do so. And today, the Teachings of the Buddha, are being verified by the most severe methods of scientific investigation.

The Buddha advises that any form of religion is proper if it contains the Four Noble Truths and the Noble Eightfold Path. This clearly shows that the Buddha did not want to form a particular religion. What He wanted was to reveal the Ultimate Truth of our life and the world. Although the Buddha expounded the Four Noble Truths and the Eightfold Noble Path, this method is not the property of Buddhists alone. This is a universal Truth.

Most people find it necessary to put forth arguments to 'prove' the validity of the religion that they are following. Some claim that their religion is the oldest and therefore contains the truth. Others claim that their religion is the latest or newest and therefore contains the truth. Some claim that their religion has the most followers and therefore contains the truth. Yet none of these arguments are valid to establish the truth of a religion. One can judge the value of a religion by using only common sense and understanding.

Some religious traditions require man to be subservient to a greater power than himself, a power which controls his creation, his actions and his final deliverance. The Buddha did not accept such powers. Rather, He assigned to man that very power by asserting that each man is his own creator, responsible for his own salvation. That is why it is said that ' There is none so godless as the Buddha and yet none so godlike '. The religion of the Buddhists gives man a great sense of dignity; at the same time it also gives him great responsibility. A Buddhist cannot put the blame on an external power when evil befalls him. But he can face misfortune with equanimity because he knows that he has the power to extricate himself from all misery.

One of the reasons why Buddhism appeals to intellectuals and those with a good education, is that the Buddha expressly discouraged His followers from accepting anything they heard (even if it came from Himself) without first testing its validity. The teachings of the Buddha have remained and survived precisely because many intellectuals have challenged every aspect of the teachings and have concluded that the Buddha had always spoken the undeniable Truth. While other religionists are trying to ' reasses ' their founders' teachings in the light of modern knowledge about the Universe, the Buddha's teachings are being verified by scientists.

# Moral and Spiritual Development

*Without a spiritual background man has no moral responsibility: man without moral responsibility poses a danger to society.*

BUDDHISM has been an admirable lighthouse for guiding many a devotee to the salvation of eternal bliss. Buddhism is especially needed in the world today which is riddled with racial, economic and ideological misunderstandings. These misunderstandings can never be effectively cleared until the spirit of benevolent tolerance is extended towards others. This spirit can be best cultivated under the guidance of Buddhism which inculcates an ethical-moral co-operation for universal good.

We know that it is easy to learn vice without a master, whereas virtue requires a tutor. There is a very great need for the teaching of virtue by precepts and examples.

Without a spiritual background, man has no moral responsibility: man without moral responsibility poses danger to society.

In the Buddha's Teaching, it is said that the spiritual development of man is more important than the development of material welfare. History has taught us that we cannot expect to gain both worldly happiness and everlasting Happiness at the same time. The lives of most people are generally regulated by spiritual values and moral principles which only religion can effectively provide. The governmental interference in the lives of people is made comparatively unnecessary if men and women can be made to realise the value of devotion and can practise the ideals of truth, justice and service.

Virtue is necessary to attain salvation, but virtue alone is not enough. Virtue must be combined with wisdom. Virtue and wisdom are like the pair of wings of a bird. Wisdom can also be compared to the eyes of a man; virtue, to his feet. Virtue can be likened to a vehicle that brings man up to the gate of salvation. But wisdom is the actual key that opens the gate. Virtue is a part of the technique of skilful and noble living. Without any ethical discipline, there cannot be a purification of the defilements of sentient existence.

Buddhism is not mere mumbo-jumbo, a myth told to entertain the human mind or to satisfy the human emotion, but a liberal and noble method for those who sincerely want to understand and experience the reality of life.

# The God-Idea

*The reality or validity of belief in God is based on man's understanding capacity and the maturity of the mind.*

## The Development of the God-idea

To trace the origin and development of the God-idea, one must go back to the time when civilisation was still in its infancy and modern science was still unknown. Primitive people, out of fear of and admiration towards natural phenomena, had believed in different spirits and gods. They used their belief in spirits and gods to form religions of their own. According to their respective circumstances and understanding capacity different people worshipped different gods and founded different faiths.

At the beginning of the God-idea, people worshipped many gods — gods of trees, streams, lightning, storm, winds, the sun and all other terrestrial phenomena. These gods were related to each and every act of nature. Then gradually man began to attribute to these gods, sex and form as well as the physical and mental characteristics of human beings. Human attributes were given to the gods: love, hate, jealousy, fear, pride, envy and other emotions found among human beings. From all these gods, there slowly grew a realisation that the phenomena of the universe were not many but were One. This understanding gave rise to the monotheistic god of recent ages.

In the process of development, the God-idea went through a variety of changing social and intellectual climates. It was regarded by different men in different ways. Some idealised god as the King of Heaven and Earth; they had a conception of god as a person. Others thought of god as an abstract principle. Some raised the ideal of Supreme deity to the highest heaven, while others brought it down to the lowest depths of the earth. Some pictured god in a paradise, while others made an idol and worshipped it. Some went so far as to say that there is no salvation without god — no matter how much good you do, you will not receive the fruits of your actions unless you act out of a faith in god. The Atheists said, 'No' and went on to affirm that god did not really exist at all. The Sceptics or Agnostics said, ' We do not or we cannot know. ' The Positivists say that the God-idea was a meaningless problem since the idea of the term god 'was not clear'. Thus there grew a variety of ideas and beliefs and names for the God-idea: pantheism, idolatory, belief in a formless god, and belief in many gods and goddesses.

Even the monotheistic god of recent times has gone through a variety of changes as it passed through different nations and people. The Hindu god is quite different from the Christian god. The Christian god is again different from gods of other faiths. Thus numerous religions came into existence; each one differed greatly from the other in the end, and each one says that 'God is One'.

**The God-idea and Creation**

As each religion came into existence and developed around the God-idea, religion developed its own particular explanation of creation. Thus the God-idea became associated with various myths. People used the God-idea as a vehicle for their explanations of the existence of man and the nature of the universe.

Today, intelligent men, who have carefully reviewed all the available facts, have come to the conclusion that, like the God-idea, the creation of myths must be regarded as an evolution of the human imagination which began with the misunderstanding of the phenomena of nature. These misunderstandings were rooted in the fear and ignorance of primitive man. Even today, man still retains his primitive interpretations of creation. In the light of recent, scientific thinking, the theological definition of god is vague and hence has no place in the contemporary creation theories or myths.

If man is created by an external source, then he must belong to that source and not to himself. According to Buddhism, man is responsible for everything he does. Thus Buddhists have no reason to believe that man came into existence in the human from through any external sources. They believe that man is here today because of his own action. He is neither punished nor rewarded by anyone but himself according to his own good and bad action. In the process of evolution, the human being came into existence. However, there are no Buddha-words to support the belief that the world was created by anybody. The scientific discovery of gradual development of the world-system conforms with the Buddha's Teachings.

## Human Weakness and the Concept of God

Both the concept of God and its associated creation myths have been protected and defended by believers who need these ideas to justify their existence and usefulness to human society. All the believers claim to have received their respective scriptures as Revelation; in other words, they all profess to come directly from the one God. Each God-religion claims that it stands for Universal Peace and Universal Brotherhood and other such high ideals.

However great the ideals of the religions might be, the history of the world shows that the religions up to the present day have also helped in spreading superstitions. Some have stood against science and the advancement of knowledge, leading to ill-feelings, murders and wars. In this respect, the God-religions have failed in their attempt to enlighten mankind. For example, in certain countries when people pray for mercy, their hands are stained with the blood of the morbid sacrifices of innocent animals and sometimes, even fellow human beings. These poor and helpless creatures were slaughtered at the desecrated altars of imaginary and imperceptible gods. It has taken a long time for people to understand the futility of such cruel practices in the name of religion. The time has come for them to realise that the path of real purification is through love and understanding.

Dr. G. Dharmasiri in his book ' Buddhist critique of the Christian Concept of God ' has mentioned, ' I see that though the notion of God contains sublime moral strands, it also has certain implications that are extremely dangerous to the humans as well as to the other beings on this planet.

'One major threat to humanity is the blindfold called ' authority' imposed on the humans by the concept of God. All theistic religions consider authority as ultimate and sacred. It was this danger that the Buddha was pointing at in the *Kalama Sutta*. At the moment, human individuality and freedom are seriously threatened by various forms of authorities. Various 'authorities' have been trying to make 'you' a follower. On top of all our 'traditional' authorities, a new form of authority has emerged in the name of 'science'. And lately, the mushrooming new religions and the menace of the Gurus (as typified by Jim Jones), have become live threats to the individual's human freedom and dignity. The Buddha's eternal plea is for you to become a Buddha, and He showed, in a clearly rational way, that each and every one of us has the perfect potentiality and capacity to attain that ideal. '

God-religions offer no salvation without God. Thus a man might conceivably have climbed to the highest pinnacle of virtue, and he might have led a righteous way of life, and he might even have climbed to the highest level of holiness, yet he is to be condemned to eternal hell just because he did not believe in the existence of God. On the other hand, a man might have sinned deeply and yet, having made a late repentance, he can be forgiven and therefore 'saved'. From the Buddhist point of view, there is no justification in this kind of doctrine.

Despite the apparent contradictions of the God-religions, it is not deemed advisable to preach a Godless doctrine since the belief in god has also done a tremendous service to mankind, especially in places where the god concept is desirable. This belief in god has helped mankind to control his animal nature. And much help has been granted to others in the name of god. At the same time, man feels insecure without the belief in god. He finds protection and inspiration when that belief is in his mind. The reality or validity of such a belief is based on man's understanding capacity and spiritual maturity.

However, religion should also concern our practical life. It is to be used as a guide to regulate our conduct in the world. Religion tells us what to do and what not to do. If we do not follow a religion sincerely, mere religious labels or belief in god do not serve us in our daily life.

On the other hand, if the followers of various religions are going to quarrel and to condemn other beliefs and practices — especially to prove or disprove the existence of God — and if they are going to harbour anger towards other religions because of their different religious views, then they are creating enormous disharmony amongst the various religious communities. Whatever religious differences we have, it is our duty to practise tolerance, patience and understanding. It is our duty to respect the other man's religious belief even if we cannot accomodate it; tolerance is necessary for the sake of harmonious and peaceful living.

However, it does not serve any purpose to introduce this concept of god to those who are not ready to appreciate it. To some people this belief is not important to lead a righteous life. There are many who lead a noble life without such belief while amongst believers there are many who violate the peace and happiness of innocent people.

Buddhists can also co-operate with those who hold this concept of god, if they use this concept for the peace, happiness and welfare of mankind but not with those who abuse this concept by threatening people in order to introduce this belief just for their own benefit and with ulterior motives.

For more than 2,500 years, all over the world, Buddhists have practised and introduced Buddhism very peacefully without the necessity of sustaining the concept of a creator God. And they will continue to sustain this religion in the same manner without disturbing the followers of other religions.

Therefore, with due respect to other religionists, it must be mentioned that any attempt to introduce this concept into Buddhism is unnecessary. Let Buddhists maintain their belief since it is harmless to others and, let the basic Teachings of the Buddha remain.

From time immemorial, Buddhists have led a peaceful religious life without incorporating the particular concept of God. They should be capable of sustaining their particular religion without the necessity, at this juncture, of someone trying to force something down their throats against their will. Having full confidence in their Buddha Dhamma, Buddhists should be permitted to work and seek their own salvation without any undue interference from other sources. Others can uphold their beliefs and concepts, Buddhists will uphold theirs, without any rancour. We do not challenge others in regard to their religious persuasions, we expect reciprocal treatment in regard to our own beliefs and practices.

# Changing of Religious Label Before Death

*Merely to believe that there is someone to wash away our sins without suppressing our evil state of mind, is not in accordance with the Teachings of the Buddha.*

VERY often we come across cases of people who change their religion at the last moment when they are about to die. By embracing another religion, some people are under the mistaken belief that they can 'wash away their sins' and gain an easy passage to heaven. They also hope to ensure themselves a simple and better burial. For people who have been living a whole life-time with a particular religion, to suddenly embrace a religion which is totally new and unfamiliar and to expect an immediate salvation through their new faith is indeed very far-fetched. This is only a dream. Some people are even known to have been converted into another faith when they are in a state of unconsciousness and in some cases, even posthumously. Those who are over zealous and crazy about converting others into their faith, have misled uneducated people into believing that theirs is the one and only faith with an easy method or short-cut to heaven. If people are led to believe that there is someone sitting somewhere up there who can wash away all the sins committed during a life-time, then this belief will only encourage others to commit evil.

According to the Teachings of the Buddha there is no such belief that there is someone who can wash away sins. It is only when people sincerely realise that what they are doing are wrong and after having realised this, try to mend their ways and do good that they can suppress or counter the bad reactions that would accrue to them for the evil they had committed.

It has become a common sight in many hospitals to see purveyors of some religions hovering around the patients promising them ' life after death '. This is exploiting the basic ignorance and phsychological fear of the patients. If they really want to help, then they must be able to work the ' miracles ' they so proudly claim lies in their holy books. If they can work miracles, we will not need hospitals. Buddhists must never become victims to these people. They must learn the basic teachings of their noble religion which tells them that all suffering is the basic lot of mankind. The only way to end suffering is by purifying the mind. The individual creates his own suffering and it is he alone who can end it. One cannot hope to eradicate the consequences of one's evil actions simply by changing one's religious label at the door-step of death.

A dying man's destiny in his next life depends on the last thoughts which appear to him according to the good and bad *kamma* he had accumulated during his current lifetime, irrespective of what type of religious label he prefers to don himself at the last moment.

# Short-cut to Paradise

*Paradise is open not only to the followers of a particular religion, but it is open to each and every person who leads a righteous and noble way of life.*

THERE is no difficulty at all for Buddhists to go to heaven if they really want to. But there are some people who go from house to house trying to convert other religionists into their faith and promising them the heaven they carry in their bags. They claim that they are the only blessed people who can go to heaven; they also claim that they have the exclusive authority to send others to the same goal. They introduce their religion like a patent medicine and this has become a nuisance to the public today. Many innocent people who lack the knowledge of their own religion, have become victims of these paradise sellers.

If Buddhists can understand the value of the Noble Teachings of the Buddha, they will not be misled by such people. These paradise sellers are also trying to mislead the people by saying that this world which is created by god, is going to end very soon. Those who want to have a wonderful everlasting life in heaven must accept their particular religion before the end of the world comes, otherwise people would miss this golden opportunity and would have to suffer in eternal hell.

This threat of the end of the world, had been going on for hundreds of years. The wonder of it all is that there are still people today who believe in such a treat which is irrational and imaginary. Some people get converted after hearing such preaching, without using their common sense.

In Buddhism, there is no personal judge either to condemn or to reward but only the working of an impersonal moral causation and natural law.

### Why wicked people enjoy while good people suffer

Some people ask, ' If good begets good and bad begets bad why should many good people suffer and some wicked people prosper in this world? ' The answer to this question, according to the Buddhist point of view, is that although some are good by nature, they have not accumulated enough good merits in their previous birth to compensate for the bad effects of unwholesome kamma in this present life; somewhere in their past there must have been some defect. On the other hand, some are wicked by nature and yet are able to enjoy this life for a short period due to some strong good kamma that they accumulated in their previous birth.

For example, there are certain people who by nature have inherited a strong constitution and as a result enjoy perfect health. Their physical power of resistence is strong and hence they are not prone to illnesses. Although they do not take special precautions to lead a hygienic life, they are able to remain strong and healthy. On the other hand, there are others who take various tonics and vitamin — enriched foods to fortify themselves, but in spite of their efforts to become strong and healthy, their health do not show any improvement.

Whatever good and bad deeds people commit within this life-time, they will definitely experience the reaction within this life or hereafter. It is impossible to escape from their results simply by praying, but by cultivating the mind and leading a noble life.

Buddhists are encouraged to do good deeds not for the sake of gaining a place in heaven. They are expected to do good in order to eradicate their selfishness and to experience peace and happiness.

# 14
## PROMOTER OF
## TRUE HUMAN CULTURE

### Modern Religion

*Buddhism is strong enough to face any modern views which pose a challenge to religion.*

BUDDHIST ideas have greatly contributed to the enrichment of both ancient and modern thought. Its teaching of causation and relativism, its doctrine of sense data, its pragmatism, its emphasis on the moral, its non-acceptance of a permanent soul, its unconcern about external supernatural forces, its denial of unnecessary rites and religious rituals, its appeal to reasoning and experience and its compatibility with modern scientific discoveries all tend to establish its superior claim to modernity.

Buddhism is able to meet all the requirements of a rational religion that suit the needs of the future world. It is so scientific, so rational, so progressive that it will be a pride for a man in the modern world to call himself a Buddhist. In fact, Buddhism is more scientific in approach than science; it is more socialistic than socialism.

Among all the great founders of religions, it was the Buddha alone who encouraged the spirit of investigation among His followers and who advised them not to accept even His Teaching with blind faith. Therefore, it is no exaggeration to say that Buddhism can be called a modern religion.

Buddhism is a well-elaborated scheme of how to lead a practical life and a carefully thought-out system of self-culture. But more than that, it is a scientific method of education. This religion is best able in any crisis to restore our peace of mind and to help us to face calmly whatever changes the future may have in store.

Without sensual pleasure, would life be endurable? Without belief in immortality, can man be moral? Without resorting to divinity, can man advance towards righteousness? YES, is the answer given by Buddhism. These ends can be attained by knowledge and by the purification of the mind. Knowledge is the key to the higher path. Purification is that which brings calmness and peace to life and renders man indifferent to and detached from the vagaries of the phenomenal world.

Buddhism is truly a religion suited to the modern, scientific world. The light which comes from nature, from science, from history, from human experience, from every point of the universe, is radiant with the Noble Teachings of the Buddha.

# Religion in a Scientific Age

*Religion without science is crippled, while science without religion is blind.*

TODAY we live in a scientific age in which almost every aspect of our lives has been affected by science. Since the scientific revolution during the seventeenth century, science has continued to exert tremendous influence on what we think and do.

The *impact of science* has been particularly strong on traditional religious beliefs. Many basic religious concepts are crumbling under the pressure of modern science and are no longer acceptable to the intellectual and the well-informed man. No longer is it possible to assert truth derived merely through theological speculations or based on the authority of religious scriptures in isolation to scientific consideration. For example, the findings of modern psychologists indicate that the human mind, like the physical body, work according to natural, causal laws without the presence of an unchanging soul as taught by some religions.

Some religionists choose to disregard scientific discoveries which conflict with their religious dogmas. Such rigid mental habits are indeed a hindrance to human progress. Since the modern man refuses to believe anything blindly, even though it had been traditionally accepted, such religionists will only succeed in increasing the ranks of non-believers with their faulty theories.

On the other hand, some religionists have found it necessary to accommodate popularly accepted scientific theories by giving new interpretations to their religious dogmas. A case in point is Darwin's Theory of Evolution. Many religionists maintain that man was directly created by God. Darwin, on the other hand, claimed that man had evolved from the ape, a theory which upset the doctrines of divine creation and the fall of man. Since all enlightened thinkers have accepted Darwin's theory, the theologians today have little choice except to give a new interpretation to their doctrines to suit this theory which they had opposed for so long.

In the light of modern scientific discoveries, it is not difficult to understand that many of the views held in many religions regarding the universe and life are merely conventional thoughts of that which have long been superceded. It is generally true to say that religions have greatly contributed to human development and progress. They have laid down values and standards and formulated principles to guide human life. But for all the good they have done, religions can no longer survive in the modern, scientific age if the followers insist on imprisoning truth into set forms and dogmas, on encouraging ceremonies and practices which have been depleted of their original meaning.

**Buddhism and Science**

Until the beginning of the last century, Buddhism was confined to countries untouched by modern science. Nevertheless, from its very beginning, the Teachings of the Buddha were always open to scientific thinking.

One reason why the Teaching can easily be embraced by the scientific spirit is that the Buddha never encouraged rigid, dogmatic belief. He did not claim to base His Teachings on faith, belief, or divine revelation, but allowed great flexibility and freedom of thought.

The second reason is that the scientific spirit can be found in the Buddha's approach to spiritual Truth. The Buddha's method for discovering and testing spiritual Truth is very similar to that of the scientist. A scientist observes the external world objectively, and would only establish a scientific theory after conducting many successful practical experiments.

Using a similar approach 25 centuries ago, the Buddha observed the inner world with detachment, and encouraged His disciples not to accept any teaching until they had critically investigated and personally verified its truth. Just as the scientist today would not claim that his experiment cannot be duplicated by others, the Buddha did not claim that His experience of Enlightenment was exclusive to Him. Thus, in His approach to Truth, the Buddha was as analytical as the present day scientist. He established a practical, scientifically worked-out method for reaching the Ultimate Truth and the experience of Enlightenment.

While Buddhism is very much in ,ine with the scientific spirit, it is *not correct to equate* Buddhism with science. It is true that the practical applications of science have enabled mankind to live more comfortable lives and experience wonderful things undreamed of before. Science has made it possible for man to swim better than the fishes, fly higher than the birds, and walk on the moon. Yet the sphere of knowledge acceptable to conventional, scientific wisdom is confined to empirical evidence. And scientific truth is subject to constant change. Science cannot give man control over his mind and neither does it offer moral control and guidance. Despite its wonders, science has indeed many limitations not shared by Buddhism.

## Limitations of Science

Often one hears so much about science and what it can do, and so little about what it cannot do. Scientific knowledge is *limited* to the data received through the sense organs. It does not recognise reality which transcends sense-data. Scientific truth is built upon logical observations of sense-data which are continually changing. Scientific truth is, therefore, relative truth not intended to stand the test of time. And a scientist, being aware of this fact, is always willing to discard a theory if it can be replaced by a better one.

Science attempts to understand the outer world and has barely scratched the surface of man's inner world. Even the science of psychology has not really fathomed the underlying cause of man's mental unrest. When a man is frustrated and disgusted with life, and his inner world is filled with disturbances and unrest, science today is very much unequipped to help him. The social sciences which cater for man's environment may bring him a certain degree of happiness. But unlike an animal man requires more than mere physical comfort and needs help to cope with his frustrations and miseries arising from his daily experiences.

Today so many people are plagued with fear, restlessness, and insecurity. Yet science fails to succour them. Science is unable to teach the common man to control his mind when he is driven by the animal nature that burns within him.

Can science make man better? If it can, why do violent acts and immoral practices abound in countries which are so advanced in science? Isn't it fair to say that despite all the scientific progress achieved and the advantages conferred on man, science leaves the inner man basically unchanged: it has only heightened man's feelings of dependence and insufficiency? In addition to its failure to bring security to mankind, science has also made everyone feel even more insecure by threatening the world with the possibility of wholesale destruction.

Science is *unable* to provide a meaningful purpose of life. It cannot provide man clear reasons for living. In fact, science is thoroughly secular in nature and unconcerned with man's spiritual goal. The materialism inherent in scientific thought denies the psyche goals higher than material satisfaction. By its selective theorizing and relative truths, science disregards some of the most essential issues and leaves many questions unanswered. For instance, when asked why great inequalities exist among men, no scientific explanation can be given to such questions which are beyond its narrow confines.

**Learned Ignorance**

The transcendental mind developed by the Buddha is not limited to sense-data and goes beyond the logic trapped within the limitation of relative perception. The human intellect, on the contrary, operates on the basis of information it collects and stores, whether in the field of religion, philosophy, science or art. The information for the mind is gathered through our sense organs which are inferior in so many ways. The very limited information perceived makes our understanding of the world distorted.

Some people are proud of the fact that they know so much. In fact, the less we know, the more certain we are in our explanations; the more we know, the more we realize our limitations.

A brilliant scholar once wrote a book which he considered as the ultimate work. He felt that the book contained all the literary gems and philosophies. Being proud of his achievement, he showed his masterpiece to a colleague of his who was equally brilliant with the request that the book be reviewed by him. Instead, his colleague asked the author to write down on a piece of paper all he knew and all he did not know. The author sat down deep in thought, but after a long while failed to write down anything he knew. Then he turned his mind to the second question, and again he failed to write down anything he did not know. Finally, with his ego at the lowest ebb, he gave up, realizing that all that he knew was really ignorance.

In this regard, Socrates, the well-known Athenian philosopher of the Ancient World, had this to say when asked what he knew: ' *I know only one thing — that I do not know* '.

**Beyond Science**

Buddhism goes beyond modern science in its acceptance of a wider field of knowledge than is allowed by the scientific mind. Buddhism admits knowledge arising from the sense organs as well as personal experiences gained through mental culture. By training and developing a highly concentrated mind, religious experience can be understood and verified. Religious experience is not something which can be understood by conducting experiments in a test-tube or examined under a microscope.

The truth discovered by science is relative and subject to changes, while that found by the Buddha is final and absolute: the Truth of Dhamma does not change according to time and space. Furthermore, in contrast to the selective theorizing of science, the Buddha encouraged the wise not to cling to theories, scientific or otherwise. Instead of theorizing, the Buddha taught mankind how to live a righteous life so as to discover Ultimate

Truths. By living a righteous life, by calming the senses, and by casting off desires, the Buddha pointed the way through which we can discover within ourselves the nature of life. And the real purpose of life can be found.

*Practice* is important in Buddhism. A person who studies much but does not practise is like one who is able to recite recipes from a huge cookery-book without trying to prepare a single dish. His hunger cannot be relieved by book knowledge alone. Practice is such an important prerequisite of enlightenment that in some schools of Buddhism, such as Zen, practice is put even ahead of knowledge.

The scientific method is outwardly directed, and modern scientists exploit nature and the elements for their own comfort, often disregarding the need to harmonise with the environment and thereby polluting the world. In contrast, Buddhism is inwardly directed and is concerned with the inner development of man. On the lower level, Buddhism teaches the individual how to adjust and cope with events and circumstances of daily life. At the higher level, it represents the human endeavour to grow beyond oneself through the practice of mental culture or mind development.

Buddhism has a complete system of mental culture concerned with gaining insight into the nature of things which leads to complete self-realization of the Ultimate Truth — *Nibbana*. This system is both practical and scientific, it involves dispassionate observation of emotional and mental states. More like a scientist than a judge, a meditator observes the inner world with mindfulness.

**Science Without Religion**

Without having moral ideals, science poses a *danger to all mankind*. Science has made the machine which in turn becomes king. The bullet and bomb are gifts of science to the few in power on whom the destiny of the world depends. Meanwhile the rest of mankind waits in anguish and fear, not knowing when the nuclear weapons, the poisonous gases, the deadly arms — all fruits of scientific research designed to kill efficiently — will be used on them. Not only is science completely unable to provide moral guidance to mankind, it has also fed fuel to the flame of human craving.

Science devoid of morality spells only destruction: it becomes the draconian monster man discovered. And unfortunately, this very monster is becoming more powerful than man himself. Unless man learns to restrain and govern the monster through the practice of religious morality, the monster will soon overpower him. Without religious guidance, science threatens the world with destruction. In contrast, science when coupled with a religion like Buddhism can transform this world into a haven of peace and security and happiness.

Never was there a time when the *co-operation* between science and religion is so desperately needed in the best interest and service of mankind. Religion without science is crippled, while science without religion is blind.

**Tribute to Buddhism**

The wisdom of Buddhism founded on compassion has the vital role of correcting the dangerous destination modern science is heading for. Buddhism can provide the spiritual leadership to guide scientific research and invention in promoting a brilliant culture of the future. Buddhism can provide worthy goals for scientific advancement which is presently facing a hopeless impasse of being enslaved by its very inventions.

Albert Einstein paid a tribute to Buddhism when he said in his autobiography: ' If there is any religion that would cope with modern scientific needs, it would be Buddhism '. Buddhism requires no revision to keep it 'up to date' with recent scientific findings. Buddhism need not surrender its views to science because it embraces science as well as goes beyond science. Buddhism is the bridge between religious and scientific thoughts by stimulating man to discover the latent potentialities within himself and his environment. *Buddhism is timeless!*

# Religion of Freedom

*This is a religion of freedom and reason for man to lead a noble life.*

BUDDHISM does not prevent anyone from learning the teachings of other religions. In fact, the Buddha encouraged His followers to learn about other religions and to compare His Teachings with other teachings. The Buddha says that if there are reasonable and rational teachings in other religions, His followers are free to respect such teachings. It seems that certain religionists try to keep their followers in the dark, some of them are not even allowed to touch other religious objects or books. They are instructed not to listen to the preachings of other religions. They are enjoined not to doubt the teachings of their own religion, however unconvincing their teachings may appear to be. The more they keep their followers on a one-track mind, the more easily they can keep them under control. If anyone of them exercises freedom of thought and realises that he had been in the dark all the time, then it is alleged that the devil has possessed his mind. The poor man is given no opportunity to use his common sense, education, or his intelligence. Those who wish to change their views on religion are taught to believe that they are not perfect enough to be allowed to use free will in judging anything for themselves.

According to the Buddha, religion should be left to one's own free choice. Religion is not a law, but a disciplinary code which should be followed with understanding. To Buddhists true religious principles are neither a divine law nor a human law, but a natural law.

In actual fact, there is no real religious freedom in any part of the world today. Man has not the freedom even to think freely. Whenever he realises that he cannot find satisfaction through his own religion to which he belongs, which cannot provide him with satisfactory answers to certain questions, he has no liberty to give it up and to accept another which appeals to him. The reason is that religious authorities, leaders, and family members have taken that freedom away from him. Man should be allowed to choose his religion which is in accordance with his own conviction. One has no right to force another to accept a particular religion. Some people surrender their religion for the sake of love, without a proper understanding of their partner's religion. Religion should not be changed to suit man's emotions and human weaknesses. One must think very carefully before changing one's religion. Religion is not a subject for bargaining; one should not change one's religion for personal, material gains. Religion is to be used for spiritual development and for self-salvation.

Buddhists never try to influence other religionists to come and embrace their religion for material gain. Nor do they try to exploit poverty, sickness, illiteracy and ignorance in order to increase the number of Buddhist population. The Buddha advised those who indicated their wish to follow Him, not to be hasty in accepting His Teachings. He advised them to consider carefully His Teaching and to determine for themselves whether it was practical or not for them to follow.

Buddhism teaches that mere belief or outward rituals are insufficient for attaining wisdom and perfection. In this sense, outward conversion becomes meaningless. To promote Buddhism by force would mean pretending to propagate justice and love by means of oppression and injustice. It is of no importance to a follower of the Buddha whether a person calls himself a Buddhist or not. Buddhists know that only through man's own understanding and exertion will they come nearer to the goal preached by the Buddha.

Amongst the followers of every religion are some fanatics. Religious fanaticism is dangerous. A fanatic is incapable of guiding himself by reason or even by the scientific principles of observation and analysis. According to the Buddha, a Buddhist must be a free man with an open mind and must not be subservient to anyone for his spiritual development. He seeks refuge in the Buddha by accepting Him as a source of supreme guidance and inspiration. He seeks refuge in the Buddha, not blindly, but with understanding. To Buddhists, the Buddha is not a saviour nor is He an anthropomorphic being who claims to possess the power of washing away others' sins. Buddhists regard the Buddha as a Teacher who shows the Path to salvation.

Buddhism has always supported the freedom and progress of mankind. Buddhism has always stood for the advancement of knowledge and freedom for humanity in every sphere of life. There is nothing in the Buddha's Teaching that has to be withdrawn in the face of modern, scientific inventions and knowledge. The more new things that scientists discover, the closer they come to the Buddha.

The Buddha emancipated man from the thraldom of religion. He also released man from the monopoly and the tyranny of the priestcraft. It was the Buddha who first advised man to exercise his reason and not to allow himself to be driven meekly like dumb cattle, following the dogma of religion. The Buddha stood for rationalism, democracy and practical, ethical conduct in religion. He introduced this religion for people to practise with human dignity.

The followers of the Buddha were advised not to believe anything without considering it properly. In the *Kalama Sutta,* the Buddha gave the following guidelines to a group of young people:-

 ' Do not accept anything based upon mere reports,
  traditions or hearsay,
  Nor upon the authority of religious texts,
  Nor upon mere reasons and arguments,

Nor upon one's own inference,
Nor upon anything which appears to be true,
Nor upon one's own speculative opinions,
Nor upon another's seeming ability,
Nor upon the consideration: ' This is our Teacher. '

'But, when you know for yourselves that certain things are unwholesome and bad: tending to harm yourself or others, reject them.

'And when you know for yourselves that certain things are wholesome and good: conducive to the spiritual welfare of yourself as well as others, accept and follow them. '

Buddhists are advised to accept religious practices only after careful observation and analysis, and only after being certain that the method agrees with reason and is conducive to the good of one and all.

A true Buddhist does not depend on external powers for his salvation. Nor does he expect to get rid of miseries through the intervention of some unknown power. He must try to eradicate all his mental impurities to find eternal Happiness. The Buddha says, ' If anyone were to speak ill of me, my teaching and my disciples, do not be upset or perturbed, for this kind of reaction will only cause you harm. On the other hand, if anyone were to speak well of me, my teaching and my disciples, do not be over-joyed, thrilled or elated, for this kind of reaction will only be an obstacle in forming a correct judgement. If you are elated, you cannot judge whether the qualities praised are real and actually found in us. ' *(Brahma Jala Sutta)* Such is the unbiased attitude of a genuine Buddhist.

The Buddha had upheld the highest degree of freedom not only in its human essence but also in its divine qualities. It is a freedom that does not deprive man of his dignity. It is a freedom that releases one from slavery to dogmas and dictatorial religious laws or religious punishments.

# Buddhist Missionaries

*' Go forth, O Bhikkhus, for the good of the many, for the happiness of the many, out of compassion for the world, for the good, benefit, and happiness of gods and men.'* (The Buddha)

WHEN we turn the pages of the history of Buddhism, we learn that Buddhist missionaries gave the noble message of the Buddha in a peaceful and respectable way. Such a peaceful mission should put to shame those who have practised violent methods in propagating their religions.

Buddhist missionaries do not compete with other religionists in converting people in the market place. No Buddhist missionary or monk would ever think of preaching ill-will against the so-called ' unbelievers '. Religious, cultural and national intolerance are unbuddhistic in attitude, to people who are imbued with the real Buddhist spirit. Aggression never finds approval in the teaching of the Buddha. The world has bled and suffered enough from the disease of dogmatism, religious fanaticism and intolerance. Whether in religion or politics, people make conscious efforts to bring humanity to accept their own way of life. In doing so, they sometimes show their hostility towards the followers of other religions.

Buddhism had no quarrel with the national traditions and customs, art and culture of the people who accepted it as a way of life but allowed them to exist with refinement. The Buddha's message of love and compassion opened the hearts of men and they willingly accepted the Teachings, thereby helping Buddhism to become a world religion. Buddhist missionaries were invited by the independent countries which welcomed them with due respect. Buddhism was never introduced to any country through the influence of colonial or any other political power.

Buddhism was the first spiritual force known to us in history which drew closely together large numbers of races which were separated by the most difficult barriers of distance, language, culture and morals. Its motive was not the acquisition of international commerce, empire-building or migratory impulse to occupy fresh territory. Its aim was to show how people could gain more peace and happiness through the practice of Dhamma.

A sparkling example of the qualities and approach of a Buddhist missionary was Emperor Asoka. It was during Emperor Asoka's time that Buddhism spread to many Asian and western countries. Emperor Asoka sent Buddhist missionaries to many parts of the world to introduce the Buddha's message of peace. Asoka respected and supported every religion at that time. His tolerance towards other religions was remarkable. One of his scripts engraved in stone on Asoka Pillars, and still standing today in India, says:

' One should not honour only one's own religion and condemn the religion of others, but one should honour others' religions for this or that reason. In so doing, one helps one's own religion to grow and renders service to the religions of others too. In acting otherwise one digs the grave of one's own religion and also does harm to other religions. Whosoever honours his own religion and condemns other religions, does so indeed through devotion to his own religion, thinking, 'I will glorify my own religion.' But on the contrary, in so doing he injures his own religion more gravely, so concord is good. Let all listen, and be willing to listen to the doctrines professed by others. '

In 268 B.C., he made the doctrines of the Buddha a living force in India. Hospitals, social service institutions, universities for men and women, public wells and recreation centres sprang up with this new movement, and the people thereby realised the cruelty of senseless wars.

The golden era in the history of India and the other countries of Asia the period when art, culture, education and civilisation reached their zenith — occurred at the time when Buddhist influence was strongest in these countries. Holy wars, crusades, inquisitions and religious discrimination do not mar the annals of Buddhist countries. This is a noble history mankind can rightly be proud of. The Great Nalanda University of India which flourished from the second to the ninth century was a product of Buddhism. It was the first university that we know of and which was opened to international students.

In the past, Buddhism was able to make itself felt in many parts of the East, although communication and transport were difficult and people had to cross hills and deserts. Despite these difficult barriers Buddhism spread far and wide. Today, this peace message is spreading in the West. Westerners are attracted to Buddhism and believe that Buddhism is the only religion that is in harmony with modern science.

Buddhist missionaries have no need or desire to convert those who already have a proper religion to practise. If people are satisfied with their own religion, then, there is no need for Buddhist missionaries to convert them. They give their full support to missionaries of other faiths if their idea is to convert the wicked, evil, and uncultured people to a religious way of life. Buddhist are happy to see the progress of other religions so long as they truly help people to lead a religious way of life according to their faith and enjoy peace, harmony and understanding. On the other hand, Buddhist missionaries deplore the attitude of certain missionaries who disturb the followers of other religions, since there is no reason for them to create an unhealthy atmosphere of competition for converts if their aim is only to teach people to lead a religious way of life.

In introducing Dhamma to others, Buddhist missionaries have never tried to use imaginary exaggerations depicting a heavenly life in order to attract human desire and arouse their craving. Instead, they have tried to explain the real nature of human and heavenly life as taught by the Buddha.

# 15

# WAR AND PEACE

## Why is there no Peace?

*Man has forgotten that he has a heart. He forgets that if he treats the world kindly, the world will treat him kindly in return.*

WE are living in a world of really amazing contradictions. On the one hand, people are afraid of war; on the other hand, they prepare for it with frenzy. They produce in abundance, but they distribute miserly. The world becomes more and more crowded, but man becomes increasingly isolated and lonely. Men are living close to each other as in a big family, but each individual finds himself more than ever before, separated from his neighbour. Mutual understanding and sincerity are lacking very badly. One man cannot trust another, however good the latter may be.

When the United Nations was formed after the horrors of the Second World War, the heads of Nations who gathered to sign the charter agreed that it should begin with the following preamble: ' *Since it is in the minds of men that wars begin, it is in the minds of men the ramparts of peace should be erected.* ' This very same sentiment is echoed in the first verse of the *Dhammapada* which states: 'All [mental] states have mind as their forerunner, mind is their chief, and they are mind-made. If one speaks or acts, with a defiled mind, suffering follows one even as the wheel follows the hoof of the draught-ox. '

The belief that the only way to fight force is by applying more force has led to the arms race between the great powers. And this competition to increase the weapons of war has brought mankind to the very brink of total self-destruction. If we do nothing about it, the next war will be the end of the world where there will be neither victors nor victims — only dead bodies.

' Hatred does not cease by hatred; by love alone does it cease. ' Such is the Buddha's advice to those who preach the doctrine of antagonism and ill-will, and who set men to war and rebellion against one another. Many people say that the Buddha's advice to return good for evil is impracticable. Actually, it is the only correct method to solve any problem. This method was introduced by the great Teacher from His own experience. Because we are proud and egoistic, we are reluctant to return good for evil, thinking that the public may treat us as cowardly people. Some people even think that kindness and gentleness are effeminate, not 'macho'! But what harm is there if we settle our problems and bring peace and happiness by adopting this cultured method and by sacrificing our dangerous pride?

Tolerance must be practised if peace is to come to this earth. Force and compulsion will only create intolerance. To establish peace and harmony among mankind, each and everyone must first learn to practise the ways leading to the extinction of hatred, greed and delusion, the roots of all evil forces. If mankind can eradicate these evil forces, tolerance and peace will come to this restless world.

Today the followers of the most compassionate Buddha have a special duty to work for the establishment of peace in the world and to show an example to others by following their Master's advice: ' All tremble at punishment, all fear death; comparing others with oneself, one should neither kill nor cause to kill. ' *(Dhammapada 129)*

Peace is always obtainable. But the way to peace is not only through prayers and rituals. Peace is the result of man's harmony with his fellow beings and with his environment. The peace that we try to introduce by force is not a lasting peace. It is an interval in between the conflict of selfish desire and worldly conditions.

Peace cannot exist on this earth without the practice of tolerance. To be tolerant, we must not allow anger and jealousy to prevail in our mind. The Buddha says, ' No enemy can harm one so much as one's own thoughts of craving, hate and jealousy. ' *(Dhammapada 42)*

Buddhism is a religion of tolerance because it preaches a life of self-restraint. Buddhism teaches a life based not on rules but on principles. Buddhism has never persecuted or maltreated those whose beliefs are different. The Teaching is such that it is not necessary for anyone to label himself as a Buddhist to practise the Noble Principles of this religion.

The world is like a mirror and if you look at the mirror with a smiling face, you can see your own, beautiful smiling face. On the other hand, if you look at it with a long face, you will invariably see ugliness. Similarly, if you treat the world kindly the world will also certainly treat you kindly. Learn to be peaceful with yourself and the world will also be peaceful with you.

Man's mind is given to so much self-deceit that he does not want to admit his own weakness. He will try to find some excuse to justify his action and to create an illusion that he is blameless. If a man really wants to be free, he must have the courage to admit his own weakness. The Buddha says:—

*"Easily seen are other's faults; hard indeed it is to see one's own faults."*

# Can We Justify War?

*The difference between a dog fight and a war or between two groups of people is only in its organisation.*

THE history of mankind is a continuous manifestation of man's greed, hatred, pride, jealousy, selfishness and delusion. During the last 3,000 years, men have fought 15,000 major wars. Is it a characteristic of man? What is his destiny? How can men bring destruction to one another?

Although men have discovered and invented many important things, they have also made great advances towards the destruction of their own kind. This is how many human civilisations have been completely erased from this earth. Modern man has become so sophisticated in his art and techniques of warfare that it is now possible for him to turn the whole of mankind into ashes within a few seconds. The world has become a storehouse of military hardware as a result of a little game called ' Military Superiority. '

We are told that the prototype of a nuclear weapon is more powerful than the atomic bomb which was dropped at Hiroshima Japan in August, 1945 is being planned. Scientists believe that a few hundred thermonuclear weapons will chart the course towards universal destruction. Just see what we are doing to our human race! Think what sort of scientific development it is! See how foolish and selfish man is!

Man should not pander to his aggressive instincts. Man should uphold the ethical teachings of the religious teachers and display justice with morality to enable peace to prevail.

Treaties, pacts and peace formulae have been adopted and millions of words have been spoken by countless world leaders throughout the world who proclaim that they have found the way to maintain and promote peace on earth. But for all their efforts, they have not succeeded in removing the threat to mankind. The reason is that we have all failed to educate our young to truly understand and respect the need for selfless service and the danger of selfishness. To guarantee true peace, we must use every method available to us to educate our young to practise love, goodwill and tolerance towards others.

## The Buddhist Attitude

A Buddhist should not be the aggressor even in protecting his religion or anything else. He must try his best to avoid any kind of violent act. Sometimes he may be forced to go to war by others who do not respect the concept of the brotherhood of man as taught by the Buddha. He may be called upon to defend his fellow men from aggression, and as long as he has not renounced the worldly life, he is duty-bound to join in the struggle for peace and freedom. Under these circumstances, he cannot be blamed for his action in becoming a soldier or being involved in defence. However, if everyone were to follow the advice of the Buddha, there would be no reason for war to take place in this world. It is the duty of every cultured man to find all possible ways and means to settle disputes in a peaceful manner, without declaring war to kill his fellow men. The Buddha did not teach His followers to surrender to any form of evil power — be it man or supernatural being.

Indeed, with reason and science, man could conquer nature, and yet man has not yet even secured his own life. Why is it that life is in danger? While devoted to reason and being ruled by science, man has forgotten that he has a heart which has been neglected and has been left to wither and be polluted by passions.

If we cannot secure our own lives, then how can world peace be possible? To obtain peace, we must train our minds to face facts. We must be objective and humble. We must realise that no one person, nor one nation is always wrong. To obtain peace, we must also share the richness of the earth, not necessarily with equality but at least with equity. There can never be absolute equality but surely there can be a greater degree of equity.

It is simply inconceivable that five percent of the world's population should enjoy fifty percent of its wealth, or that twenty-five percent of the world should be fairly well-fed and some overfed, while seventy-five percent of the world is always hungry. Peace will only come when nations are willing to share and share equitably, the rich to help the poor and the strong to help the weak, thus creating international goodwill. Only if and when these conditions are met, can we envision a world with no excuse for wars.

The madness of the armaments race must stop! We must try to build schools instead of cruisers, hospitals instead of nuclear weapons. The amount of money and human lives that various governments waste in the battlefield should be diverted to build up the economies to elevate the standard of living.

The world cannot have peace until men and nations renounce selfish desires, give up racial arrogance, and eradicate egoistical lust for possession and power. Wealth cannot secure happiness. Religion alone can effect the necessary change of heart and bring about the only real disarmament — that of the mind.

All religions teach people not to kill; but unfortunately this important precept is conveniently ignored. Today, with modern armaments, man can kill millions within one second, that is, more than primitive tribes did in a century.

Very unfortunately some people in certain countries bring religious labels, slogans and banners into their battlefields. They do not know that they are disgracing the good name of religion.

' Verily, O monk, ' said the Buddha, ' due to sensuous craving, kings fight with kings, princes with princes, priests with priests, citizens with citizens, the mother quarrels with the son, the son quarrels with the father, brother with brother, brother with sister, sister with brother, friend with friend. ' *(Majjihima Nikaya)*

We can happily say that for the last 2,500 years there has never been any serious discord or conflict created by Buddhists that led to war in the name of this religion. This is a result of the dynamic character of the concept of tolerance contained in the Buddha's teaching.

# Can a Buddhist Join the Army?

*You can be a soldier of Truth, but not the aggressor.*

ONE day, Sinha, the general of the army, went to the Buddha and said, ' I am a soldier, O Blessed One. I am appointed by the King to enforce his laws and to wage his wars. The Buddha teaches infinite love, kindness and compassion for all sufferers: Does the Buddha permit the punishment of the criminal? And also, does the Buddha declare that it is wrong to go to war for the protection of our homes, our wives, our children and our property? Does the Buddha teach the doctrine of complete self-surrender? Should I suffer the evil-doer to do what he pleases and yield submissively to him who threatens to take by violence what is my own? Does the Buddha maintain that all strife including warfare waged for a righteous cause should be forbidden? '

The Buddha replied, ' He who deserves punishment must be punished. And he who is worthy of favour must be favoured. Do not do injury to any living being but be just, filled with love and kindness. ' These injunctions are not contradictory because the person who is punished for his crimes will suffer his injury not through the ill-will of the judge but through the evil act itself. His own acts have brought upon him the injury that the executors of the law inflict. When a magistrate punishes, he must not harbour hatred in his heart. When a murderer is put to death, he should realise that his punishment is the result of his own act.

With his understanding, he will no longer lament his fate but can console his mind. And the Blessed One continued, ' The Buddha teaches that all warfare in which man tries to slay his brothers is lamentable. But he does not teach that those who are involved in war to maintain peace and order, after having exhausted all means to avoid conflict, are blameworthy.

' Struggle must exist, for all life is a struggle of some kind. But make certain that you do not struggle in the interest of self against truth and justice. He who struggles out of self-interest to make himself great or powerful or rich or famous, will have no reward. But he who struggles for peace and truth will have great reward; even his defeat will be deemed a victory.

' If a person goes to battle even for a righteous cause, then Sinha, he must be prepared to be slain by his enemies because death is the destiny of warriors. And should his fate overtake him, he has no reason to complain. But if he is victorious his success may be deemed great, but no matter how great it is, the wheel of fortune may turn again and bring his life down into the dust. However, if he moderates himself and extinguishes all hatred in his heart, if he lifts his down-trodden adversary up and says to him, ' Come now and make peace and let us be brothers, ' then he will gain a victory that is not a transient success; for the fruits of that victory will remain forever.

' Great is a successful general, Sinha, but he who conquers self is the greater victor. This teaching of conquest of self, Sinha, is not taught to destroy the lives of others, but to protect them. The person who has conquered himself is more fit to live, to be successful and to gain victories than is the person who is the slave of self. The person whose mind is free from the illusion of self, will stand and not fall in the battle of life. He whose intentions are righteousness and justice, will meet with no failures. He will be successful in his enterprise and his success will endure. He who harbours love of truth in his heart will live and not suffer, for he has drunk the water of immortality. So struggle courageously and wisely. Then you can be a soldier of Truth. '

There is no justice in war or violence. When we declare war, we justify it, when others declare war, we say, it is unjust. Then who can justify war? Man should not follow the law of the jungle to overcome human problems.

# Mercy Killing

*Mercy and Killing can never go together.*

ACCORDING to Buddhism mercy killing cannot be justified. Mercy and killing can never go together. Some people kill their pets on the grounds that they do not like to see the pets suffer. However, if mercy killing is the correct method to be practised on pets and other animals, then why are people so reluctant to do the same to their beloved ones?

When some people see their dogs or cats suffer from some skin disease, they arrange to kill those poor animals. They call this action, mercy killing. Actually it is not that they have mercy towards those animals, but they kill them for their own precaution and to get rid of an awful sight. And even if they do have real mercy towards a suffering animal, they still have no right to take away its life. No matter how sincere one may be, mercy killing is not the correct approach. The consequences of this killing, however, are different from killing with hatred towards the animal. Buddhists have no grounds to say that any kind of killing is justified.

Some people try to justify mercy killing with the misconception that if the motive or reason is good, then the act itself is good. They then claim that by killing their pet, they have the intention to relieve the unhappy animal from its suffering and so the action is good. No doubt their original intention or motive is good. But the evil act of killing which occurs through a later thought, will certainly bring about unwholesome results.

Keeping away from mercy killing can become a nuisance to many. Nevertheless, the Buddhist religion cannot justify mercy killing as completely free from bad reaction. However, to kill out of necessity and without any anger or hatred has less bad reaction than to kill out of intense anger or jealousy.

On the other hand, a being (man or animal) may suffer owing to his bad *kamma*. If by mercy killing, we prevent the working out of one's bad *kamma,* the debt will have to be paid in another existence. As Buddhists, all that we can do is to help to reduce the pain of suffering in others.

**Killing for Self Protection**

The Buddha has advised everyone to abstain from killing. If everybody accepts this advice, human beings would not kill each other. In the case where a person's life is threatened, the Buddha says even then it is not advisable to kill out of self-protection. The weapon for self-protection is loving-kindness. One who practises this kindness very seldom comes across such misfortune. However, man loves his life so much that he is not prepared to surrender himself to others; in actual practice, most people would struggle for self-protection. It is natural and every living being struggles and kills others for self-protection but kammic effect depends on their mental attitude. During the struggle to protect himself, if he happens to kill his opponent although he has no intention to kill, then he is not responsible for that action. On the other hand, if he kills another person under any circumstances with the intention to kill, then he is not free from the kammic reaction; he has to face the consequences. We must remember that killing is killing; when we disapprove of it, we call it 'murder'. When we punish man for murdering, we call it 'capital punishment'. If our own soldiers are killed by an ' enemy ' we call it 'slaughter'. However, if we approve a killing, we call it 'war'. But if we remove the emotional content from these words, we can understand that killing is killing.

In recent years many scientists and some religionists have used the expressions like ' humane killing ', ' mercy killing ', ' gentle killing ' and ' painless killing ' to justify the ending of a life. They argue that if the victim feels no pain, if the knife is sharp, killing is justified. Buddhism can never accept these arguments because it is not *how* the killing occurs that is important, but the fact that a life of one being is terminated by another. No one has any right to do that for whatever reason.

PART SIX

# THIS WORLD AND OTHER WORLDS

# 16

# REALMS OF EXISTENCE

## The Origin of the World

*'There is no reason to suppose that the world had a beginning at all. The idea that things must have a beginning is really due to the poverty of our thoughts.'* (Bertrand Russell)

THERE are three schools of thought regarding the origin of the world. The first school of thought claims that this world came into existence by nature and that nature is not an intelligent force. However, nature works on its own accord and goes on changing.

The second school of thought says that the world was created by an almighty God who is responsible for everything.

The third school of thought says that the beginning of this world and of life is inconceivable since they have neither beginning nor end. Buddhism is in accordance with this third school of thought. Bertrand Russell supports this school of thought by saying, ' There is no reason to suppose that the world had a beginning at all. The idea that things must have a beginning is really due to the poverty of our thoughts. '

Modern science says that some millions of years ago, the newly cooled earth was lifeless and that life originated in the ocean. Buddhism never claimed that the world, sun, moon, stars, wind, water, days and nights were created by a powerful god or by a Buddha. Buddhists believe that the world was not created once upon a time, but that the world has been created millions of times every second and will continue to do so by itself and will break away by itself. According to Buddhism, world systems always appear and disappear in the universe.

H.G. Wells, in *A Short History of the World,* says 'It is universally recognised that the universe in which we live, has to all appearance, existed for an enormous period of time and possibly for endless time. But that the universe in which we live, has existed only for six or seven thousand years may be regarded as an altogether exploded idea. No life seems to have happened suddenly upon earth. '

The efforts made by many religions to explain the beginning and the end of the universe are indeed ill-conceived. The position of religions which propound the view that the universe was created by god in an exactly fixed year, has become a difficult one to maintain in the light of modern and scientific knowledge.

Today scientists, historians, astronomers, biologists, botanists, anthropologists and great thinkers have all contributed vast new knowledge about the origin of the world. This latest discovery and knowledge is not at all contradictory to the Teachings of the Buddha. Bertrand Russell again says that he respects the Buddha for not making false statements like others who committed themselves regarding the origin of the world.

The speculative explanations of the origin of the universe that are presented by various religions are not acceptable to the modern scientists and intellectuals. Even the commentaries of the Buddhist Scriptures, written by certain Buddhist writers, cannot be challenged by scientific thinking in regard to this question. The

Buddha did not waste His time on this issue. The reason for His silence was that this issue has no religious value for gaining spiritual wisdom. The explanation of the origin of the universe is not the concern of religion. Such theorizing is not necessary for living a righteous way of life and for shaping our future life. However, if one insists on studying this subject, then one must investigate the sciences, astronomy, geology, biology and anthropology. These sciences can offer more reliable and tested information on this subject than can be supplied by any religion. The purpose of a religion is to cultivate the life here in this world and hereafter until liberation is gained.

In the eyes of the Buddha, the world is nothing but *Samsara* — the cycle of repeated births and deaths. To Him, the beginning of the world and the end of the world is within this *Samsara*. Since elements and energies are relative and inter-dependent, it is meaningless to single out anything as the beginning. Whatever speculation we make regarding the origin of the world, there is no absolute truth in our notion.

' Infinite is the sky, infinite is the number of beings,
  Infinite are the worlds in the vast universe,
  Infinite in wisdom the Buddha teaches these,
  Infinite are the virtues of Him who teaches these. '

*(Sri Ramachandra)*

One day a man called Malunkyaputta approached the Master and demanded that He explain the origin of the Universe to him. He even threatened to cease to be His follower if the Buddha's answer was not satisfactory. The Buddha calmly retorted that it was of no consequence to Him whether or not Malunkyaputta followed Him, because the Truth did not need anyone's support. Then the Buddha said that He would not go into a discussion of the origin of the Universe. To Him, gaining knowledge about such matters was a waste of time because a man's task was to liberate himself from the present, not the past or the future. To illustrate this, the Enlightened One related the parable of a man who was shot by a poisoned arrow. This foolish man refused to have the arrow removed until he found out all about the person who shot the arrow. By the time his attendants discovered these unnecessary details, the man was dead. Similarly, our immediate task is to attain Nibbana, not to worry about our beginnings.

# Other World Systems

*In the light of modern, scientific discoveries, we can appreciate the limitations of the human world and the hypothesis that other world systems might exist in other parts of the universe.*

ON certain occasions, the Buddha has commented on the nature and composition of the universe. According to the Buddha, there are some other forms of life existing in other parts of the universe. The Buddha has mentioned that there are thirty-one planes of existence within the universes. They are:—

4   States of unhappiness or sub human realms: (life in hells, animal life, ghost-worlds and demon-worlds)
1   Human world.
6   Devalokas or heavenly realms.
16  Rupalokas or Realms of Fine-Material Forms.
4   Arupalokas or Formless Realms.*

The existence of these other-world systems is yet to be confirmed by modern science. However, modern scientists are now working with the hypothesis that there is a possibility of other forms of life existing on other planets. As a result of today's rapid scientific progress, we may soon find some living beings on other planets in the remotest parts of the galaxy system. Perhaps, we will find them subject to the same laws as ourselves. They might be physically quite different in both appearance, elements and chemical composition and exist in different dimensions. They might be far superior to us or they might be far inferior.

*For further details read 'The 31 Planes of Existence' by E. Baptist.*

Why should the planet earth be the only planet to contain life forms? Earth is a tiny speck in a huge universe. Sir James Jeans, the distinguished astrophysicist, estimates the whole universe to be about one thousand million times as big as the area of space that is visible through the telescope. In his book, *The Mysterious Universe,* he states that the total number of universes is probably something like the total number of grains of sand on all the sea shores of the world. In such a universe, the planet Earth is only one-millionth of a grain of sand. He also informs us that the light from the sun which takes a seventh of a second to reach the earth, takes probably something like 100,000 million years to travel across the universe! Such is the vastness of the cosmos. When we consider the vastness of the many universes making up what is popularly known as 'outer space', the hypothesis that other-world systems might exist is scientifically feasible.

In the light of modern scientific discoveries, we can appreciate the limitations of the human world. Today, science has demonstrated that our human world exists within the limitations of the vibrational frequencies that can be received by our sense organs. And science has also shown us that there are other vibrational frequencies which are above or below our range of reception. With the discovery of radio waves, X-rays, T.V. waves, and micro waves, we can appreciate the extremely limited vision that is imposed on us by our sense organs. We peep out at the universe through the 'crack' allowed by our sense organs, just as a little child peeps out through the crack in the door. This awareness of our limited perception demonstrates to us the possibility that other world systems may exist that are separate from ours or that interpenetrate with ours.

As to the nature of the universe, the Buddha said that the beginning and ending of the universe is inconceivable. Buddhists do not believe that the world will suddenly end in complete and utter destruction. There is no such thing as complete destruction of the whole universe at once. When a certain section of the universe disappears, another section remains. When the other section disappears, another section reappears or evolves out of the dispersed matters of the previous universe. This is formed by the accumulation of molecules, basic elements, gas and numerous energies, a combination supported by cosmic impulsion and gravity. Then some other new world systems appear and exist for sometime. This is the nature of the cosmic energies. This is why the Buddha says that the beginning and the end of the universe is inconceivable.

It was only on certain, special occasions, that the Buddha commented on the nature and composition of the universe. When He spoke, He had to address Himself to the understanding capacity of the enquirer. The Buddha was not interested in this kind of metaphysical speculation that did not lead to the higher spiritual development.

Buddhists do not share the view held by some people that the world will be destroyed by a god, when there are more non-believers and more corruptions taking place amongst the human beings. With regard to this belief people can ask, instead of destroying with his power, why can't this god use the same power to influence people to become believers and to wipe out all immoral practices from men's mind? Whether the god destroys or not, it is natural that one day there will be an end to everything that comes into existence. However, in the language of the Buddha, the world is nothing more than the combination, existence, disappearance, and recombination of mind and matter *(nama-rupa)*.

In the final analysis, the Teaching of the Buddha goes beyond the discoveries of modern science however startling or impressive they may be. In science, the knowledge of the universe is to enable man to master it for his material comfort and personal safety. But the Buddha teaches that no amount of factual knowledge will ultimately free man from the pain of existence. He must strive alone and diligently until he arrives at a true understanding of his own nature and of the changeable nature of the cosmos. To be truly free a man must seek to tame his mind, to destroy his craving for sensual pleasure. When a man truly understands that the universe he is trying to conquer is impermanent, he will see himself as Don Quixote fighting windmills. With this Right View of himself he will spend his time and energy conquering his mind and destroying his illusion of self without wasting his effort on unimportant and unnecessary issues.

# The Buddhist Concept of Heaven and Hell

*The wise man makes his own heaven while the foolish man creates his own hell here and hereafter.*

THE Buddhist concept of heaven and hell is entirely different from that in other religions. Buddhists do not accept that these places are eternal. It is unreasonable to condemn a man to eternal hell for his human weakness but quite reasonable to give him every chance to develop himself. From the Buddhist point of view, those who go to hell can work themselves upwards by making use of the merit that they had acquired previously. There are no locks on the gates of hell. Hell is a temporary place and there is no reason for those beings to suffer there forever.

The Buddha's Teaching shows us that there are heavens and hells not only beyond this world, but in this very world itself. Thus the Buddhist conception of heaven and hell is very reasonable. For instance, the Buddha once said, ' When the average ignorant person makes an assertion to the effect that there is a Hell *(patala)* under the ocean he is making a statement which is false and without basis. The word 'Hell' is a term for painful sensations. ' The idea of one particular ready-made place or a place created by god as heaven and hell is not acceptable to the Buddhist concept.

The fire of hell in this world is hotter than that of the hell in the world-beyond. There is no fire equal to anger, lust or greed and ignorance. According to the Buddha, we are burning from eleven kinds of physical pain and mental agony: lust, hatred, illusion sickness, decay, death, worry, lamentation, pain (physical and mental), melancholy and grief. People can burn the entire world with some of these fires of mental discord. From a Buddhist point of view, the easiest way to define hell and heaven is that wherever there is more suffering, either in this world or any other plane, that place is a hell to those who suffer. And where there is more pleasure or happiness, either in this world or any other plane of existence, that place is a heaven to those who enjoy their worldly life in that particular place. However, as the human realm is a mixture of both pain and happiness, human beings experience both pain and happiness and will be able to realise the real nature of life. But in many other planes of existence inhabitants have less chance for this realisation. In certain places there is more suffering than pleasure while in some other places there is more pleasure than suffering.

Buddhists believe that after death rebirth can take place in any one of a number of possible existences. This future existence is conditioned by the last thought-moment a person experiences at the point of death. This last thought which determines the next existence results from the past actions of a man either in this life or before that. Hence, if the predominant thought reflects meritorious action, then he will find his future existence in a happy state. But that state is temporary and when it is exhausted a new life must begin all over again, determined by another dominating ' kammic ' energy. This repetitious process goes on endlessly unless one arrives at ' Right View ' and makes a firm resolve to follow the Noble Path which produces the ultimate happiness of *Nibbana*.

Heaven is a temporary place where those who have done good deeds experience more sensual pleasures for a longer period. Hell is another temporary place where those evil doers experience more physical and mental suffering. It is not justifiable to believe that such places are permanent. There is no god behind the scene of heaven and hell. Each and every person experiences according to his good and bad *kamma*. Buddhists never try to introduce Buddhism by frightening people through hell-fire or enticing people by pointing to paradise. Their main idea is character building and mental training. Buddhists can practise their religion without aiming at heaven or without developing fear of hell. Their duty is to lead righteous lives by upholding humane qualities and peace of mind.

# Belief in Deities (Devas)

*Buddhists do not deny the existence of various gods or deities.*

DEVAS are more fortunate than human beings as far as sensual pleasures are concerned. They also possess certain powers which human beings usually lack. However, the powers of these deities are limited because they are also transitory beings. They exist in happy abodes and enjoy their life for a longer period than human beings do. When they have exhausted all the good *kamma,* that they have gathered during previous births, these deities pass away and are reborn somewhere else according to their good and bad *kamma.* According to the Buddha, human beings have more opportunities to accrue merits to be born in a better condition, and the deities have less chances in this respect.

Buddhists do not attribute any specific importance to such gods. They do not regard the deities as a support for the moral development or as a support for the attainment of salvation of *Nibbana.* Whether they are great or small, both human beings and deities are perishable and subject to rebirth.

It is a common belief amongst the Buddhist public that such deities can be influenced to grant their favours by transferring merits to them whenever meritorious deeds are performed. This belief is based on the Buddha's injunction to the deities to protect those human beings who lead a religious way of life. This is the reason why Buddhists transfer the merits to such deities or remember them whenever they do some meritorious deeds. However, making of offerings to and worshipping such deities are not encouraged, although some Buddhist customs centre around such activities. When people are in great difficulties, they naturally turn to the deities to express their grievances in a place of worship. By doing this, they gain some relief and consolation; in their hearts, they feel much better. However, to an intellectual who has strong will power, sound education and understanding, such beliefs and actions need not be resorted to. There is definitely no Teaching in Buddhism to the effect that Buddhists can attain *Nibbana* by praying to any deity. Buddhists believe that ' purity and impurity depend on oneself. No one from outside can purify another. ' *(Dhammapada 165)*

*Buddhahood* and *Nibbana* can be attained without any help from an external source. Therefore, Buddhists can practise their religion with or without the deities.

# Spirit World

*There are visible and invisible beings or spirits in the same way as there are visible and invisible lights.*

BUDDHISM does not deny the existence of good and evil spirits. There are visible and invisible beings or spirits in the same way as there are visible and invisible lights. We need special instruments to see the invisible light and we need a special sense to see the invisible beings. One cannot deny the existence of such spirits just because one is unable to see them with one's naked eyes. These spirits are also subject to birth and death. They are not going to stay permanently in the spirit form. They too exist in the same world where we live.

A genuine Buddhist is one who moulds his life according to moral causation discovered by the Buddha. He should not be concerned with the worshipping of these gods and spirits. However, this kind of worshipping is of some interest and fascination to the multitude and has naturally brought some Buddhists into contact with these activities.

Regarding protection from evil spirits, goodness is a shield against evil. Goodness is a wall through which evil cannot penetrate unless the good person opens the door to an evil influence. Even though a person leads a truly virtuous and holy life and has a good shield of moral and noble living that person can still lower his shield of protection by believing in the power of evil that would do harm to him.

The Buddha has never advised His followers to worship such spirits and to be frightened of them. The Buddhist attitude towards them is to transfer merits and to radiate loving-kindness to them. Buddhists do not harm them. On the other hand, if man is religious, virtuous and pure in mind, and if he is also intelligent and possesses strong will-power and understanding capacity, then such a person could be deemed to be much stronger than spirits. The evil spirits would keep away from him, the good spirits would protect him.

# The Significance of Transference of Merits to the Departed

*If you really want to honour and help your departed ones, then do some meritorious deeds in their name and transfer the merits to them.*

ACCORDING to Buddhism, good deeds or 'acts of merit' bring happiness to the doer both in this world and in the hereafter. Acts of merit are also believed to lead towards the final goal of everlasting happiness. The acts of merit can be performed through body, speech or mind. Every good deed produces 'merit' which accumulates to the 'credit' of the doer. Buddhism also teaches that the acquired merit can be transferred to others; it can be shared vicariously with others. In other words, the merit is 'reversible' and so can be shared with other persons. The persons who receive the merit can be either living or departed ones.

The method for transferring merits is quite simple. First some good deeds are performed. The doer of the good deeds has merely to wish that the merit he has gained accrues to someone in particular, or to 'all beings'. This wish can be purely mental or it can be accompanied by an expression of words.

The wish could be made with the beneficiary being aware of it. When the beneficiary is aware of the act or wish, then a mutual 'rejoicing in' merit takes place. Here the beneficiary becomes a participant of the original deed by associating himself with the deed done. If the beneficiary identifies himself with both the deed and the doer, he can sometimes acquire even greater merit than the original doer, either because his elation is greater or because his appreciation of the value of the deed is based on his understanding of Dhamma and, hence, more meritorious. Buddhist texts contain several stories of such instances.

The 'joy of transference of merits' can also take place with or without the knowledge of the doer of the meritorious act. All that is necessary is for the beneficiary to feel gladness in his heart when he becomes aware of the good deed. If he wishes, he can express his joy by saying *'sadhu'* which means 'well done'. What he is doing is creating a kind of mental or verbal applause. In order to share the good deed done by another, what is important is that there must be actual approval of the deed and joy arising in the beneficiary's heart.

Even if he so desires, the doer of a good deed cannot prevent another's 'rejoicing in the merit' because he has no power over another's thoughts. According to the Buddha, in all actions, thought is what really matters. Transference is primarily an act of the mind.

To transfer merit does not mean that a person is deprived of the merit he had originally acquired by his good deed. On the contrary, the very act of 'transference' is a good deed in itself and hence enhances the merit already earned.

## Highest Gift to the Departed

The Buddha says that the greatest gift one can confer on one's dead ancestors is to perform 'acts of merit' and to transfer these merits so acquired. He also says that those who give also receive the fruits of their deeds. The Buddha encouraged those who did good deeds such as offering alms to holy men, to transfer the merits which they received to their departed ones. Alms should be given in the name of the departed by recalling to mind such things as, ' When he was alive, he gave me this wealth; he did this for me; he was my relative, my companion,' etc. *(Tirokudda Sutta — Khuddakapatha).* There is no use weeping, feeling sorry, lamenting and bewailing; such attitudes are of no consequence to the departed ones.

Transferring merits to the departed is based on the popular belief that on a person's death, his 'merits' and 'demerits' are weighed against one another and his destiny determined, his actions determine whether he is to be reborn in a sphere of happiness or a realm of woe. The belief is that the departed one might have gone to the world of the departed spirits. The beings in these lower forms of existence cannot generate fresh merits, and have to live on with the merits which are earned from this world.

Those who did not harm others and who performed many good deeds during their life time, will certainly have the chance to be reborn in a happy place. Such persons do not require the help of living relatives. However, those who have no chance to be reborn in a happy abode are always waiting to receive merits from their living relatives to offset their deficiency and to enable them to be born in a happy abode.

Those who are reborn in an unfortunate spirit form could be released from their suffering condition through the transferring of merits to them by friends and relatives who do some meritorious deeds.

This injunction of the Buddha to transfer merits to departed ones is the counterpart of the Hindu custom which has come down through the ages. Various ceremonies are performed so that the spirits of dead ancestors might live in peace. This custom has been a tremendous influence on the social life of certain Buddhist countries. The dead are always remembered when any good deed is done, and more on occasions connected with their lives, such as their birth or death anniversaries. On such occasions, there is a ritual which is generally practised. The transferrer pours water from a jug or other similar vessel into a receptacle, while repeating a Pali formula which is translated as follows:

> As rivers, when full must flow
> and reach and fill the distant main,
> so indeed what is given here will
> reach and bless the spirits there.
> As water poured on mountain top must
> soon descend and fill the plain
> So indeed what is given here will reach
> and bless the spirits there.
>
> *(Nidhikanda Sutta in Khuddakapatha)*

The origin and the significance of transference of merit is open to scholarly debate. Although this ancient custom still exists today in many Buddhists countries, very few Buddhists who follow this ancient custom have understood the meaning of transference of merits and the proper way to do that.

Some people are simply wasting time and money on · meaningless ceremonies and performances in memory of departed ones. These people do not realise that it is impossible to help the departed ones simply by building big graveyards, tombs, paper-houses and other paraphernalia. Neither is it possible to help the departed by burning joss-sticks, joss-paper, etc.; nor is it possible to help the departed by slaughtering animals and offering them along with other kinds of food. Also one should not waste by burning things used by the departed ones on the assumption that the deceased persons would somehow benefit by the act, when such articles can in fact be distributed among the needy.

The only way to help the departed ones is to do some meritorious deeds in a religious way in memory of them. The meritorious deeds include such acts as giving alms to others, building schools, temples, orphanages, libraries, hospitals, printing religious books for free distribution and similar charitable deeds.

The followers of the Buddha should act wisely and should not follow anything blindly. While others pray to god for the departed ones, Buddhists radiate their loving-kindness directly to them. By doing meritorious deeds, they can transfer the merits to their beloved ones for their well-being. This is the best way of remembering and giving real honour to and perpetuating the names of the departed ones. In their state of happiness, the departed ones will reciprocate their blessings on their living relatives. It is, therefore, the duty of relatives to remember their departed ones by transferring merits and by radiating loving-kindness directly to them.

# 17

# DIVINATION AND DREAMS

## Astrology and Astronomy

*' I believe in astrology but not astrologers.'*

FROM the very beginning of time man has been fascinated by the stars and he has always tried to find some links between them and his own destiny. His observation of the stars and their movements gave rise to two very important areas of study, namely, Astronomy and Astrology. Astronomy can be considered a pure science which is concerned with the measurements of distances, the evolution and destruction of stars, their movements, and so on. Of course all these calculations are always made in relation to planet earth and how these interplanetary movements affect mankind on a physical level. Modern astronomy seeks to find answers to the still unanswered questions regarding the origin of man and the final, possible end of his existence as a member of the human race. It is a fascinating area of study and our new knowledge of the universe and the galaxies has put much pressure on many religions to evaluate their age-old postulations regarding the creator and the creation of life.

Buddhism does not face any dilemma, simply because the Buddha did not encourage His followers to speculate on things beyond their comprehension. However, He has made many allusions which in the light of our new knowledge gained through science, shows us that the Buddha was very much aware of the true nature of the Universe, that it was never created in one glorious moment, that the earth is merely a tiny, even unimportant speck in all of space, that there is constant creation and destruction, and that everything is in constant motion.

Astrology, however, is a completely different area of study altogether. Ever since early man began to think, he was deeply concerned about his relationship with the universe. When human societies became involved in agricultural activities man progressed from hunting as a livelihood and began to notice a link between the movement of the sun through the years and his own activities of planting, harvesting, and similar projects. As he became more sophisticated he was able to predict the movement of the sun and he invented time measurement, dividing it into years, months, days, hours, minutes and seconds.

He associated this knowledge with his existence whereby he felt that there was a relationship between his own life cycle and the movement of the planets. That gave rise to the Zodiac — the apparent path of the sun. It contained twelve constellations. A study of these movements in relation to a human being's personal life is called a horoscope.

The study of astrology involves a great understanding of human nature, an ability to assess planetary movements precisely, together with an insight into the seemingly unexplainable phenomena in the universe. There have been many brilliant astrologers in the past and some exist even today. Unfortunately there are an even larger number of charlatans who give astrology a bad name. They hood-wink people by predicting seemingly true events about their future. They make large sums of money by exploiting the ignorance and fear of the gullible. As a result, for a long time scientists scoffed at astrology and did not depend on it. However their hostile attitude is not really justifiable. The main purpose of reading a horoscope should be to give one an insight into one's own character, in the same way that an X-ray photograph can show the physical make-up of a man.

Statistics have shown that the influence of the sun in the signs of the Zodiac accounts for the birth of unusual people during certain months. Certain crimes have been found to correspond with Zodiac signs in which the sun is moving during certain months of the year.

Thus an understanding of this relationship will help a man to plot his life more meaningfully in harmony with his innate tendencies, so that there is less friction as he goes through life.

A new-born baby is like a seed. It contains within itself all the ingredients which will make it a similar, yet completely different individual from all its fellow human beings. How its potential is developed depends, like the seed, on the kind of nurture it receives. The nature of a man is born within him, but his own free will determines whether he will make really good use of his talents and abilities. Whether he will overcome his potential for vice or weakness depends on how he is trained in his youth. If we recognise our nature — our tendency towards laziness, irritability, worries, frustrations, wickedness, cunningness, jealousy — we can take positive steps to overcome them. The first step in solving problems is to recognize them for what they are.

Astrological interpretations indicate our inclinations and tendencies. Once pointed out, we must take the necessary steps to chart our lives in a manner that will make us useful citizens of the world. Even a person with criminal tendencies can become a saint, if he recognizes his nature and takes steps to lead a good life.

A horoscope is a chart drawn to show the karmic force a man carries, calculated from the time of his birth. The force determines the time of birth and knowing this time, a skilful astrologer can accurately chart a man's destiny within a given life-span.

Everybody knows that the earth takes approximately one year to move around the sun. This movement, viewed from the earth, places the sun in various zodiacal areas during the year. A person is born (not accidentally, but as a result of karmic influence) when the sun is on transit in one of the twelve Zodiacal signs.

Through the horoscope you can determine certain times in your life when you have to slow down, or push yourself to great levels of creativity, or when you have to watch your activities and health.

## Buddhist Attitude Towards Astrology

The question most people ask is whether Buddhism accepts or rejects astrology. Strictly speaking, the Buddha did not make any direct pronouncement on this subject because as in many other cases, He stated that discussion on matters such as these do not pertain to spiritual development. Buddhism, unlike some other religions, does not condemn astrology and people are free to use the knowledge they can get from it to make their lives more meaningful. However, if we study the Buddha's teaching carefully, we will come to accept that a proper and intelligent understanding of astrology can be a useful tool. There is a direct link between the life of an individual human being and the vast workings of the cosmos. Modern science is in accordance with the teachings of Buddhism. We know for example that there is a close link between the movement of the moon and our own behaviour. This is seen especially among mentally disturbed and abnormally violent people. It is also true that certain sicknesses like asthma and bronchitis are aggravated when the moon waxes. There is, therefore, sufficient basis for us to believe that other planets can also influence our lives.

Buddhism accepts that there is an immense cosmic energy which pulsates through every living thing, including plants. This energy interacts with the karmic energy which an individual generates and determines the course that a life will take. The birth of an individual is not the first creation of a life but the continuation of one that had always existed and will continue to exist so long as the karmic energy is not quelled through final liberation in the unconditioned state. Now, for a life to manifest itself in a new existence, certain factors, namely seasons, germinal order and nature must be fulfilled. These are supported by mental energy and karmic energy and all these elements are in constant interaction and interdependent with each other resulting in constant changes to a human being's life.

According to astrologers, the time at which a person is born is predetermined by the cosmic energy and the karmic energy. Hence, it can be concluded that life is not merely accidental: it is the result of the interaction between an individual's karma and the universal energy force. The course of a human life is predetermined, caused partly by a being's own actions in the past and the energies that activate the cosmos. Once started, a life is controlled by the interaction between these two forces even to the moment at which a birth takes place. A skilful astrologer then, as one who understands cosmic as well as karmic influence, can chart the course of one's life, based on the moment of the person's birth.

While we are in one sense at the mercy of these forces, the Buddha has pointed out a way through which we can escape its influence. All karmic energies are stored in the subconscious mind normally described as mental purities and impurities. Since karmic forces influence one's destiny, a person can develop his mind and negate certain evil influences caused by previous bad kamma. A person can also ' purify ' his mind and rid himself of all karmic energies and thus prevent rebirth. When there is no rebirth, there is no potential life and there will consequently be no ' future ' existence which can be predicated or charted. At such a stage of spiritual and mental development, one will have transcended the need to know about his life because most imperfections and unsatisfactoriness would have been removed. A highly developed human being will have no need for a horoscope.

Since the beginning of the 20th century, psychologists and psychiatrists have come to recognize that there is much more to the human mind than the hard core materialists have been ready to accept. There is more to the world than can be seen and touched. The famous Swiss psychologist, Carl Jung, used to cast the horoscopes of his patients. On one occasion when he made an astrological analysis of about 500 marriages, he discovered that the findings of Ptolemy, on which modern Western astrology is based, were still valid, that favourable aspects between the sun and the moon of the different partners did produce happy marriages.

The well-known French psychologist, Michel Gauguelin, who originally held a negative view of astrology, made a survey of about 20,000 horoscopical analyses and found to his surprise that the characteristics of the persons studied coincided with characterization produced by modern psychological methods.

The planting of certain flowers, trees and vegetables at different times of a year will produce differences in strength or appearance of the plants. So there is no reason to doubt that people born in certain times of the year will have different characteristics from people born at other times. By knowing his weaknesses, failures and short-comings, a man can do his best to overcome them and make himself a better and more useful person to society. It will also help him a great deal to get rid of unhappiness and disappointments. (Going away from the country where a person is born for example, can sometimes help one avoid the influence of the stars).

Shakespeare says: 'The fault is not in our stars but in ourselves'. A well known astrologer has said: 'The stars impel; they do not compel'. St. Thomas Aquinas says: 'The planets influence the more elemental part of man than passions', but through his intellect man can arrange his life in harmony with the planets, and also cultivate his inherent talents and manipulate them for his betterment.

Astrology cannot automatically solve all your problems. You must do that yourself. Just like a doctor who can diagnose the nature of diseases, an astrologer can only show certain aspects of your life and character. After that it is left to you to adjust your way of life. Of course, the task will be made easier, knowing what it is you are up against. Some people are too dependent on astrology. They run to the astrologer everytime something happens or if they have a dream. Remember, even today astrology is very much an imperfect science and even the best astrologers can make serious mistakes. Use astrology intelligently, just as you would use any tool which would make your life more comfortable and more enjoyable. Above all, beware of fake astrologers who are out to cheat you by telling you not the truth, but what you want to hear.

Do not expect good luck to come to you or be handed to you easily without any effort on your part. If you want to reap the harvest, you must sow the seed and it must be the right seed. Remember, ' Opportunity knocks at the door, but never break the lock to gain entrance '.

# Fortune-Telling and Charms

*Hard work is the luckiest star.*

ALTHOUGH Buddhism does not refute belief in deities, spirits, astrology and fortune-telling, the Buddha's advice was that people should not be slaves to any of those forces. A good Buddhist can overcome all his difficulties if he knows how to make use of his intelligence and will-power. The above mentioned beliefs

---

*Read ' Stress and Mental Health in Malaysian Society ' by Dr. Tan Chee Khuan.*

have no spiritual significance or value. Man must overcome all his problems and difficulties by his own efforts and not through the medium of deities, spirits, astrology or fortune-telling.

In one of the Buddhist Jataka stories, the Bodhisatta said:

    ' The fool may watch for lucky days,
    Yet luck he shall always miss,
    The luck itself is luck's own star,
    What can mere stars achieve? '

He believed that hard work was the luckiest star and one should not waste time by consulting stars and lucky days in order to achieve success. To do your best to help yourself is better than to rely solely on the stars or external sources.

Although some Buddhists practise fortune-telling and dispense some forms of charms or amulets under the guise of religion, the Buddha at no time encouraged anyone to practise such things. Like fortune-telling, charms come under the category of superstition, and have no religious value. Yet there are many people today who, because of sickness and misfortunes attribute the cause of their illness and ill-luck to the power of charms. When the cause of certain sicknesses and misfortunes cannot be ascertained or traced, many people tend to believe that their problems are due to charms or some other external causes. They have forgotten that they are now living in the twentieth century. This is the modern age of scientific development and achievement. Our leading scientists have thrown aside many superstitious beliefs and they have even placed men on the moon!

All sicknessess owe their origin to either mental or physical causes. In Shakespeare, Macbeth asked a doctor if there was any medicine that could cure his wife and the doctor replied: ' More needs she the divine than the physician. ' What he meant was that some diseases could only be cured if the mind was purified. Some severe mental disorders manifest themselves in a physical manner — ulcers, stomach aches, and so on.

Of course diseases are purely physical and can be cured by a competent doctor. And finally, some inexplicable disorders could be caused by what Buddhists call the ripening of the kammic fruit. This means we would have to pay for some evil deed that we have committed in a past life. If we can understand this in the case of some incurable diseases, we can bear it with greater patience, knowing its real cause.

People who cannot be cured of their sickness are advised to consult a medical specialist and obtain specialised attention. If after having gone through a medical check-up, a person still feels in need of attention, then he may want to seek spiritual guidance from a proper religious teacher.

Buddhists are strongly advised against falling into the miserable pit of superstitious beliefs and allowing the mind to be troubled by unnecessary and unfounded fears. Cultivate a strong will-power by refusing to believe in the influence of charms.

A short meditation course may also prove very helpful to clear the mind of unwholesome thoughts. Meditation leads to the purification of the mind. A purified mind automatically leads to a purified and healthy body. The Buddha-Dhamma is a soothing balm to get rid of sickness of this nature.

# Consulting Mediums

*Consulting mediums is not a Buddhist practice: it is just a traditional and psychological belief.*

IN many countries, people seek the advice and guidance of mediums to overcome their problems in situations which they consider as beyond their comprehension.

The medium's help is sought in many ways and for various reasons. In time of sickness when medical help is apparently ineffective, some people may become desperate and turn anywhere to seek solace. At such times, mediums are often consulted. Some people also turn to mediums when they are faced with a complex problem and are unable to find an acceptable solution. Others consult mediums out of greed in order to get rich quickly.

Some people believe that when a medium is in a trance, the spirit of a certain god or deity communicates through the medium and offers advice or guidance to those seeking help. Others believe that the trance-state is the work of the subconscious mind which surfaces and takes over the conscious mind.

Consulting mediums is a fairly common practice amongst the public. The Buddhist attitude towards consulting mediums is one of neutrality. It is difficult to verify whether what the medium conveys is correct or not. The practice of consulting mediums is not a Buddhist practice; it is just a traditional practice.

Consulting mediums is for worldly material gain; the Teaching of the Buddha is for spiritual development. However, if people believe what the medium conveys is true, there is no reason for Buddhists to object to such practices.

If a person really understands and practices the Teachings of the Buddha, he can realise the nature of his problems. He can overcome his own problems without consulting any medium.

# Dreams and Their Significance

*' Life is nothing but a dream.'*

ONE of man's greatest unsolved problems is the mystery of dreams. From the very earliest of times man has tried to analyse dreams and has tried to explain them in prophetic and psychological terms, but while there has been some measure of success recently, we are probably no nearer the answers to the baffling question: ' What is a dream? '

The great English Romantic poet William Wordsworth had a startling concept: that this life we live is merely a dream and that we will ' awake ' to the ' real ' reality when we die, when our ' dream ' ends.

'  Our birth is but a sleep and forgetting:
   The Soul, that rises with us, our life's star,
   Hath had elsewhere its setting,
   And cometh from afar. '

A similar concept is expressed in a charming old Buddhist tale which tells of a deva who was playing with some other devas. Being tired, he lay down to take a short nap and passed away. He was reborn as a girl on earth. There she got married, had a few children and lived to be very old. After her death again she was born as a deva amongst the same companions who had just finished playing their game. (This story also illustrates the relativity of time, that is, how the concept of time in the human world is very different from time in another plane of existence).

What has Buddhism to say about dreams? Just as in every other culture, Buddhism has had its fair share of people who claimed to be skilled in interpreting dreams. Such people earn a lot of money exploiting the ignorance of men and women who believe that every dream has a spiritual or prophetic significance.

According to Buddhist psychology dreams are ideational processes which occur as activities of the mind. In considering the occurrence of dreams it is relevant to remember that the process of sleeping can be regarded as falling into five stages.

1. drowsiness,             · 4. light slumber and
2. light slumber,            5. awakening.
3. deep slumber,

The significance and the cause of dreams were the subject of discussion in the famous book ' Milinda Panha ' or ' The Questions of King Milinda ', in which Ven. Nagasena has stated that there are six causes of dreams, three of them being organic, wind, bile and phlegm. The fourth is due to the intervention of supernatural forces, fifth, revival of past experience and sixth, the influence of future events. It is categorically stated that dreams occur only in light slumber which is said to be like the sleep of the monkey. Of the six causes given Ven. Nagasena has stated positively that the last, namely prophetic dreams are the only important ones and the others are relatively insignificant.

Dreams are mind-created phenomena and they are activities of the mind. All human beings dream, although some people cannot remember. Buddhism teaches that some dreams have psychological significance. The six causes mentioned earlier can also be classified in the following manner:

I.   Every single thought · that is created is stored in our subconscious mind and some of them strongly influence the mind according to our anxieties. When we sleep, some of these thoughts are activated and appear to us as ' pictures ' moving before us. This happens because during sleep, the five senses which constitute our contact with the outside world, are temporarily arrested. The subconscious mind then is free to become dominant and to ' re-play ' thoughts that are stored. These dreams may be of value to psychiatry but cannot be classified as prophetic. They are merely the reflections of the mind at rest.

II.   The second type of dream also has no significance. These are caused by internal and external provocations which set off a train of ' visual thoughts ' which are ' seen ' by the mind at rest. Internal factors are those which disturb the body (e.g. a heavy meal which does not allow one to have a restful slumber or imbalance and friction between elements that constitute the body). External provocation is when the mind is disturbed (although the sleeper may be unaware of it) by natural phenomena like the weather, wind, cold, rain, leaves rustling, windows rattling etc. The subconscious mind reacts to these disturbances and creates pictures to ' explain ' them away. The mind accomodates the irritation in a seemingly rational way so that the dreamer can continue to sleep undisturbed. These dreams too have no importance and need no interpretation.

III.   Then there are the prophetic dreams. These are important. They are seldom experienced and only when there is an impending event which is of great relevance to the dreamer. Buddhism teaches that besides the tangible world we can experience, there are devas who exist on another plane or some spirits who are bound to this earth and are invisible to us. They could be our relatives or friends who have passed away and who have been reborn. They maintain their former mental relationships and attachments to us. When Buddhists transfer merits to devas and departed ones, they remember them and invite them to share the happiness accrued in the merit. Thus they develop a mental relationship with their departed ones. The devas in turn are pleased and they keep a watch over us and indicate something in dreams when we are facing certain big problems and they try to protect us from harm.

So, when there is something important that is going to happen in our lives they activate certain mental energies in our minds which are seen as dreams. These dreams can warn of impending danger or even prepare us for sudden over-whelming good news. These messages are given in symbolic terms (much like the negatives of photographs) and have to be interpreted skilfully and with intelligence. Unfortunately too many people confuse the first two kinds of dreams with these and end up wasting valuable time and money consulting fake mediums and dream-interpreters. The Buddha was aware that this could be exploited for personal gain and He therefore warned the monks against practising soothsaying, astrology and interpreting dreams in the name of Buddhism.

IV. Finally, our mind is the depository of all kammic energies accumulated in the past. Sometimes, when a kamma is about to ripen (that is, when the action we did in a previous life or early part of our life, is going to experience its reaction) the mind which is at rest during sleep can trigger off a ' picture ' of what is going to happen. Again the impending action has to be of great importance and must be so strongly charged that the mind ' releases ' the extra energy in the form of a vivid dream. Such dreams occur only very rarely and only to certain people with a special kind of mental make up. The sign of the effect of certain kammas also appears in our minds at the last moment when we are going to depart from this world.

Dreams can occur when two living human beings send strong mental telepathic messages to each other. When one person has an intense desire to communicate with another, he concentrates strongly on the message and the person with whom he wishes to communicate. When the mind is at rest, it is in an ideal state to receive these messages which are seen as dreams. Usually these dreams only appear in one intense moment because the human mind is not strong enough to sustain such messages over a long period of time.

All worldlings are dreamers, and they see as permanent, what is essentially impermanent. They do not see that youth ends in old age, beauty in ugliness, health in sickness, and life itself in death. In this dream-world, what is truly without substance is seen as reality. Dreaming during sleep is but another dimension of the dream-world. The only ones who are awake are the Buddhas and Arahats as they have seen reality.

Buddhas and arahants never dream. The first three kinds of dream cannot occur in their minds, because their minds have been permanently ' stilled ' and cannot be activated to dream. The last kind of dream cannot happen to them because they have eradicated all their craving energy completely, and there is no ' residual ' energy of anxiety or unsatisfied desire to activate the mind to produce dreams. The Buddha is also known as the Awakened One because His way of relaxing the physical body is not the way we sleep which results in dreams. Great artists and thinkers, like the German Goethe, have often said they get some of their best inspiration through dreams. This could be because when their minds are cut off from the five senses during sleep, they produce clear thoughts which are creative in the highest degree. Wordsworth meant the same thing when he said that good poetry results from ' powerful emotions recollected in tranquillity '.

# Faith Healing

*Faith healing — a psychological approach.*

The practice of faith-healing is prevalent in many countries. Many people are trying to influence the public through emotional persuasion designated as faith-healing. In order to impress on their patients the efficacy of their healing powers, some faith-healers use the name of a god or a religious object to introduce a religious flavour into their faith healing methods. The introduction of religion into faith-healing is actually a guise or a decoy to beguile the patient into developing more devotion and enhance the confidence or faith of the patient in the faith-healer. This healing act, if performed in public is intended to get converts to a particular religious denomination.

In actual fact, in so far as faith-healing is concerned, religion is not all that important. There are numerous cases of faith-healers performing their faith-healing acts without using religion at all. A case in point is the science of hypnotism, the practice of which involves no religious aspects at all. Those who associate religion with faith-healing are in a way engaging in a subtle form of illusion trying to attract converts to their particular religion by making use of faith healing and describing certain cures as miraculous acts.

The methods employed by faith healers are to condition the minds of patients into having a certain mental attitude with the result that certain favourable psychological and physiological changes invariably take place. This attracts the condition of the mind, the heart, the consequent blood circulation and other related organic functions of the body, thus creating a feeling of a sense of well-being. If sickness is attributed to the condition

*Read ' The Significance of Paritta Chanting '.*

of the mind, then the mind can certainly be properly conditioned to assist in eradicating whatever illness that may occur.

In this context, it is to be noted that the constant and regular practice of meditation can help to minimise, if not to completely eradicate, various forms of illnesses. There are many discourses in the Teaching of the Buddha where it was indicated that various forms of sicknesses were eradicated through the conditioning of the mind. Thus it is worthwhile to practise meditation in order to attain mental and physical well-being.

# Superstitions and Dogmas

*' People ridicule the superstitions of others, while cherishing their own. '*

ALL ailments have cures but not superstitions. And if for some reason or other, any superstition crystallises into a religion, it easily becomes an almost incurable malady. In the performance of certain religious functions, even educated people of today forget their human dignity to accept the most ridiculous, super-stitious beliefs.

Superstitious beliefs and rituals were adopted to decorate a religion in order to attract the multitude. But after sometime, the creeper which is planted to decorate the shrine as it were, outgrows and outshines the shrine, with the result that religious tenets are relegated to the background and superstitious beliefs and rituals become predominant — the creeper eclipsing the shrine.

Like superstition dogmatic belief also chokes the healthy growth of religion. Dogmatic belief and intolerance go hand-in-hand. One is reminded of the Middle Ages with its pitiless inquisitions, cruel murders, violence, infamy, tortures and burning of innocent beings. One is also reminded of the barbaric and ruthless crusades.

All these events were stimulated by dogmatic beliefs in religious authority and the intolerance resulting therefrom.

Before the development of scientific knowledge, ignorant people had many superstitious beliefs. For example a lot of people believed that the eclipse of the sun and moon brought bad luck and pestilence. Today we know that such beliefs are not true. Again some unscrupulous religionists encourage people to believe in superstitions so that they can make use of their followers for their own benefit. When people have truly purified their minds of ignorance, they will see the universe as it really is and they will not suffer from superstition and dogmatism. This is the ' salvation ' that Buddhists aspire to.

It is extremely difficult for us to break up the emotional feeling that is attached to superstition or dogmatic belief. Even the light of scientific knowledge is often not strong enough to cause us to give up the misconceptions. For example, we have noticed for generations that the earth moves round the sun; but experientially we still behold the sun rising, moving across the sky, and setting in the evening. We still have to make an intellectual leap to imagine that we are, in fact, hurtling at great speed around the sun.

We must understand that the dangers of dogmatism and superstition go hand-in-hand with religion. The time has come for wise people to separate religion from dogmatism and superstition. Otherwise, the good name of religion will be polluted and the number of non-believers will be increased, as they have already.

# INDEX

# About this book......

**What Buddhists Believe** answers many questions which are asked about Buddhism by Buddhists and non-Buddhists alike. There are so many misconceptions regarding superstitions and misinterpretations which are associated with this noble religion that it has become imperative to explain the Teachings in a manner which has contemporary relevance.

Ven. Dr. K. Sri Dhammananda's **What Buddhists Believe** is already a classic in that it has proved to be extremely popular not only with practising Buddhists who are born into the religion, but also those who are really interested in knowing what the Buddha taught. Its popularity can be attested by the fact that it has run into four editions and it has been translated into Chinese, Korean and Indonesian. This revised and enlarged volume covers almost every aspect of Buddhism, and is written in clear and precise language which will appeal not only to the casual reader but also to the intellectual student of the Dhamma. Directed mainly to an average person, this book adopts a non-textual approach to explain the Buddhist viewpoint on a wide range of doctrinal and contemporary topics, including those not normally touched upon by traditional Buddhist writers.

*The author of this book is a graduate in Buddhist philosophy and literature as well as oriental languages from both Indian and Sri Lankan universities. He is a prolific writer and is well known for his dhammaduta activities. He is amply qualified to explain Buddhism to those who are culturally, socially and academically unfamiliar with the Teachings.*

*Cover design by Chong Hong Choo*

ISBN 967-9920-29-1

*"Wherever the Buddha's teachings have flourished,*

*either in cities or countrysides,*

*people would gain inconceivable benefits.*

*The land and pepole would be enveloped in peace.*

*The sun and moon will shine clear and bright.*

*Wind and rain would appear accordingly,*

*and there will be no disasters.*

*Nations would be prosperous*

*and there would be no use for soldiers or weapons.*

*People would abide by morality and accord with laws.*

*They would be courteous and humble,*

*and everyone would be content without injustices.*

*There would be no thefts or violence.*

*The strong would not dominate the weak*

*and everyone would get their fair share."*

~THE BUDDHA SPEAKS OF
THE INFINITE LIFE SUTRA OF
ADORNMENT, PURITY, EQUALITY
AND ENLIGHTENMENT OF
THE MAHAYANA SCHOOL~

With bad advisors forever left behind,
From paths of evil he departs for eternity,
Soon to see the Buddha of Limitless Light
And perfect Samantabhadra's Supreme Vows.

The supreme and endless blessings
of Samantabhadra's deeds,
I now universally transfer.
May every living being, drowning and adrift,
Soon return to the Pure Land of
Limitless Light!

~The Vows of Samantabhadra~

I vow that when my life approaches its end,
All obstructions will be swept away;
I will see Amitabha Buddha,
And be born in His Western Pure Land of
Ultimate Bliss and Peace.

When reborn in the Western Pure Land,
I will perfect and completely fulfill
Without exception these Great Vows,
To delight and benefit all beings.

~The Vows of Samantabhadra
Avatamsaka Sutra~

# NAME OF SPONSOR

## 助 印 功 德 芳 名

Document Serial No : 95218

委印文號：95218

書　名：What Buddhists Believe
Book Serial No.,書號：EN049

## N.T.Dollars :

35,000：楊新德（迴向韓長庸、韓李國珍、楊萬和、蕭運明、韓桂渝，
業障消除，增福增慧，發菩提心，早生淨土）。

87,500：佛陀教育基金會。
The Corporate Body of the Buddha Educational Foundation

Amount: N.T.Dollars 122,500 , 3,500 copies.
以上合計新台幣：122,500 元 ，恭印 3,500 冊。

# DEDICATION OF MERIT

May the merit and virtue
accrued from this work
adorn Amitabha Buddha's Pure Land,
repay the four great kindnesses above,
and relieve the suffering of
those on the three paths below.

May those who see or hear of these efforts
generate Bodhi-mind,
spend their lives devoted to the Buddha Dharma,
and finally be reborn together in
the Land of Ultimate Bliss.
Homage to Amita Buddha!

## NAMO AMITABHA
## 南 無 阿 彌 陀 佛

財團法人佛陀教育基金會　印贈
台北市杭州南路一段五十五號十一樓

Printed and donated for free distribution by
**The Corporate Body of the Buddha Educational Foundation**
11F., 55 Hang Chow South Road Sec 1, Taipei, Taiwan, R.O.C.
Tel: 886-2-23951198 , Fax: 886-2-23913415
Email: overseas@budaedu.org
Website:http://www.budaedu.org
**This book is strictly for free distribution, it is not for sale.**
Printed in Taiwan
3,500 copies; September 2006
EN049-6183